BIOLOGY

BIOLOGY

Trends in Science

BIOLOGY

Overview by
Martin Walters and Phill Watts

Copyright © Helicon Publishing 2001

Helicon Publishing Ltd
42 Hythe Bridge Street
Oxford OX1 2EP
United Kingdom
E-mail: admin@helicon.co.uk
Web site: http://www.helicon.co.uk

First published 2001

ISBN: 1–85986–367–1

British Library Cataloguing in Publication Data
A catalogue record for this book is available from the
British Library.

Typeset by
Florence Production Ltd, Stoodleigh, Devon
Printed and bound in Great Britain by
Clays Ltd, Bungay, Suffolk

Acknowledgements

Overview
Martin Walters, freelance writer specializing in life sciences and environmental issues

Dr Phill Watts,
School of Biological Sciences
University of Liverpool

Editors
Editorial Director
Hilary McGlynn

Managing Editor
Elena Softley

Editor
Catherine Thompson

Editorial Assistant
Ruth Collier

Content Fulfilment Manager
Tracey Auden

Production Manager
John Normansell

Production Assistant
Stacey Penny

Picture Editor
Sophie Evans

Contents

Preface

There is never a right time to take stock of biology, so the recent turn of the century is as good a moment as any. The problem, if it is a problem, is that the 20th century was unparalleled for scientific advance and the unremitting pace of discovery shows no sign of letting up. Science does not pause for us to take stock – we have to do it on the fly.

So this book does not set out to be a definitive account of the state of biology. Rather it is a collection of resources, which will give you the necessary grounding to pursue your own studies in biology into the 21st century.

The **chronology** is a year-by-year account of important advances since 1900. Here you will learn how biology has unfolded since the beginning of the last century and be able to trace the many strands of discovery as they unwind throughout the 20th century.

In science it has been customary to associate advances in knowledge with individual scientists – one thinks of Darwin, Mendel, Watson and Crick – so in the **biography** section you can read about some of the biologists, geneticists, biochemists, and other life scientists who have contributed in some important way to their discipline in the 20th century. Yet in biology, as in other disciplines, the luminaries seem to shine less intensely towards the end of the century than at the beginning. Biology is now "big science", almost wholly reliant on state funding, and the days when a determined individual could dominate a field are almost gone – there are no more Darwins.

Parallel trends are at work in the **organizations and institutions** of biology. In 1900 a mere handful of institutions were doing serious research in biology, and they were essentially all in Europe and North America. Today, such is the proliferation of research, that we have have been hard pressed to list the institutions that one might regard as key.

One obstacle to the public appreciation of any science is the specialized language, which is why we have included a **glossary** of definitions of hundreds of terms from the life sciences, from abiotic factor to zoology, that will inform and enrich your reading.

But where should you start your study of biology? To orient the reader, the book begins with an overview of the field since 1900. Here are the big ideas of the 20th century, and the seed corn for the 21st.

BIOLOGY

Part One

1 Overview

Introduction

Developments in several important fields of biology have been rapid during the 20th century, with a number of originally relatively separate disciplines coming together, to the benefit of our overall knowledge. In a few instances, this amalgamation of research fields has created new and distinct areas of research. Some advances have been largely the result of technological improvements, such as the increasing power and resolution of microscopes, culminating in the electron microscope, leading to rapid advances in cell biology. Others have been based more on advances in theoretical guidelines – for example the strides made in evolutionary studies of behaviour and ecology. Amongst the more important of these developments have been discoveries in genetics, and in the related fields of developmental and molecular biology. For example, we now know that many diseases have a genetic component, and techniques in biotechnology and genetic engineering enable us to detect the responsible genes and to suggest ways in which such diseases may be treated. Prenatal screening for a variety of inherited conditions is also now possible, both for the parents and the unborn child. Genetics has also had a productive impact on ecology and behavioural biology, providing them with a theoretical underpinning which has helped, for example, to explain the evolution of particular strategies in reproduction. There have been major advances in the study of mammalian, including human, reproduction, with techniques such as in-vitro fertilization becoming almost routine.

Biotechnology and genetic engineering are new biological disciplines, born during the 20th century, mainly from a fusion of techniques from genetics and biochemistry. These fields are having a significant impact on agriculture and medicine, with new varieties of crop plants being produced by genetic engineering, and techniques perfected for the biological manufacture of drugs. The 20th century has also seen significant advances in our understanding of evolution as seen through the fossil record, shedding light not least upon the origins of our own species. Awareness of the global environment has gradually come more and more to the fore throughout the 20th century, with a realization of the sensitivity of the environment and planet to the destructive effects of pollution.

In all fields of biological research there have been technological advances which have had a considerable impact on progress. Not least has been the rapid rise and development of computers, which have become more and more powerful and portable, and which are now an essential tool in most biological research. The increase in computer speed and analytical power has allowed detailed and very rapid analysis of scientific data, and also the intricate modelling of biological systems. Indeed, it is the rapid increase in computing technology that has provided scientists with computers that have memories which are large enough to cope with databases that, for example, store data on DNA and protein sequences, genetic maps, and also human genes and inherited diseases. Many of these databases may be freely accessed over the Internet, which itself has allowed biologists to collaborate across the globe in a way unimaginable earlier this century.

The unravelling of genetics

The first half of the 20th century was notable for several great steps forward in our understanding of the mechanisms underlying genetics. The spark for this was actually based on the rediscovery and reinterpretation of much earlier findings: those of the Czech monk Gregor Mendel (1822–1884). Mendel's work on the inheritance patterns of flower and seed colour in peas was published in 1866, but had little influence on biological thinking for over thirty years. At the start of the 20th century Hugo de Vries in Holland, Karl Erich Correns in Germany, and Gustav Tschermak von Seysenegg in Austria all independently rediscovered Mendel's work. Their work signalled the start of serious research into heredity. Key stages here were the observation and study of genetic mutations, and the discovery of the basic unit of inheritance, the gene. This discovery pointed to a physical mechanism which helped to explain the observed patterns of inheritance of particular traits, such as flower colour in plants and eye colour in humans, to name but two examples. In 1906, English biologist William Bateson (1861–1926) introduced the word 'genetics' and in 1909, Wilhelm L Johanssen (1857–1927), from Denmark, coined the term 'gene'. Bateson demonstrated that certain inherited traits tend to be transmitted as a group, thus establishing the concept of genetic linkage and in 1909 he used the term 'allele' for alternate forms of a gene.

Early geneticists

The US biologist Thomas Henry Morgan (1866–1945) published his influential book *The Theory of the Gene* in 1926. Morgan had many important insights into genetics, and remarked, among other things, upon the phenomenon of sex-linked inheritance and on the significance of the crossing over of chromosomes. Morgan considered the genes, the units of inheritance, to be sited at particular places on the chromosomes, and by determining some of these positions, he began the process of mapping them. Between 1930 and 1932 English geneticist Ronald Fisher (1890–1962),

Model of the DNA double helix. Roger Ressmeyer/CORBIS

Anglo-Indian physiologist and geneticist John Haldane (1892–1964), and US geneticist Sewall Wright (1889–1988) published a series of papers and books that formed the basis of modern population genetics. However, it was only later that scientists attributed a link behind the inheritance of single-particle traits, as originally described by Mendel, and features that vary in a discontinuous way, such as height, weight, and milk production. We now know that it is a mixture of an organism's genes and the environment that controls the expression of many continuously variable or 'quantitative' traits. Identifying the genes behind quantitative traits, such as meat quality, litter size, and disease resistance, now forms the basis of many crop and livestock improvement programmes. Thus, although humans have been improving the qualities of numerous domestic species for thousands of years, the 20th century has seen a rapid development in crop and animal science through our vastly improved understanding of heredity.

Mention should be made here of the work of the Soviet biologist Trofim Lysenko (1898–1976), who championed the erroneous view that physical traits acquired during life, such as increased muscle mass, could be inherited, basing his ideas partly on the thoughts of the French naturalist Jean Lamarck (1744–1829). Lysenko controlled Soviet biological research from 1928 until 1965, and was strongly supported by the dictator Stalin, who used Lysenko's theories to underpin and support his own philosophy of social and political control. In this way an incorrect view of evolution become enmeshed with an imposed political system, and this view of evolution affected many decades of biology in the former Soviet Union.

One-gene–one-enzyme and the double helix

In the mid-20th century, the chemical link between the gene and the expression of that gene in the organism was beginning to be unravelled. This link proved to be the production by the gene of a specific protein,

The fruit fly Drosophila melanogaster, *a species to which our knowledge of genetics is much indebted.* Robert Pickett/CORBIS

called an enzyme, which has a particular effect in the cell in which it is produced. In 1941, US geneticists George W Beadle (1903–1989) and Edward L Tatum (1909–1975) established the one-gene–one-enzyme hypothesis, showing that one gene was responsible for the production of one specific enzyme. Work of this kind was part of the rapidly developing discipline of biochemistry, which was to become more and more dominant in 20th century biology. A further piece of the genetic jigsaw was to fall into place with the discovery of the chemical nature of the genetic material itself: the elucidation of the structure of deoxyribonucleic acid (DNA), the compound containing the fundamental genetic information. The unravelling of the structure of DNA began in 1951 when English biophysicist Rosalind Franklin (1920–1958) produced X-ray diffraction photographs of DNA; later, in April 1953, James Watson (1928–) and Francis Crick (1916–) solved the three-dimensional structural model for DNA, thus providing a physical mechanism for the storage and transmission of genetic information from one generation to the next.

4

Biologists still had the problem of translating the genetic information because DNA is composed of only 4 nucleotide bases, yet some 20 different amino acids each required their own code. A sequence of three bases (called a codon) is the minimum number of bases required to provide a specific code for every amino acid, and this 'triplet code' is indeed the way by which each amino acid is specified. The precise way in which this genetic information is coded began to be clarified when, in 1961, US geneticist Marshall W Nirenberg (1927–) cracked the first letter of the genetic code, and by the mid-1960s the entire 'alphabet' of DNA sequences that represent each amino acid had been deciphered.

Debt to the fruit fly

Research into genetics has continued apace through the 20th century and much of this research has relied heavily upon a small insect, the fruit fly, *Drosophila melanogaster*. The fruit fly is admirably suited for this role: it is easy to culture in the laboratory; it has a rapid reproductive rate; conveniently large chromosomes; and many of its mutations are easily visible, for example causing changes in the shape of legs or wing structures. Such work began as early as 1927 when Hermann Muller used X-rays to cause artificial gene mutations in *Drosophila*. Mutations, which represent sudden changes in the transfer of inherited characters, began to be seen as playing a central role in the mechanism of evolution. Analysis of mutations in the fruit fly, which, for example, caused bizarre characteristics such as an extra set of wings or legs replacing the antennae, lead to the discovery of homeotic genes. We now know that homeotic genes control the development of cells and hence the overall body plan of an organism, and that the sequence of DNA is virtually the same in all eukaryotic organisms – from the humble baker's yeast to ourselves. Nowadays geneticists employ a variety of different species, such as yeast, worms, fish, and mice, to unravel the workings of genetics and act as models to improve our understanding of the ways by which genes regulate our development.

Sequencing DNA

A major step forward in genetics took place in 1977 when English biochemist Fred Sanger (1918–) and US microbiologists Alan Maxam and Walter Gilbert (1932–) developed the 'chain termination' and the 'chemical' methods of sequencing DNA, respectively. This technology rapidly took genetic research in a new direction because it allowed scientists to directly read large chunks of DNA sequence for the first time. Sanger's chain-termination system forms the basis of modern automated sequencing machines that have been developed during the last 20 years. Initially, the goals of sequencing projects were to obtain the whole DNA sequence of organelles such as mitochondria or organisms such as viruses and bacteria, because they all contain only small amounts of DNA. The first breakthrough in determining the genetic makeup of more complex organisms came in 1992 when a consortium of more than 30 European laboratories published the complete DNA sequence of chromosome 3 of the yeast *Saccharomyces cerevisiae*. Six years later a nematode worm became the first animal to have its entire DNA sequence known. In addition to the work by academic institutions, there are now an increasing number of private companies that are sequencing commercially and medically important organisms. The complete DNA sequences of over 600 organisms are now listed in the National Centre for Biotechnology Information (NCBI) database on the Internet. Together with sequencing, perhaps the most important development in genetics during the latter half of the 20th century was that in 1985 when the polymerase chain reaction (PCR) was described for the first time, after its concept two years earlier by Kary Mullis (1944–   ). PCR uses an enzyme to make many millions of copies of DNA from tiny starting amounts, even as small as a single strand of DNA, within a few hours. In this way PCR has revolutionized genetic research because prior to its development large starting quantities of DNA were required. It is now possible to analyse DNA samples from, for example, crime scenes, archaeological sites, single cells, and even ancient specimens.

New science of genetic engineering

Perhaps the most notable – or notorious – of all areas in which biology has progressed in the 20th century has been in the field of genetic engineering. This involves altering the genetic makeup of an organism so as to change the type or quantity of the proteins that it produces. Selective breeding of animals and plants has effectively been doing this passively for thousands of years, but genetic engineering now allows scientists to modify an organism's genetic makeup more directly. Genetic engineering relies on certain specific techniques which were discovered in the 20th century. A key discovery in genetic engineering was made by US geneticist Joshua Lederberg (1925–   ) in 1952. This was that bacteria come together and exchange genetic material by a process known as conjugation. At about the same time it was realized that many bacteria were evolving resistance to drugs and antibiotics. If resistant bacteria were introduced to a culture of unresistant forms, this resistance could be established rapidly through the colony as the resistant genes were spread by this process. Another key stage was the study of viruses which infect bacteria – bacteriophages, or 'phages' for short. In 1946, German-born US biologist Max Delbrück (1906–1981) and US biochemist Alfred Hershey (1908–1997) showed that genes from different phages could combine.

Recombinant DNA and gene splicing

Perhaps one of the most essential tools in genetic engineering was discovered by Swiss biochemist Werner Arber (1929–) who identified that bacteria resist phage attack by using their enzymes, termed restriction enzymes, to split the phage's DNA. By 1968, Arber had located the enzymes which cut the DNA at specific sequences and found that if the split strands of different genes are put together in the absence of the enzyme they will recombine. The product of this process become known as recombinant DNA, and the process is now a central technique in genetic engineering. By 1970 the first restriction enzyme (*Hind* III) was isolated and a general method for inserting DNA into the bacterium *Escherichia coli* was subsequently developed. The first researchers to undertake true genetic engineering in this manner were US chemists Stanley H Cohen (1922–) and Herbert W Brown (1912–) in 1973. These scientists removed a piece of DNA from a bacterium, and then inserted a gene from a different bacterium. The engineered bacterium then reproduced, using its altered genetic makeup. Soon scientists had inserted into bacteria not just genes from other bacteria, but genes from other unrelated organisms, such as frogs and fruit flies. A logical progression from such research resulted in the production of genetically engineered useful products. However, such research was not without concern among molecular biologists and geneticists and in 1975 prompted a scientific meeting at Asilomar, California, during which a historic set of guidelines were written to regulate experimentation with recombinant DNA.

In 1977, the US scientist Herbert Boyer (1936–), of the first genetic engineering company, Genentech, fused a segment of human DNA (deoxyribonucleic acid) into the bacterium *Escherichia coli*, allowing it to produce a human protein (in this case the hormone somatostatin); this was the first commercially produced genetically engineered product. The commercial prospect of genetically engineered products was significantly increased in 1980 when the United States Supreme Court ruled that genetically modified organisms (GMOs) could be patented. General Electric obtained a patent for a bacterium that had been genetically modified to be capable of degrading oil slicks. Now, this technology has moved on to the point where genetically engineered bacteria and yeasts are used almost routinely to produce useful products such as human growth hormone and insulin. These essential drugs were amongst the first genetically engineered products to go on sale.

Advent of genetically modified crops

In recent years it has become possible to use genetic engineering techniques to alter the genetic makeup of plants. This offers the possibility of creating new varieties of species that possess specific characteristics and important agricultural benefits; for example, resistance to low temperatures can be introduced to crops from warm climates, so they may be grown successfully elsewhere, as can resistance to insect pests and virus diseases. Work is under way with cassava (a staple tropical crop) to introduce disease resistance, and to increase its protein content. Genetically modified (GM) crops are now produced in many parts of the world. In 1993 the first gene-spliced fruit to be approved by the FDA – tomatoes genetically engineered for a longer shelf life – were marketed. Today GM products such as soybean, sugar beet, maize and corn are commonplace in supermarkets alongside their more 'natural' relatives. The marketing of such products or their derivatives has not remained uncontroversial and after extensive media coverage there was a public backlash against these so-called 'Frankenstein foods' towards the end of the 20th century and into the start of the new millennium.

A genetically modified seedling ready for planting. Ted Spiegel/CORBIS

Transgenic animals and xenotransplantation

The final years of the 20th century saw further developments in genetic engineering, many of which have important implications for medicine. It is now possible to produce what are known as transgenic animals, by injecting genes from one animal into the fertilized egg of another. This technique was first perfected in 1981 by scientists at Ohio University, USA, who injected genes from one animal into the fertilized egg of a mouse. The resulting transgenic mouse then has the foreign gene in many of its cells and the gene is passed on to its offspring, creating permanently altered (transgenic) animals. In 1982, for example, a gene controlling growth was transferred from a rat to a mouse, producing a transgenic mouse that grew to double its normal size. Such transgenic techniques promise to benefit medicine, and in particular transplant surgery. One of the major problems in surgery has been in transplanting organs – the main difficulties being the supply of suitable organs, and the process of rejection by the host. Transgenic pigs have now been bred which incorporate human genes that reduce the risk of tissue rejection when pigs' organs are transplanted into human patients, in a process called xenotransplantation. Xenotransplantation brings its own problems, however, including the possible risk of the transmission of porcine (or simian, in the case of primate organs) viruses to the human recipient.

Parallel research has established that it may soon be possible to grow kidneys in humans which are derived from embryo kidney cells. If successful, these techniques could simultaneously address the twin problems of supply and rejection of human organs. Nevertheless, such research has raised difficult ethical problems that have yet to be fully resolved. Many of the rapid advances in animal genetic engineering are of direct medical benefit to humans. Examples of products that can now be manufactured from engineered animals are: human blood clotting factors from sheep and goats; human growth hormone and beta-interferon (used to treat multiple sclerosis) from cattle; and humanized organs for transplant from pigs. Genetic engineering technology is also being used in the plant kingdom to the benefit of medical science. For example, a canola oil has already been developed that contains an increased amount of antioxidants. It is clear that as we proceed through the 21st century, genetically engineered plants – or 'nutraceuticals' – will be used increasingly to deliver medically useful compounds.

Advances in human genetics

At the turn of the 20th century operations were considered risky because the medical community could not understand why some blood transfusions worked and others failed. A landmark discovery was made in 1901 by Karl Landsteiner who identified and described the ABC blood system (later changed to the A, B, and O blood groups); the importance of this work was not fully realized until World War I when blood was collected and stored for wounded soldiers. We now know that blood groups are genetically determined; however, it was only in the last few decades of the 20th century, with the development of more sophisticated sequencing machines and advances in recombinant DNA technology, that biological research into human genetics gathered pace at an impressive rate. In 1954, for example, when V A McKusick published 'Mendelian Inheritance in Man', there were 1,487 genetic disorders listed, and by 1994 the number of entries listed in this catalogue had risen to 6,678. During 1981 three independent research teams announced that they had discovered human oncogenes (cancer genes) and by 1983 Kay Davies and Robert Williamson located the first marker for a human genetic disease, in this case Duchenne muscular dystrophy. Mapping genes involves studying the DNA from affected and unaffected members of a family, and identifying a piece of DNA which is inherited with the disease. By 1987, the actual gene for this condition was found, and copies were made of it – a process known as gene cloning. By the early 1990s it was found that this gene failed to produce a particular protein which is needed by the skeletal muscles, thus establishing a cause for the disease.

In 1989 Francis Collins and Lap-Chee Tsui identified the gene which codes for the cystic fibrosis transmembrane conducter regulator protein (CFTR) on human chromosome 7; mutations of this gene can cause cystic fibrosis. Several other genetic diseases can now be detected by analysis of DNA, in some cases before birth. In the mid 1980s, the British geneticist Alec Jeffreys (1950–) made an important discovery, leading to the development of so-called 'genetic fingerprinting'. He found that each person carries a unique sequence of short base sequences in their DNA, and that these sequences can be revealed by laboratory analysis, even with only tiny starting samples of DNA. This technique has found a number of uses, such as in the resolution of cases of disputed parenthood, and to identify criminals from traces of their body fluids, hair, and tissues. In September 2000 the UK government announced plans for DNA testing to be compulsory for all criminal offences. Once again, genetic science has been perceived as threatening or intrusive and technological advances have raised ethical concerns. Who has access to the DNA profiles once they have become available? Should DNA fingerprints be filed indefinitely or destroyed?

Gene therapy

The start of the final decade of the 20th century saw the first successful use of human gene replacement therapy – the treatment or prevention of a disease by gene transfer. In this case, T-lymphocytes (a type of white blood cell) from a four-year-old girl suffering from an enzyme (adenosine deaminase or ADA) deficiency were cultured and then incubated with a harmless retrovirus that carried DNA which codes for the normally functioning gene. The virus transfers the normal gene into the lymphocytes, which, after being reinjected into the patient, allowed her immune system to begin functioning. Gene therapy raised hopes for the effective treatment of single gene diseases and some cancers and has become the focus of a whole new industry. Despite this early success, however, introducing other genes into target tissue and getting them to work proved much harder than previously anticipated. Gene therapy has always been subject to intensive regulation but the future of research into this medical practice is now uncertain after the tragic death of a research subject, US teenager Jesse Gelsinger, in 1999.

Human Genome Project

Perhaps one of the most important developments in genetics is the Human Genome Project (HGP), which is a publicly funded project that is being conducted in 16 centres around the world, coordinated by the Human Genome Organization. This ambitious project, which began in October 1990, aims to map and sequence the whole of the human genome, and discover all of the estimated 80,000 to 140,000 human genes. As part of the HGP, parallel studies are being carried out on selected 'model' organisms that are much easier to study than humans but share a lot of genetic information with us. Species such as baker's yeast *Sacchromyces cerevisiae*, the fruit fly *Drosophila melangaster*, the nematode worm *Caenorhabditis elegans*, and the mouse *Mus musculus*, are all being used to help develop the technology and interpret the functions of numerous genes.

The complete sequencing of the 3 billion base-pairs that make up the entire human genome was completed as a working draft in June 2000. After completing the job of determining the sequence of the letters in

US geneticist and businessman Craig Venter (right) of Celera Genomics at the 1999 Human Genome meeting in Brisbane, Australia. Applied Biosystems

our genetic alphabet comes the next stage or 'annotation'. Annotation is the hard part where scientists must decode the meaning of the genetic instruction book and discover where a gene works, how it does so and in what network of genes it interacts. Currently, research is simply attempting to find the parts of DNA that belong to a gene and distinguish this from the roughly 96% of 'junk DNA' that appears to have no function. One perceived benefit deriving in part from this effort is the detection of inherited genetic disorders and diseases, and treatment of people who may be carriers of such conditions, even of the fetus during pregnancy. It is hoped that the HGP will also improve our understanding of genetic diseases, such as cystic fibrosis, and perhaps pave the way towards more effective treatment.

A major controversy in the race to sequence the human genome is the formation of the private company Celera Genomics, headed by the US businessman Craig Venter. In April 2000 Celera Genomics claimed that they had completed a first draft of the human genome. Critics have raised objections to the commercial ethics behind Celera – who wish to patent chunks of DNA sequence for which no biological function has yet been identified – and argue that the information from the human DNA sequence should be freely available to the scientific community without any legal restrictions.

Birth of biochemistry and cell biology

During the 20th century, biology gained enormously by absorbing the findings of the chemists, and in particular from the study of organic compounds which provide the building materials of all living organisms. This led to the rise of a new discipline, biochemistry, concerned with the chemistry of living organisms. Improvements in the quality and power of lenses led also to advances in the field of cell biology. A major step forward here was provided by the invention of the electron microscope, which revealed structures previously invisible to the human eye, enabling even intracellular structures to be examined clearly. Through the 20th century, biologists became increasingly aware of the role of specific chemicals in controlling bodily processes. The first such chemical to be discovered, and then synthesized, was the heart stimulant adrenaline. Adrenaline was discovered by the Japanese-born US biochemist Jokichi Takamine (1854–1922) in 1901. This was soon followed, in 1902, by the discovery of peristalsis (the involuntary action involved in hormonal secretion) and of the hormone secretin by English physiologists Ernest Starling (1866–1927) and William Bayliss (1860–1924). In 1921 Frederick Banting (1891–1941) and Charles Best (1899–1978) began researching into a cure for diabetes and had isolated insulin a year later. Scientists also started to comprehend and

An early electron microscope built under the direction of Russian-born US electronics engineer Vladimir Zworykin.
CORBIS–Bettmann

describe the relationships between these chemicals and the intracellular structures that act as the machinery of cells.

Our understanding of cell biology was greatly improved during the 1930s when the German-born British scientist Hans Krebs clarified the cycle through which energy is released to fuel work – the Krebs or tricarboxylic acid (TCA) cycle.

Arrival of antibiotics

At the turn of the 20th century, people began to realize that soil, although it is full of bacteria and fungi, does not generally cause diseases. Something in the soil seems to stop disease-producing bacteria from thriving there, and scientists began to search for this magic factor. In 1922, Scottish bacteriologist Alexander Fleming (1881–1955) isolated a substance, he called lysozyme, from tears, which he demonstrated could kill bacteria. Then in 1928, an accidental event in his laboratory led to a major biological discovery that was to have a huge impact. A mould had grown on a petri dish in which there was a culture of *Staphylococcus* bacteria. Around each speck of mould was a ring of dead bacteria. Fleming isolated a substance from the mould, and found that it killed certain bacteria, but not others, nor did it damage white blood cells. He called this substance penicillin. Eventually, methods were perfected (by Australian pathologist Howard Florey and German-born British biochemist Ernst Chain) for extracting large quantities of penicillin from cultures of mould, and this drug was then used to save thousands of lives during World War II. Around the same time a German doctor Gerhard Domagk (1895–1964) was researching into drugs that kill bacteria. Domagk found that prontosil rubrum, an orange-red sulfonamide dye developed by two colleagues at a dye company, was both safe and effective at curing streptococcal infections. Prontosil was the first medication that was effective against many different bacteria. However, the adverse side-effects associated with many of the sulfa drugs led to increased research into penicillin.

Since 1943, other natural antibiotics, such as streptomycin and aure-omycin, have been discovered. More recently, many more antibiotics have been synthesized by biochemists. However, although they are an effective way of combating infection, the liberal use of antibiotics has promoted the evolution by the target bacteria of resistant strains, and this posed an increasing problem for disease control in the latter years of the 20th century.

The natural world has been the single most productive source of drug leads, and with less than 10% of the Earth's biodiversity tested for biolog-ically active compounds, our environment still represents a huge reservoir of new medicinal reagents. Research into developing new drugs from the environment, however, has raised both ecological and political concerns. Firstly, slow-growing organisms or species that are not able to be cultured, such as certain corals, snails, and trees, may easily be over-exploited and thus be driven to extinction. Secondly, the source country may not receive any financial benefit from its biological resource being taken and subse-quently used in the marketplace. Legislation has partially solved the latter problem, but we have to look forward to advances in techniques such as cloning and the genetic engineering of useful genes to reduce adverse effects of 'mining' our environment.

Developmental biology

In developmental biology, great strides forward have also been made, the main one being the realization that all the cells of an organism undergo a process of differentiation, with only a small fraction of the genes in a single cell being active at a given time. Around 1900, the distinction was made between tissues that seem to develop according to an intrinsic genetic programme (determinate development) and those that are affected by adjacent tissues or structures (regulative development). This led to the new concept of 'induction', where one tissue affects the development of another. Induction was first shown clearly in 1901 by German embryologist Hans Spemann (1869–1941), using the eye of a frog embryo. These early findings in developmental biology continued through the 20th century and gradually the position-dependent development of cells is being teased apart. In this new field of topobiology, the cell membranes are being investigated ever more closely, to decipher the precise mechanisms involved.

A marriage between genetics and developmental biology came about with the demonstration, by Canadian bacteriologist Oswald Avery (1877–1955) in 1944, that DNA was the carrier of the genetic information, controlling the production of the proteins forming the organism. Development consists of the marshalling of these proteins, and their combination to form the different organ systems in the body, in an ordered sequence of gene expression. Through the 20th century there has been a steady increase in our knowledge of the processes controlling reproduction, and in particular human reproduction.

Oral contraceptives, first produced during the mid 1950s, have been refined, and are now routinely used by millions of women as an effective means of family planning. Globally, this control has helped to begin to stem the problem of over-population, arguably the greatest problem to face humanity, with its knock-on effects of famine and poverty, and on our environment in general. Significant further advances in oral contraceptive technology were made towards the end of the 20th century with the development of the 'morning after' pill for women and the first effective contraceptive pills for men; current research into drugs that regulate genes may pave the way for non-hormonal birth control in men.

A major event in reproductive biology, this time in the late 1960s, was the successful fertilization of human egg cells outside the body – the so-called test-tube baby technique, or in-vitro fertilization. 1978 saw the first baby, Louise Joy Brown, born using this technique. Having been unable to remove a blockage from her mother's Fallopian tube, English obstetrician Patrick Steptoe (1913–1988) and Welsh physiologist Robert Edwards (1925–) removed an egg from her ovary, fertilized it with her husband's sperm, and implanted it in her uterus.

Since the 1970s there have been several further advances in our knowledge of reproduction, including the development of some controversial techniques. These include the successful cloning of animals, first undertaken with a rabbit in 1975. Eventually, in 1996, two monkeys were successfully cloned from embryo cells, indicating that cloning techniques would probably be possible in humans as well.

It may be possible in the near future to allow fetal development to continue outside the mother's body. In a key experiment, in 1997, the

Japanese scientist Yoshinori Kuwabara announced that his team had successfully grown goat embryos in an acrylic tank. The embryos, which were removed from their mother at 17 weeks into pregnancy, were placed in the tank which was filled with liquid simulating amniotic fluid. The role of the placenta was replaced by a machine to pump oxygen and nutrients into the embryo's blood. At 20 weeks' gestation the goat was 'born'. At present the procedure can only be done late in development. Were it to be extended to people, it could be used to rescue babies that are at risk early in a pregnancy, or who are born very prematurely.

Cloning

In 1997, British geneticists successfully cloned an adult sheep. In this process, a cell was taken from the udder of the mother sheep and its DNA combined with an unfertilized egg that had had its DNA removed. The fused cells were grown in the laboratory and then implanted into the uterus of a surrogate mother sheep. The resulting lamb, Dolly, became famous as the first animal cloned using cells other than reproductive cells. Theoretically at least, a similar process could clone members of our own species, and this realization has resulted in international calls to prevent the cloning of humans. Despite the potential benefits of cloning technology, there are major concerns about the ethics of extending its use to humans. The artificial production of cloned humans may be possible, but it raises obvious moral problems. In June 1997, the US National Bioethics Advisory Commission proposed a five-year ban on human cloning, and in 1998, 19 European countries also signed an international ban on human cloning. In August 2000 the UK government promised a new law explicitly banning human cloning; however, it is likely that research into 'therapeutic cloning' – where a patient's cells are used to create an embryo for use as a store of material for treatment – will be allowed. An alternative to therapeutic cloning may have been provided by US scientists who have managed to grow nerve cells from bone marrow and hope to advance this technology as a treatment for conditions including Alzheimer's disease and paralysis.

Ecology and animal behaviour

Ecologists study animals and plants in their habitats, and much of this involves seeing how populations change with changing conditions. The term 'ecology' was coined in the 1860s, by the German zoologist Ernst Haeckel, for the study of the interrelations of animals and plants. But it is only in the 20th century that ecology developed into an active field of biological research. In the 18th and 19th centuries, ecology (or natural history as it was then known) was mainly a descriptive cataloguing of God's ordered natural world, and no need was felt to search for underlying mechanisms. In the 20th century, however, the major innovation in ecology was mainly that its investigations become explanatory – biologists began to search for reasons to explain their observations, by experiment and by the testing of theories. As elsewhere in biology, Darwin's *Origin of Species* had a huge influence on ecology and gave it a secure theoretical support. Another big influence here was the publication in 1927 of British ecologist Charles Elton's *Animal Ecology*, which set out a population biology approach to ecology. Before the rise of the computer, such studies were difficult and time-consuming, but the increase in power and sophistication of computers has allowed ecologists to analyse much more data, with far greater accuracy, and to model the behaviour of natural populations, and to compare these models with reality. Many ecological field studies investigate how different species compete with each other for resources, and have shown differences in reproductive strategy, related to environment and habitat.

Ecologists have also been responsible for unravelling some of the many complex feeding relations – food chains and webs – highlighting the interdependence of organisms in nature. Thus it is through ecological research and studying the biological interactions between species that we now understand, for example, how energy flows through ecosystems, and the carbon and nitrogen cycles. Such knowledge is essential if we are to successfully manage our exploitation of the environment.

Effective ecological work is impossible without a sound knowledge of the identities of the species involved. In the 19th century, taxonomy and natural history tended to go hand in hand, but in recent decades species description and naming have often come to be regarded as unglamorous pursuits. Nevertheless, it is essential to increase our knowledge in this area and to attempt to expand our inventory of species, especially now so many of them are under threat. It is a sobering thought that despite the efforts of taxonomists, there is still no reliable estimate of the number of species that exist today. To take the case of animals, about 1.5 million species have been described, of a minimum of some 10 million species estimated to exist, representing just 15%. Advances in our understanding of genetics and of evolution also had a significant impact on ecology, resulting in the disciplines of evolutionary and behavioural ecology. In particular, the application of the study of genetics and inheritance proved powerful in explaining and predicting the behaviour of many species of animals.

Sociobiology

The incorporation of evolutionary thinking into studies of animal behaviour gave rise to the science of sociobiology, heralded by the publication of *Sociobiology: The New Synthesis* by US zoologist Edward O Wilson in

1975. Wilson and others showed that many different patterns of social behaviour in animals can be explained in terms of the evolution of behaviour 'designed' to promote the survival of their genes. This analytical method proved particularly powerful in explaining the many examples of altruistic behaviour, in which individuals behave, or appear to behave, in an unselfish manner. Close study has revealed that in many such cases the danger to the altruistic individual may be offset by other advantages. In other cases, individual behaviour may be truly altruistic, but the beneficiaries are nearly always closely related genetically.

During the 20th century there have been many important field studies which have carefully observed the behaviour of animals in the wild. In particular the observations of chimpanzees and their close relative the bonobo (or pygmy chimpanzee) have shed a great deal of light on the complex patterns of social behaviour of these primates. Amongst the most important of such studies has been the detailed work on wild chimpanzees by English primatologist Jane Goodall (1934–) since 1960. Thanks to this research we now know that chimpanzees have highly complex and elaborate social lives, with many parallels to human behaviour, and that they are omnivorous, not strictly vegetarians as once thought. Similar studies were made by US primatologist Dian Fossey (1938–1985) on gorillas in Rwanda, revealing these powerful apes to have peaceful, family-based lives, browsing on forest vegetation. Goodall and Fossey also pointed out the growing need for effective conservation policies to protect the great apes – indeed Dian Fossey died at the hands of illegal poachers, whose traps she had interfered with, becoming a martyr to the cause of conservation.

Of course, developments in genetics have played their role in the study of the natural population starting largely in 1966 when Hubby and Lewontin used the technique of enzyme electrophoresis to reveal the paradox that many natural populations contain much more genetic variation than had been expected. Prior to this many geneticists had expected genetic variation to be low because it was primarily under the influence of natural selection. These findings led to a huge scientific debate about the relative importance of natural selection and more random events in shaping the evolution of populations and species. Nowadays, with the advent of PCR (polymerase chain reaction), genetic studies are commonplace for the analysis of populations and have created the new research field of 'molecular ecology' or 'ecological genetics'.

The environment

The 20th century saw the birth of awareness about the need to care for our environment, and of the destructive effects of pollution. Influential here was the publication in 1962 of a book called *Silent Spring*, written by US ecologist Rachel Carson (1907–1964), which perhaps more than any other event launched the environmental movement. This awareness has continued to gather pace through the 20th century as we have realized more and more that the Earth is a closed system with its own often delicate balance of physical and biological factors supporting the living organisms which thrive and in turn influence its makeup. This whole-Earth view gained its most famous expression with the formulation of the Gaia hypothesis, by British scientist James Lovelock (1919–), in the mid 1960s. This view regards the planet Earth as a complex, self-regulating system, easily disturbed, but able to adjust, almost like a giant single organism. The Gaia concept has undoubtedly helped focus peoples' thoughts on the importance of a global ecological view of our planet, and has highlighted the damage caused by human activity on the natural ecological pathways, damage that potentially threatens the future of the Earth itself. While the Gaia hypothesis has helped to focus biological thought, it has also attracted a less critical, almost mystical, following, perhaps because of its name, after an ancient Greek Earth goddess.

In recent decades, environmental ideas have become established, and have now started to feed through into a new environmental ethic that recognizes our responsibility for the rest of the natural world. In 1972, the United Nations Conference on the Human Environment was held in Stockholm, Sweden. This was the first international conference on the environment, and its stated aim was to improve the world's environment through monitoring, resource management, and education. Put at its starkest, the problem faced by human society today, and recognized clearly for the first time during the 20th century, is a conflict between individual freedom and the health of the planet. Unsustainable exploitation of the natural world and overpopulation are two of the biggest problems we face, and perhaps the best hope for the future lies in a view of life that recognizes our responsibilities and states that we as individuals should strive not to do anything to our environment that would make life more difficult for future generations. In essence, we all share a responsibility for the future of our species, and also for the diversity of life on the whole planet. A true and deep understanding of biology, of evolution, and of our place in nature leads naturally to this world view which, if widely implemented, gives us the best hope of a healthy future. Particularly dangerous amongst the threats to the environment are global warming, the destruction of the rainforests, and desertification.

During the final decades of the 20th century, biologists became increasingly concerned about the effects of pollution, particularly on the atmosphere. It is now well established that chemical pollution in the atmosphere has thinned the naturally occurring layer of high-level ozone. The latter protects the Earth from much harmful radiation. At the same time, accumulated pollutants, notably carbon dioxide, have increased the green-house effect by trapping heat in the atmosphere, threatening a warming of global average temperatures. Scientists are now broadly in agreement that global warming (that is, human-induced recent global warming) is a reality. The dangers are the unpredictable effects of alterations to global climate patterns, but also the raising of sea levels caused largely by a melting of polar ice. Average world temperatures are expected to have risen by 1.5°C by the year 2025, with a 20 cm/7.8 in rise in sea level.

During August 2000 a US researcher claimed that the ice cap at the North Pole had completely melted for the first time in 50 million years and had been replaced by a mile-wide area of ocean. Other Arctic scientists, however, argue that the emergence of ice-free areas is not new and that it has been happening for thousands of years. What seems certain though is that the extent of open water during summer is increasing, as is the thinning of the Arctic ice. Clearly global warming will continue to be a great cause for concern during the 21st century.

Evolution of human origins

Even though earlier biologists, most notably Lamarck in 1809, had postulated various methods of evolution and the descent of humans from primates it was not until the last decades of the 19th century that evolution began to enter into the mainstream of biological thought and research. Since then evolution has become very much a central skeleton supporting many varied branches of biological research and spawning disciplines such as human biology, rooted in physical and cultural anthropology, anatomy, physiology, and genetics. Thus, in the 20th century, our own species, although obviously unique and special, was no longer regarded as separate from the rest of life and evolutionary processes, and biologists increasingly applied evolutionary principles to many different areas of their research, perhaps most notably in ecology and animal behaviour. In 1859, with the publication of *On the Origin Of Species by Means of Natural Selection or the Preservation Of Favoured Races in the Struggle for Life* (*The Origin of Species*, for short), Darwin revolutionized our understanding of evolution.

In 1912 German meteorologist and geophysiscist Alfred Wegener (1880–1930) proposed his theory of continental drift, which we now know has extremely important implications for the distribution of life on Earth. His ideas, however, were almost completely ignored until the 1960s, but now the theory of continental drift plays a huge role in our understanding of the current distribution of species diversity.

Indeed Darwin's theory of natural selection was not generally accepted until the early 1930s, when the findings of the geneticists and evolutionary biologists began to be reconciled. In 1930, the English geneticist Ronald Fisher (1890–1962) published *The Genetical Theory of Natural Selection*, in which he synthesized Mendelian genetics and Darwinian evolution. This synthesis was also due in no small part to Ukrainian-born US geneticist Theodosius Dobzhansky (1900–1975), who was both naturalist and geneticist. In 1937 he distilled his thinking in the seminal work *Genetics and the Origin of Species*. Slightly later, during the 1940s, a group of scientists, including Theodosius Dobzhansky, Ernst Mayr, G Ledyard Stebbins, and George Gaylord Simpson, brought together ideas from many different fields such as palaeontology, genetics, and taxonomy. The result of this amalgamation was a new theory of evolution that is now known as the evolutionary (or modern) synthesis. Although some of its early ideas have been modified and some evolutionary biologists are still challenging its claims and assumptions, the modern synthesis had a profound effect upon 20th-century thinking and biological research.

Fossils of early humans

This century has seen major discoveries of human fossils, which have helped to shed light on the evolution of our own species and also provided us with a famous scientific hoax. Around the turn of the 20th century, fossils of a species called *Homo erectus* (Java Man) were discovered. This human-like creature (hominid) lived between 0.5 and 1.5 million years ago. Just after the start of the 20th century the first molar tooth of 'Peking Man' was found, but a definite site of human origin still remained unclear because of a lack of substantial evidence. Then, in 1912, the theory that humans originated in the east was placed in serious doubt because the apparent fossilized remains of an ancient Pleistocene hominid were reported from the Piltdown quarries in Sussex by the amateur naturalist Charles Dawson. During the next two decades more hominid fossils were discovered in Africa and China. During this time some of the major discoveries were made by English anthropologist and archaeologist Mary Leakey (1913–1996), including a form from Africa that was about 1.6 million years old and was named as the separate genus *Australopithecus*. This hominid was thought to have lived between about 1 and 2 million years ago. Since the 1950s, even older forms of *Australopithecus* have come to light in Africa. The controversy concerning the authenticicty of the Piltdown man continued until 1953 when it was finally declared to be a deliberate fraud.

More recently, in 1994, *A. ramidus* has been dated at 4.4 million years old. This form was probably mainly vegetarian and lived in a woodland habitat. Like humans, it walked upright on its hind legs. In the 1960s and 70s, a form regarded as intermediate between the modern human (*Homo sapiens*) and *Australopithecus* was found in Africa. This was named in 1964, by Louis Leakey, Philip Tobias, and John Napier, Handy Man (*Homo habilis*), after its apparent use of stone tools. The fossils came from the now famous Olduvai Gorge in Tanzania, and have been dated at between 1.6 and 2 million years old. Various further finds of *Homo erectus* (named after its human-like upright stance) have been made, in Africa and in Europe, mainly in northern Kenya, but also in Algeria, Morocco, Ethiopia, and South Africa. The most likely story emerging is that this form originated in Africa, then spread to Europe and Asia.

Molecular evolution

Homo erectus probably used tools made of wood, such as hand axes, and were hunters and gatherers with a mixed diet. The techniques of genetics and biochemistry were also applied to physical anthropology, and analyses of protein and DNA from fossils and living humans and apes were undertaken as early as 1972 when DNA hybridization experiments suggested that chimpanzees were the closest living relatives to humans. Subsequent and more sophisticated genetic analyses have confirmed that modern humans are more closely related to chimpanzees and bonobos (pygmy chimpanzees) than either are to gorillas, gibbons, and orang utans. They also helped shed light on the evolutionary pathways on the fossil hominid line. Analysis of DNA and fossils suggests that modern humans are only a few hundred thousand years old, and that the evolutionary split between humans and apes occurred between 5 and 8 million years ago, probably in Africa. Our own species, *Homo sapiens* (Wise Man) emerged as recently as around 400,000 years ago. All living peoples are closely related, and probably share a common ancestor in Africa. A form of human, *Homo neanderthalensis*, known as Neanderthal Man (from the Neander valley in Germany where the first fossils were discovered) evolved in Europe around 200,000 years ago. A genetic analysis carried out on DNA extracted from fossil Neanderthal bones indicated in 1997 that Neanderthals shared a common ancestor with modern humans no later than 600,000 years ago, and proved conclusively that they were not our direct ancestors but represent a separate evolutionary line.

Eugenics – abuse of science

The influx of evolutionary thinking into human biology has not been without its problems, however, and most notoriously these have been applied to aspects of racial differences, and in the pseudo-science of eugenics. Since humans have so clearly evolved, can the 'quality' of the species be improved? This is a question that has been asked by many people, and distorted sometimes for socio-political ends. It was Darwin's cousin Francis Galton (1822–1911) who first coined the term 'eugenics', suggesting that selection be used to improve humankind, to the benefit of future generations of people. Sadly, most attempts to do so have been disastrous and misguided. There are a number of reasons why eugenics is undesirable, not least the undemocratic nature of the processes that would be required – who is to decide which individuals deserve to contribute their genes to the future?

We now realize that such aims are not beneficial, and that to function effectively human society needs a rich mixture of individuals of different genetic makeup. Thankfully perhaps, eugenic improvement is probably impossible, and is now largely discredited. Modern human society operates largely outside the constraints of natural selection, and the human gene pool is highly variable. Nevertheless, our increasing knowledge of genetically based disorders does allow voluntary decisions to be taken, for example by parents who may be carrying certain genes that markedly increase the likelihood of their having a disabled child. This could be seen as a kind of voluntary, limited form of eugenics.

Extinction and the discovery of new species

More than 99.9% of all evolutionary lines that once existed on Earth have become extinct, so extinction has loomed large in the history of life on Earth, and continues to feature in the natural world today. On the other hand, our knowledge of the natural world remains so sparse that species are still being discovered and described.

Discoveries by palaeontologists and geologists have helped to explain the apparently catastrophic extinctions which seem to have occurred from time to time in the distant past. The best known of these was the relatively sudden demise of the dinosaurs towards the end of the Cretaceous period. Analysis of a clay layer in deposits dated at the boundary of the Cretaceous and Tertiary periods by US physicists Walter and Luis Alvarez in 1980 revealed unusually rich traces of the heavy metal iridium. It was then found that this enriched iridium layer was present in deposits of similar age worldwide. The Alvarezes proposed the theory that this was caused by the impact on the Earth of a large asteroid, which might have had other ecological effects and possibly explain the sudden extinction of many creatures, including the dinosaurs. David Raup and John Sepkoski, Jr, looked at other mass extinctions of the past, and found that these were periodic, happening around every 26 million years. They developed the theory that something periodically disturbed the cloud of comets (known as the Oort cloud) at the edge of our Solar System, causing some of the comets to fall towards the Sun, occasionally hitting the Earth or other planets.

Humans, however, are having a notable effect upon their environment and we are undoubtedly causing many species to become prematurely extinct. International attempts to protect species began in 1948 when UN officials formed the International Union for the Protection of Nature, which was later renamed the International Union for the Conservation of Nature and Natural Resources (IUCN). The IUCN promotes worldwide conservation and gathers information on endangered species that is published in the Red Data Book.

The next major step forward took place in 1975, when ten nations signed the Convention on International Trade in Endangered Species of Wild Fauna and Flora (CITES). This agreement regulates trade in wildlife and prohibits the international sale of endangered species or products derived from them, such as ivory and furs. By 1995, 128 nations had joined CITES.

Some extinctions, however, have been actively sought; for example, in 1980 the World Health Assembly officially declared the world to be free from endemic smallpox after a programme of vaccination.

At the beginning of the 21st century, new species of animals and plants are still being discovered and described. Expeditions to tropical rainforests routinely find undescribed insects, notably beetles, but there have also been recent discoveries of new vertebrates. One of the most exciting animal discoveries in the 20th century was that of the coelacanth, *Latermeria chalumnae*, in 1938 off the coast of southern Africa by Marjorie Courtney-Latimer. Coelacanths, sometimes described as 'living fossils', represent an ancient order of fishes believed to be extinct for about 70 million years. These fish generated much scientific interest because, unlike all other species of fish living today, the structure of the bones in their caudal fins is the same as the animal group that gave rise to the land vertebrates – amphibians, reptiles, birds, and mammals – some 350 million years ago. An extensive search programme was undertaken to try to find the source population, although it was not until 1952 that coelacanths were rediscovered off the Comoro Islands to the north of Madagascar. Since then some 200 other specimens have been caught and there are fears that the demand for scientific specimens may be endangering this population. Now active conservation measures are in place to protect the future of this important link to the past.

A new population of coelacanths was identified in 1998 by at least two specimens caught off North Sulawesi, Indonesia, some 10,000 km from the Comoro Islands. The observed specimens appear identical to the Comoran coelacanth, except that they are brown rather than blue and possess gold flecks on their sides, although genetic comparisons appear to confirm the Indonesian fish to be new species of coelacanth, *Latimeria menadoensis*. The Indonesian authorities are also enforcing conservation measures, with only by-catches being kept for scientific research. Because much of the marine realm, especially in the deep sea, still remains to be explored, it is perhaps not surprising that new discoveries of large animals are still being made, such as a new species of whale that was described from Chile in 1996. By contrast, humans have encroached upon virtually all of the inhabitable land on the Earth and it is therefore extremely unlikely that we will make many more findings of large, land-dwelling animals. Despite this, however, several species of muntjac deer were found in Vietnam in the late 1990s.

How life on Earth began

The problem of how life began on the Earth has intrigued biologists for centuries, but in the 20th century some of the mystery of this process was removed. In the early 1900s, Swedish scientist Svante Arrhenius (1859–1927) suggested that life may have been seeded from elsewhere in the universe (panspermia), and this idea was revived most notably by English astronomer Fred Hoyle (1915–   ) in the 1970s. In the 1950s it was becoming clear that the early atmosphere of the Earth probably consisted mainly of methane, ammonia, hydrogen, and water, but with little free oxygen. By passing an electric current through this mixture in the laboratory, US chemist Stanley Miller (1930–   ) produced at least 25 different amino acids, the precursors of the proteins that are so central to living things. However, the discovery of DNA as the central, and probably in some sense ancestral, molecule of life made it hard to see how life could have evolved from a soup of these early chemicals. How could this mixture organize itself into the complexity required for replication? Most biologists now agree that RNA (ribonucleic acid – a simpler form of DNA) probably formed at some stage and led to the evolution of simple replicating organisms, although no one has yet explained how this might have happened. So, although advances have been made in the last century, speculation remains on this fundamental topic in biology. What we do know is that the earliest forms of life were simple, single-celled bacteria, dating from 3.5 billion years ago. From these organisms, the whole of the rest of life on Earth gradually evolved. Although the mechanism and possible routes for evolution are generally agreed and understood, we still do not know precisely how the whole process began.

'Genomic Era'

The ability to sequence the entire genetic makeup of any organism (its 'genome') quickly and effectively gave rise to the 'Genomic Era'. Sequences are now catalogued in online databases and thus the future challenge is for computer scientists and biologists to begin the daunting task of using and understanding these data. Analysis of such large datasets has been enhanced by the development of the new field of bioinformatics – an integration of mathematics and computer algorithms to process biological data. For example, bioinformaticists are attempting to identify genes and their roles, unravel the network of interacting genes in a particular enzyme pathway, and also predict the complex, three-dimensional structure of the protein that a particular gene codes for directly from the sequence data. With an increased understanding of the interactions between genes and their enzyme products it is hoped that medicines can be optimized according to a person's individual genetic profile; research into this field has, of course, led to another new scientific discipline – pharmaco-genomics. Although it has long been realized that people show different positive responses and side-effects to certain medicines, it is only since the genomic era that we have been able to gather relevant data. The next phase of analysing the complex interactions between genes and drugs will hope-fully result in an increase in drug efficiency and also prevent many of the thousands of unnecessary deaths that take place each year due to adverse reactions to pharmaceutical treatment.

Martin Walters and Phill Watts

2   Chronology

1900

Dutch geneticist Hugo Marie de Vries, German botanist Carl Erich Correns, and Austrian botanist Erich Tschermak von Seysenegg, simultaneously and independently, rediscover the Austrian monk Gregor Mendel's 1865 work on heredity.

The Kral Collection of micro-organisms is established in Prague, Czechoslovakia; the first collection of pure cultures of micro-organisms to be used for research purposes.

1901

Austrian immunologist Karl Landsteiner discovers the ABO blood group system.

English biochemist Frederick Gowland Hopkins isolates the amino acid tryptophan.

Japanese-born US biochemist Jokichi Takamine first synthesizes the heart stimulant adrenaline (epinephrine) from the suprarenal gland. It is the first pure hormone to be synthesized from natural sources.

1902

British physiologists William Bayliss and Ernest Starling discover that a substance, which they call secretin, is released into the bloodstream by cells in the duodenum. It stimulates the secretion of digestive juices by the pancreas and is the first hormone to be discovered.

French physiologist Charles Richet discovers cases of acute sensitiveness to antidiphtheria serum, which he calls 'anaphylaxis'. His work leads to a greater understanding of problems of asthma, hay fever, and other allergic reactions.

German chemists Emil Fischer and Franz Hofmeister discover that proteins are polypeptides consisting of amino acids.

1902–1904

US geneticist Walter Sutton and the German zoologist Theodor Boveri found the chromosomal theory of inheritance when they show that cell division is connected with heredity.

1903

Russian physiologist Ivan Pavlov describes learning by conditioning. He trains dogs to expect food when they hear a bell and eventually they salivate every time the bell rings.

1904

Spanish physiologist Santiago Ramón y Cajal demonstrates that the neuron is the basis of the nervous system.

c. 1905

English biochemist Frederick Gowland Hopkins shows that the amino acid tryptophan and other essential amino acids cannot be manufactured from other nutrients but must be supplied in the diet.

1905

Danish botanist Wilhelm Johannsen introduces the terms 'genotype' and 'phenotype' to explain how genetically identical plants differ in external characteristics.

English physiologist Ernest Starling coins the word 'hormone' (from Greek *hormon* 'impel') to describe chemicals that stimulate an organ from a distance.

Scottish physiologist John Scott Haldane discovers that breathing is regulated by the concentration of carbon dioxide in the blood affecting the respiratory centre of the brain.

1906

British biochemists Arthur Harden and William Young discover catalysis among enzymes.

English biologist William Bateson introduces the term 'genetics'.

Russian botanist Mikhail Semyonovich Tsvet develops chromatography for separating plant pigments.

1907

English biochemists Frederick Gowland Hopkins and Walter Fletcher show that working muscle accumulates lactic acid, which leads to a greater understanding of the chemistry of muscular contraction.

German chemist Emil Fischer publishes *Researches on the Chemistry of Proteins*, in which he describes the synthesis of amino acid chains in proteins.

US zoologist Granville Ross Harrison develops the first successful animal tissue cultures; they prove vital in cancer research.

1908

English mathematician Godfrey Hardy and German physician Wilhelm Weinberg establish the mathematical basis for population genetics, now known as the Hardy–Weinberg equilibrium.

1909

Danish botanist Wilhelm Ludvig Johannsen introduces the term 'gene'.

English biologist William Bateson publishes *Mendel's Principles of Genetics*, which introduces Mendelian genetics to the English-speaking world.

German botanist Carl Correns shows that certain hereditary characteristics of plants are determined by factors in the cytoplasm of the female sex cell. It is the first example of non-Mendelian heredity.

Russian-born US chemist Phoebus Levene discovers D-ribose, the five-carbon sugar that forms the basis of RNA.

1910

US geneticist Thomas Hunt Morgan discovers that certain inherited characteristics of the fruit fly *Drosophila melanogaster* are sex linked. He later argues that because all sex-related characteristics are inherited together they are linearly arranged on the X-chromosome.

1912

English biochemist Frederick Gowland Hopkins publishes the results of his experiments that prove that 'accessory substances' (vitamins) are essential for health and growth and that their absence may lead to diseases such as scurvy or beriberi. In the same year, Polish-born US biochemist Casimir Funk discovers that pigeons fed on rice polishings can be cured of beriberi, and suggests that the absence of a vital nitrogen-containing substance known as an amine causes such diseases. He calls these substances 'vitamines'.

1913

German chemist Richard Willstätter determines the composition of chlorophyll.

US biochemist Elmer Verner McCollum isolates vitamin A.

US physiologist John Abel invents the first artificial kidney.

1914

German biochemist Fritz Albert Lepmann explains the role of adenosine triphosphate (ATP) as the carrier of chemical energy from the oxidation of food to the energy consumption processes in the cells.

US biochemist Edward Kendall isolates the hormone thyroxine from the thyroid gland. It regulates metabolism by stimulating all cells to consume oxygen.

1915

US geneticists Thomas Hunt Morgan, Alfred Sturtevant, Calvin Bridges, and Hermann Muller publish *The Mechanism of Mendelian Heredity*, which outlines their work on the fruit fly *Drosophila* demonstrating that genes can be mapped on chromosomes.

1917

US researcher Donald Jones discovers the 'double cross' technique of hybridizing corn; four inbred lines, instead of two, are crossbred.

1918

Scottish geneticist Ronald Fisher shows that both genes and environmental factors affect an individual's behaviour.

1919

Austrian zoologist Karl von Frisch discovers that bees communicate the location of nectar through wagging body movements and rhythmic dances.

Austrian zoologist Karl von Frisch, whose most renowned work concerned communication among honey bees. By marking bees and following their movements in special observation hives, he found that foraging bees that had returned from a food source often perform a dance, either a relatively simple round dance or a more complex waggle dance.
Bettmann/CORBIS

1920

Russian botanist Nikolay Ivanovich Vavilov states that a plant's place of origin is the region where its greatest diversity is found. He identifies 12 world centres of plant origin.

1921

Canadian microbiologist Félix-Hubert D'Hérelle publishes *Le Bactériophage, son rôle dans l'immunité/The Bacteriophage, Its Role in Immunity*, in which he describes the discovery of bacteriophages, viruses that infect bacteria.

Canadian physiologists Frederick Banting, Charles Best, and John James MacLeod isolate insulin. A diabetic patient in Toronto, Canada, receives the first insulin injection.

Scottish bacteriologist Alexander Fleming discovers the antibacterial enzyme lysozyme, which is found in tears and saliva.

US botanist Edward Murray East develops a high-yield hybrid corn.

1922

English biochemist Frederick Gowland Hopkins isolates glutathione and demonstrates its vital role in the cell's utilization of oxygen.

French surgeon Alexis Carrel discovers white blood cells (leucocytes).

US chemist Herbert McLean Evans discovers vitamin E.

1923

French bacteriologists Albert Calmette and Camille Guérin develop the tuberculosis vaccine, known as Bacillus Calmette-Guérin (BCG), and use it to vaccinate newborns at a hospital in Paris, France.

1924

English physiologist Ernest Starling finds that bicarbonates, chlorides, glucose, and water excreted by the kidney are reabsorbed by the glomeruli at the lower end of the kidney tubules.

1925

English geneticist Ronald Fisher publishes *Statistical Methods for Research Workers*, in which he demonstrates experimental techniques and statistical methods to be used in biology.

US geneticists Thomas Hunt Morgan, Alfred Sturtevant, and Calvin Blackman Bridges publish the results of their genetic experiments with the fruit fly *Drosophila melanogaster*, showing that genes can be mapped onto chromosomes.

US pathologist George Whipple demonstrates that iron is the most important factor involved in the formation of red blood cells.

1926

US biochemist Elmer McCollum isolates vitamin D and uses it to successfully treat rickets.

US biochemist James Sumner crystallizes the enzyme urease. It is the first enzyme to be crystallized. Sumner's achievement demonstrates that enzymes are proteins.

US geneticist Thomas Hunt Morgan publishes *The Theory of the Gene*, in which he demonstrates that the gene will form the foundation of all future genetic research.

US physiologist John Jacob Abel isolates and crystallizes insulin.

1927

Austrian-born US immunologist Karl Landsteiner discovers the M and N blood groups.

US geneticist Hermann Muller uses X-rays to cause mutations in the fruit fly. It permits a greater understanding of the mechanisms of variation.

1928

English neurologists Edgar Douglas Adrian and Charles Sherrington publish *The Basis of Sensation*, which discusses how the nerves transmit messages to and from the brain.

Scottish bacteriologist Alexander Fleming discovers penicillin when he notices that the mould *Penicillium notatum*, which has invaded a culture of staphylococci, inhibits the bacteria's growth.

US biochemist Charles King and Hungarian biochemist Albert Szent-Györgyi, independently discover vitamin C.

1929

British neurologist Edgar Douglas Adrian, using an ultra-sensitive galvanometer, is able to follow a single impulse in a single nerve fibre. It aids understanding of the physical basis of sensation.

German biochemist Adolf Butenandt and, simultaneously and independently, US biochemist Edward Doisy isolate the hormone oestrone, which is involved in the growth and development of females.

1930

English geneticist Ronald Fisher publishes *The Genetical Theory of Natural Selection* in which he synthesizes Mendelian genetics and Darwinian evolution.

Swiss biochemist Paul Karrer formulates the structure of betacarotene, the precursor to vitamin A.

US biochemist Edward Doisy crystallizes the hormone oestriol, the first oestrogen hormone to be crystallized.

US biochemist John Northrop crystallizes pepsin and trypsin, demonstrating that they are proteins.

1931

German biochemist Adolf Butenandt isolates the male sex hormone androgen.

US biologist Ernest Goodpasture grows viruses in eggs, making possible the production of vaccines for such viral diseases as polio.

1932

German-born British biochemist Hans Krebs discovers the urea cycle, in which ammonia is turned into urea in mammals.

1933

Canadian biologist Ludwig von Bertalanffy writes *Theoretical Biology* in which he attempts to develop a common methodological approach to all sciences based on the tenets of organismic biology.

1934

German biochemist Adolph Butenandt isolates the female sex hormone progesterone.

Norwegian biochemist Asbjörn Fölling discovers the genetic metabolic defect phenylketonuria, which can cause retardation; his discovery stimulates research in biochemical genetics and the development of screening tests for carriers of deleterious genes.

1935

Austrian zoologist Konrad Lorenz founds the discipline of ethology by describing the learning behaviour of young ducklings; visual and auditory stimuli from the parent object cause them to 'imprint' on the parent.

US biochemist Edward Calvin Kendall isolates the steroid hormone cortisone from the adrenal cortex.

1936

US chemist Robert Runnels Williams synthesizes vitamin B_1 (thiamine).

Vitamin E is obtained in pure form by the US biochemists Herbert Evans and Oliver and Gladys Emerson.

1937

The Austrian zoologist Konrad Lorenz becomes editor of the *Zeitschrift für Tierpsychologie/Journal of Animal Psychology*, published by the newly formed German Society for Animal Psychology. His work as editor plays a major role in founding the discipline of ethology.

The French microbiologist Max Theiler develops a vaccine against yellow fever; it is the first antiviral vaccine.

The German-born British biochemist Hans Krebs describes the citric acid cycle in cells, which converts sugars, fats, and proteins into carbon dioxide, water, and energy – the 'Krebs cycle'.

1938

A coelacanth, an ancient fish assumed to be extinct, is discovered in the Indian Ocean.

1939

The US microbiologist René J Dubos is the first to search systematically for, and discover, natural antibiotics. He looks for soil bacteria that kill other bacteria and discovers the antibiotics gramicidin and tyrocidine.

1940

Austrian-born US immunologist Karl Landsteiner and US physician and immunohaematologist Alexander Wiener discover the rhesus (Rh) factor in blood.

The US physiologist Herbert M Evans uses radioactive iodine to prove that iodine is used by the thyroid gland.

1941

US biologist George Beadle and US microbiologist Edward Tatum establish the one-gene–one-enzyme hypothesis, showing that one gene is responsible for the production of one specific enzyme.

1944

The British chemists Archer J P Martin and Richard L M Synge separate amino acids by using a solvent in a column of silica gel. The beginnings of partition chromatography, the technique that leads to further advances in chemical, medical, and biological research.

1945

Scottish biochemist Alexander Fleming, German-born British biochemist Ernst Chain, and Australian pathologist Howard Florey share the Nobel Prize for Physiology or Medicine for their discovery of penicillin.

1946

The US biologists Max Delbrück and Alfred D Hershey discover recombinant DNA (deoxyribonucleic acid) when they observe that genetic material from different viruses can combine to create new viruses.

US geneticists Joshua Lederberg and Edward Lawrie Tatum pioneer the field of bacterial genetics with their discovery that sexual reproduction occurs in the bacterium *Escherichia coli*.

1947

English physiologists Alan Hodgkin and Andrew Huxley insert microelectrodes into the giant nerve fibres of the squid *Loligo forbesi* to discover the chemical and electrical properties of the transmission of nerve impulses.

The US educator and agricultural chemist Karl Paul Link develops the rat poison warfarin; an anticoagulant, it causes rats to bleed to death.

1948

Soviet biologist Trofim D Lysenko outlaws orthodox genetics in favour of 'Michurin' genetics in the USSR. Purges of geneticists (and assertions that, for example, wheat plants can produce rye seeds) obstruct agricultural development.

Swiss biochemist Paul Müller receives the Nobel Prize for Physiology or Medicine for his work on the properties of DDT.

The Swiss physiologist Walter Hess describes using fine electrodes to stimulate or destroy specific regions of the brain in cats and dogs; it allows him to discover the role played by various parts of the brain.

US biologist Alfred Mirsky discovers ribonucleic acid (RNA) in chromosomes.

5 October
IUCN (International Union for the Conservation of Nature) is established as the International Union for the Protection of Nature, or IUPN.

1949

US researchers synthesize adrenocorticotropic hormone (ACTH) which the pituitary gland secrets to stimulate the adrenal glands.

1952

English biophysicist Rosalind Franklin uses X-ray diffraction to study the structure of DNA. She suggests that its sugar-phosphate backbone is on the outside – an important clue that leads to the elucidation of the structure of DNA the following year.

The Austrian zoologist Konrad Lorenz publishes *King Solomon's Ring*, in which he argues that natural selection works on behavioural as well as physical characteristics.

US biologists Alfred Day Hershey and Martha Chase use radioactive tracers to show that bacteriophages infect bacteria with DNA and not protein.

1953

British biochemists Archer Martin and A T James, develop gas chromatography, a technique for separating the elements of a gaseous compound through differential absorption in a permeable solid.

English biochemist Frederick Sanger determines the structure of the insulin molecule. The largest protein molecule to have its chemical structure determined to date, it is essential in the laboratory synthesis of insulin.

The US biochemist Stanley Lloyd Miller shows that amino acids can be formed when simulated lightning is passed through containers of water, methane, ammonia, and hydrogen – conditions under which life may have arisen.

The US physiologists Eugene Aserinsky and Nathaniel Kleitman discover the rapid eye movements (REM) that characterize a very active period of sleep. It causes a revolution in the understanding of sleep processes since it is at odds with prevailing concepts of sleep which are thought to be quiet.

25 April
English molecular biologist Francis Crick and US biologist James Watson announce the discovery of the double helix structure of DNA, the basic material of heredity. They also theorize that if the strands are separated then each can form the template for the synthesis of an identical DNA molecule. It is perhaps the most important discovery in biology.

1954

US entomologist Edward Knipling air-drops thousands of sterilized male screwworm flies over the Caribbean island of Curaçao in an effort to control the pest. The insect is wiped out within six months and the test is followed by two successful experiments in the USA. Biological control of pests continues to be developed.

US scientists Gregory G Pincus, Hudson Hoagland, and Min-Cheh Chang, of the Worcester Foundation, develop an oral contraceptive using the hormone norethisterone.

February
US physician Jonas E Salk, developer of the poliomyelitis vaccine, inoculates children against polio in Pittsburgh, Pennsylvania.

1955

English biochemist Dorothy Hodgkin elucidates the structure of vitamin B_{12}, a liver extract used in the treatment of pernicious anaemia.

Spanish-born US molecular biologist Severo Ochoa discovers polynucleotide phosphorylase, the enzyme responsible for the synthesis of RNA (ribonucleic acid), which allows him to synthesize RNA.

The US geneticists Joshua Lederberg and Norton Zinder discover that some viruses carry part of the chromosome of one bacterium to another; called transduction it becomes an important tool in genetics research.

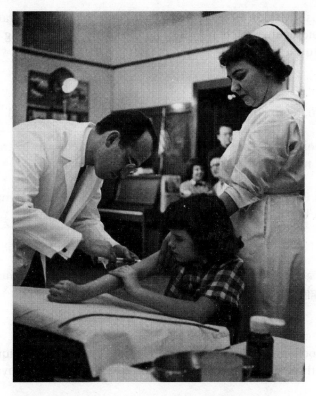

US physician and microbiologist Jonas Salk injects a child with the Salk polio vaccine during the 1954 field trials involving nearly 2 million five to nine year olds.
CORBIS–Bettmann

April

US physician Jonas E Salk proclaims the success of his poliomyelitis vaccine, which has been tested in 44 states. It is released for general use in the USA.

1956

Romanian-born US biologist George Palade discovers ribosomes, which contain RNA (ribonucleic acid).

US biochemist Arthur Kornberg, using radioactively-tagged nucleotides, discovers that the bacteria *Escherichia coli* uses an enzyme, now known as DNA polymerase, to replicate DNA (deoxyribonucleic acid). It allows him to synthesize DNA in the test tube.

US biologists Maklon Hoagland and Paul Zamecnik discover transfer RNA (ribonucleic acid), which transfers amino acids, the building blocks of proteins, to the correct site on the messenger RNA.

1957

Gibberellin, a growth-producing hormone in plants, is isolated.

Russian-born US engineer Vladimir Zworykin patents an instrument for observing microscopic organisms on a television screen.

Worcester Foundation scientist Gregory Pincus and Boston gynaecologist John Rock begin a birth control pill trial in Puerto Rico.

1959

The Austrian-born British biochemist Max Perutz determines the structure of haemoglobin.

1960

English biochemist John Kendrew, using X-ray diffraction techniques, elucidates the three-dimensional structure of the muscle protein myoglobin.

German chemist K H Hofman synthesizes pituitary hormone.

The English anthropologist Jane Goodall discovers that chimpanzees can make tools, something only humans were thought capable of. She watches a chimpanzee fashion a blade of grass into a probe that can be poked into a termite mound to remove termites.

US biochemist Robert Woodward and German biochemist Martin Strell independently synthesize chlorophyll.

1961

English molecular biologist Francis Crick and South African chemist Sydney Brenner discover that each base triplet on the DNA strand codes for a specific amino acid in a protein molecule.

French biochemists François Jacob and Jacques Monod discover messenger ribonucleic acid (mRNA), which transfers genetic information to the ribosomes, where proteins are synthesized.

1962

US biologist Rachel Carson, in her book *Silent Spring*, draws attention to the dangers of chemical pesticides.

1963

US biochemist Robert Woodward synthesizes the plant chemical colchicine.

1964

The living brain of a rhesus monkey is isolated from its body by neurosurgeons at Cleveland General Hospital, Ohio.

US zoologist William Hamilton recognizes the importance of altruistic behaviour in animals, paving the way for the development of sociobiology.

US biologist, writer, and conservationist Rachel Carson whilst working at the US Bureau of Fisheries where she had gone to work after family commitments to her widowed mother and orphaned nieces had forced her to abandon her academic career. She wrote in her spare time and was eventually able to become a full-time writer. Underwood & Underwood/CORBIS

1965

Kuru and Creutzfeld-Jakob disease are transmitted to primates by the US virologists Daniel Gajdusek and Clarence Gibbs.

1966

Enzyme electrophoresis begins to be used to study genetic variation in natural populations following two landmark papers on genetic variation, one by US geneticists Richard Lewontin and John Hobby, and one by Harry Harris.

Molecular biologists discover that DNA is not confined to chromosomes but is also contained within the mitochondria.

1967

The US biochemist Marshall Nirenberg establishes that mammals, amphibians, and bacteria all share a common genetic code.

1968

October

US geneticists Mark Ptashne and Walter Gilbert separately identify the first repressor genes.

1969

US geneticist Jonathan Beckwith and associates at the Harvard Medical School isolate a single gene for the first time.

15 February

English physiologist Robert Edwards of the Cambridge Physiological Laboratory, Cambridge, England, completes the first in vitro fertilization of human egg cells.

1970

US biochemists Howard Temin and David Baltimore separately discover the enzyme reverse transcriptase, which allows some cancer viruses to transfer their RNA to the DNA of their hosts turning them cancerous – a reversal of the common pattern in which genetic information always passes from DNA to RNA.

US geneticist Hamilton Smith discovers type II restriction enzyme that breaks the DNA strand at predictable places, making it an invaluable tool in recombinant DNA technology.

September
Indian-born US biochemist Har Gobind Khorana assembles an artificial yeast gene from its chemical components.

1971
Polish-born US endocrinologist Andrew Schally isolates the luteinizing hormone-releasing hormone (LH-RH), essential to human ovulation.

The English primatologist Jane Goodall publishes *In the Shadow of Man*, a study of chimpanzee behaviour.

6 January
Choh Hao Li and associates at the University of California Medical Centre announce the synthesis of the human growth hormone somatotrophin.

1972
The French mathematician René Frédéric Thom formulates catastrophe theory, an attempt to describe biological processes mathematically.

The USA restricts the use of DDT because it is discovered that it thins the eggshells of predatory birds, lowering their reproductive rates.

The Venezuelan-born US immunologist Baruj Benacerraf and the US microbiologist Hugh O'Neill McDevitt show immune response to be genetically determined.

US microbiologist Daniel Nathans uses a restriction enzyme that splits DNA (deoxyribonucleic acid) molecules to produce a genetic map of the monkey virus (SV40), the simplest virus known to produce cancer; it is the first application of these enzymes to an understanding of the molecular basis of cancer.

US palaeontologists Stephen Jay Gould and Nils Eldridge propose the punctuated equilibrium model – the idea that evolution progresses in fits and starts rather than at a uniform rate.

1973
Representatives from 80 nations sign the Convention on International Trade in Endangered Species (CITES) that prohibits trade in 375 endangered species of plants and animals and the products derived from them, such as ivory; the USA does not sign.

1974

The British-born Danish immunologist Niels Jerne proposes a network theory of the immune system.

The Parque Nacional da Amazonia is established in Brazil; with an area of 10,000 sq km/4,000 sq mi, it preserves a large area of tropical rainforest.

July
The National Academy of Sciences advises a worldwide ban on recombinant DNA (deoxyribonucleic acid) experiments on the bacterium *Escherichia coli* for fear that a more virulent form may be created.

1975

Argentine immunologist César Milstein and German immunologist Georges Köhler develop the first monoclonal antibodies – lymphocyte and myeloma tumour cell hybrids that are cloned to secrete unlimited amounts of specific antibodies – in Cambridge, England.

British scientist Derek Brownhall produces the first clone of a rabbit, in Oxford, England.

Swiss scientists publish details of the first chemically directed synthesis of insulin.

The gel-transfer hybridization technique for the detection of specific DNA (deoxyribonucleic acid) sequences is developed; it is a key development in genetic engineering.

US physiologist John Hughes discovers endorphins (morphine-like chemicals) in the brain.

24 February
The Asilomar conference on recombinant DNA in Pacific Grove, California, USA is held, attended by 153 participants from 16 countries. The Recombinant DNA Advisory Committee of the National Institutes of Health (RNA–NIH) is established, and the NIH guidelines for containment measures are issued.

1976

Japanese molecular biologist Susumu Tonegawa demonstrates that antibodies are produced by large numbers of genes working in combination.

The first prenatal diagnosis using a gene-specific probe in amniotic fluid is performed.

US biochemist Herbert Boyer and venture capitalist Robert Swanson found Genentech in San Francisco, California, the world's first genetic engineering company.

28 August
Indian-born US biochemist Har Gobind Khorana and his colleagues announce the construction of the first artificial gene to function naturally when inserted into a bacterial cell. This is a major breakthrough in genetic engineering.

1977

English biochemist Frederick Sanger describes the full sequence of 5,386 bases in the DNA of virus *phi*X174 in Cambridge, England; the first sequencing of an entire genome.

Scientists discover chemosynthetically based animal communities around sulphurous thermal springs deep under the sea near the Galápagos Islands, Ecuador.

Swedish neurologist Tomas Hökfelt discovers that most neurons contain not one but several neurotransmitters.

The USA signs the Convention on International Trade in Endangered Species (CITES).

UK biochemists Frederick Sanger and Alan Coulson and US molecular biologists Walter Gilbert and Allan Maxam develop a rapid gene-sequencing technique that uses gel electrophoresis.

US scientist Herbert Boyer, of the firm Genentech, fuses a segment of human DNA into the bacterium *Escherichia coli,* which begins to produce the human protein somatostatin; this is the first commercially produced genetically engineered product.

12 July
US medical researcher Raymond Damadian produces the first images of human tissues using an NMR (nuclear magnetic resonance) scanner; used to detect cancer and other diseases without the need for X-rays, the scanner is based on the fact that electromagnetic fields cause some atomic nuclei to align themselves. The scanners become commercially available in the USA in 1984.

1978

25 July

Louise Brown is born at Oldham Hospital, London, England; she is the first 'test tube' baby. Having been unable to remove a blockage from her mother's Fallopian tube, gynaecologist Patrick Steptoe and physiologist Robert Edwards removed an egg from her ovary, fertilized it with her husband's sperm, and re-implanted it in her uterus.

1980

A gene is transferred from one mouse to another by US geneticist Martin Cline and colleagues.

The US Supreme Court rules that genetically modified organisms can be patented.

May

The World Health Organization announces the eradication of smallpox.

1981

Chinese scientists make the first clone of a fish (a golden carp).

The US Food and Drug Administration grants permission to Eli Lilley and Co to market insulin produced by bacteria, the first genetically engineered product to go on sale.

US geneticists J W Gordon and F H Ruddle of the University of Ohio inject genes from one animal into the fertilized egg of a mouse that develop into mice with the foreign gene in many of the cells; the gene is then passed on to their offspring creating permanently altered (transgenic) animals; it is the first transfer of a gene from one animal species to another.

US geneticists Robert Weinberg, Geoffrey Cooper, and Michael Wigler discover that oncogenes (genes that cause cancer) are integrated into the genome of normal cells.

1982

Dolphins are discovered to possess magnetized tissues that aid in navigation; they are the first mammals discovered to have such tissues.

US geneticist Ralph Brinster of the University of Pennsylvania transfers the rat gene controlling the growth hormone somatotrophin into a mouse; the mouse grows to double its normal size.

US researcher Stanley Prusiner discovers prions (proteinaceous infectious particles); they are responsible for several neurological diseases including 'mad cow disease' (first identified in 1986).

1983

The US biologist Lynn Margulis discovers that cells with nuclei form by the synthesis of nonnucleated cells.

US biologists Andrew Murray and Jack Szostak create the first artificial chromosome; it is grafted onto a yeast cell.

April

US biochemist Kary Mullis invents the polymerase chain reaction (PCR); a method of multiplying genes or known sections of the DNA molecule a million times without the need for the living cell.

1984

Allan Wilson and Russell Higuchi of the University of California, Berkeley, USA, clone genes from an extinct animal, the quagga.

British geneticist Alec Jeffreys discovers that a core sequence of DNA is almost unique to each person; this examination of DNA, known as 'genetic fingerprinting', can be used in criminal investigations and to establish family relationships.

Robert Sinsheimer, the chancellor of the University of California at Santa Cruz, California, proposes that all human genes be mapped; the proposal eventually leads to the development of the Human Genome Project.

1985

French-born US endocrinologist Roger Guillemin discovers inhibin, which suppresses follicle-stimulating hormone secretion involved in male testicular function.

German researcher Bert Vallee and associates discover angiogenin, the factor which stimulates the growth of new blood vessels.

Researchers locate gene markers on chromosomes for cystic fibrosis and polycystic kidney disease.

The US zoologist Dian Fossey, who tried to protect endangered gorillas in Rwanda, is murdered. Poachers are suspected.

1987

German-born British geneticist Walter Bodmer and associates announce the discovery of a marker for a gene that causes cancer of the colon.

The development of the first bio-insecticides is announced in the USA; they eliminate insects without harming the environment.

The first genetically altered bacteria are released into the environment in the USA; they protect crops against frost.

US biomedical reasearcher David Page and associates announce the discovery of a gene that initiates the development of male features in mammals.

April

The US Patent and Trademark Office announces its intention to allow the patenting of animals produced by genetic engineering.

10 October

The *New York Times* announces Dr Helen Donis-Keller's mapping of all 23 pairs of human chromosomes, allowing the location of specific genes for the prevention and treatment of genetic disorders.

1988

The Human Genome Organization (HUGO) is established in Washington, DC, USA; scientists announce a project to compile a complete 'map' of human genes.

US researchers graft tissues from the bone marrow, spleen, thymus, and lymph nodes of human fetuses into mice lacking an immune system; the mice then develop an immune system identical to that of humans – a valuable tool in the development of vaccines.

1989

Researchers in Toronto, Canada, identify a gene responsible for cystic fibrosis.

The first visual image of a DNA molecule is obtained by US scientists.

The United Nations Environment Programme (UNEP) reports that the number of species, and the amount of genetic variation within individual species, is decreasing due to the rapid destruction of natural environments.

1990

A four-year-old girl in the USA has the gene for adenosine deaminase inserted into her DNA; she is the first person to receive gene therapy.

French geneticist Pierre Chambon and associates announce the discovery of a gene that may be important in the development of breast cancer.

1991

The British geneticists Peter Goodfellow and Robin Lovell-Badge discover the gene on the Y chromosome that determines sex.

1992

Sperm cells are discovered, by US physician David Garbers of the University of Texas, to have odour receptors and may therefore reach eggs by detecting scent.

The US biologist Philip Leder receives a patent for the first genetically engineered animal, the oncomouse, which is sensitive to carcinogens.

1994

A new species of kangaroo is discovered in Papua New Guinea. Known locally as the bondegezou, it weighs 15 kg/7 lb and is 1.2 m/3.9 ft in height.

The oldest surviving fungi are found as dormant spores in the hay lining the boots of the 'iceman' Ötzi who died 5,300 years ago and whose body was preserved in a glacier in the Alps (found in 1991).

May
The first genetically engineered food goes on sale in California and Chicago, Illinois. The 'Flavr Savr' tomato is produced by the US biotechnology company Calgene.

1995

A genetically engineered potato is developed in the USA that contains the gene for Bt toxin, a natural pesticide produced by the soil bacterium *Bacillus thuringiensis* (Bt). The potato plant produces Bt within its leaves. By 1997 over a quarter of a million acres of the potatoes are planted.

US scientists successfully germinate bacterial spores extracted from the gut of a bee fossilized in amber 40 million years ago.

1996

Palaeontologists from the Institute of Vertebrate Palaeontology and Palaeoanthropology in Beijing, China, discover the remains of a 135-million-year-old fossil bird in northeast China. Called the 'Confucius bird' (*Confusciusornis sactus*), it had a modern-looking beak with no teeth, unlike *Archaeopteryx*.

Researchers from the University of California discover anemones in the Bahamas that have been alive for 1,500 to 2,000 years – longer than any other known marine creature.

18 January
New Zealand ornithologist Gavin Hunt reveals that crows on the island of New Caledonia in the South Pacific make tools out of leaves and twigs which they use to reach insects in dead wood – something only chimpanzees and humans were thought capable of.

4 October
The World Conservation Union (IUCN) publishes the latest Red List of endangered species. Over 1,000 mammals are listed, far more than on previous lists. The organization believes it has underestimated the risks to habitats from pollution and that the number of endangered species is greater than previously thought.

1997
February
The US genetic scientist Don Wolf announces the production of monkeys cloned from embryos. It is a step closer to cloning humans and raises acute philosophical issues.

February
The US zoologists Bill Detrich and Kirk Malloy show that the increased ultraviolet radiation caused by the hole in the ozone layer above Antarctica kills large numbers of fish in the Southern Ocean. Because their transparent eggs and larvae stay near the surface for up to a year, they are exposed to the full force of the ultraviolet rays. It is the first time ozone depletion in the Antarctic has been shown to harm organisms larger than one-celled marine plants.

24 February
The US president Bill Clinton announces a ban on using federal funds to support human cloning research, and calls for a moratorium on this type

of scientific research. He also asks the National Bioethics Advisory Commission to review and issue a report on the ramifications that cloning would have on humans.

27 February
Scottish researcher Ian Wilmut of the Roslin Institute in Edinburgh, Scotland, announces that British geneticists have cloned an adult sheep. A cell was taken from the udder of the mother sheep and its DNA combined with an unfertilized egg that had had its DNA removed. The fused cells were grown in the laboratory and then implanted into the uterus of a surrogate mother sheep. The resulting lamb, Dolly, came from an animal that was six years old. This is the first time cloning has been achieved using cells other than reproductive cells. The news is met with international calls to prevent the cloning of humans.

16 May
US geneticists identify a gene *clock* in chromosome 5 in mice that regulates the circadian rhythm.

Dolly the sheep, the first animal to be cloned using adult body cells rather than reproductive cells. Roslin Institute

3 June

The US geneticist Huntington F Wilard constructs the first artificial human chromosome. He inserts telomeres (which consist of DNA and protein on the tips of chromosomes) and centromeres (specialized regions of DNA within a chromosome) removed from white blood cells, into human cancer cells which are then assembled into chromosomes about one-tenth the size of normal chromosomes. The artificial chromosome is successfully passed on to all daughter cells.

3 June

US computer scientists announce the construction of logic gates from DNA, which simulate the functions of an OR gate and an AND gate. Rather than responding to an electronic signal, the DNA gates respond to nucleotide sequences.

9–29 June

At the tenth Convention on International Trade in Endangered Species (CITES) convention in Harare, Zimbabwe, the elephant is downlisted to CITES Appendix II (vulnerable) and the ban on ivory exportation in Botswana, Namibia, and Zimbabwe is lifted.

27 June

US scientists at the National Human Genome Research Institute in Bethesda, Maryland, announce the discovery of a gene that causes Parkinson's disease. The gene produces a protein called alpha synuclein. When the instructions of the gene go wrong, the protein's structure is affected and this causes the build-up of deposits on brain cells that is usually seen in Parkinson's sufferers.

August

The US geneticist Craig Venter and colleagues publish the genome of the bacterium *Helicobacter pylori*, a bacterium that infects half the world's population and which is the leading cause of stomach ulcers. It is the sixth bacterium to have its genome published, but is clinically the most important. It has 1,603 putative genes, encoded in a single circular chromosome that is 1,667,867 nucleotide base-pairs of DNA long. Complete genomes are increasingly being published as gene-sequencing techniques improve.

4 August

The US researchers Sidney Altman, Cecilia Guerreir-Takada, and Reza Salavati discover a gene-transfer method of disabling the genes in disease organisms which allow them to neutralize common antibiotics. This makes the bacteria vulnerable, once again, to treatment with antibiotics and combats the growing problem of bacterial drug-resistance. The biomedical company Innovir Laboratories works on developing the process to combat viruses such as those responsible for hepatitis B and C.

7 August
The Canadian researcher Suzanne W Simard and colleagues announce the discovery that trees use mycorrhizae, the threadlike growths of fungi that infest their roots to connect the trees together underground to exchange food resources. It suggests that forest trees succeed as cooperative communities rather than competing individuals.

22 August
Scientists from the Worldwide Fund for Nature (WWF) announce the discovery of a new species of muntjac deer in Vietnam. A dwarf species weighing only about 16 kg/35 lb, it has antlers the length of a thumbnail and lives at altitudes of 457–914 m/1,500–3,000 ft.

18 September
The US geneticist Bert Vogelstein and colleagues demonstrate that the *p53* gene, which is activated by the presence of carcinogens, induces cells to commit suicide by stimulating them to produce large quantities of poisonous chemicals, called 'reactive oxygen species' (ROS). The cells literally poison themselves. It is perhaps the human body's most effective way of combating cancer. Many cancers consist of cells with a malfunctioning *p53* gene.

2 October
The UK scientists Moira Bruce and, independently, John Collinge, and their colleagues show that the new variant form of the brain-wasting Creutzfeldt-Jakob disease (CJD) in humans is the same disease as bovine spongiform encephalopathy (BSE or 'mad cow disease') in cows.

1998
7 January
Doctors meeting at the World Medical Association's conference in Hamburg, Germany, call for a worldwide ban on human cloning. US president Bill Clinton calls for legislation banning cloning the following day.

July
China's Academy of Sciences announces a project to clone the panda by 2003. This involves transferring the nucleus of a panda cell into that of another bear species, with the same species being used as a surrogate mother.

July

A new population of coelacanths is discovered off Sulawesi, Indonesia. Genetic studies show this population to consist of a different species of coelacanth to those off Cormoros.

10 December

In a joint effort by scientists around the world, the first genetic blueprint for a whole multicellular animal – a nematode worm – is completed. The 97 million-letter code, which is published on the Internet, is for a tiny worm called *Caenorhabditis elegans*. The study began 15 years ago and cost £30 million.

1999

October

A Russian expedition led by scientist Bernard Buigues discovers the carcass of a 23,000 year-old woolly mammoth frozen in Siberia. The carcass is flown to Khatanga, Russia, where scientists plan to clone the mammoth using an elephant as a surrogate mother.

17 November

US teenager Jesse Gelsinger dies during a gene therapy trial. All similar experiments are halted.

9 December

US scientists at the Institute for Genomic Research (TIGR) in Rockville, Maryland, announce plans to create a new life form in the laboratory. They will use a microbe *Mycoplasma genitalium*, which contains the smallest number of genes of any living creature known.

2000

26 June

Scientists working on the Human Genome Project in London, England, and Washington, DC, announce that they have completed the first draft of the entire structure of human DNA.

3 Biographical Sketches

Arber, Werner (1929–)

Swiss biochemist who was awarded the Nobel Prize for Physiology or Medicine in 1978 for his discovery of restriction enzymes (bacterial enzymes that can break a chain of DNA in two at a specific point). Restriction enzymes are used in genetic engineering.

Arber was born in Granichen, Switzerland, and studied at the Swiss Federal Institute of Technology. In 1949, he left for Geneva to work on bacteriophages (viruses that attack and grow in bacteria). By 1962, Arber had conducted a series of experiments to show the genetic basis of 'host-induced' variation (the phenomenon by which a bacteriophage adapts to the particular strain of bacteria that it grows in).

In Arber's theory, certain bacterial strains were postulated to contain restriction enzymes which were able to cleave unprotected (bacteriophage) DNA. Furthermore, these restriction enzymes must have the ability to recognize a specific sequence of nucleotides within a bacteriophage DNA molecule in order not to destroy the bacteria's own DNA. These enzymes would protect bacteria from infection since bacteriophage DNA would be broken before it could replicate and destroy a cell.

Arber went on to purify and characterize a sequence-specific restriction enzyme. Today such enzymes are routinely used by molecular biologists in genetic engineering to create pieces of DNA of a specified length.

Avery, Oswald Theodore (1877–1955)

Canadian-born US bacteriologist. His work on transformation in bacteria established in 1944 that DNA is responsible for the transmission of heritable characteristics. He also proved that polysaccharides play an important part in immunity.

Avery was born in Halifax, Nova Scotia, but spent most of his life in New York. He studied medicine at Columbia University, and worked at the Rockefeller Institute Hospital 1913–48.

Avery's work on transformation – a process by which heritable characteristics of one species are incorporated into another species – was stimulated by the research of British Medical Officer Frederick Griffith (1877–1941), who in 1928 published the results of his studies on *Diplococcus pneumoniae*, a bacterium that causes pneumonia in mice.

Avery proved conclusively that DNA was the transforming principle responsible for the development of polysaccharide capsules in unencapsulated bacteria that had been in contact with dead encapsulated bacteria. This implicated DNA as the basic genetic material of the cell.

Avery's early work also involved pneumococcus, but was in the field of immunology. He demonstrated that pneumococci bacteria could be classified according to their immunological response to specific antibodies and that this immunological specificity is due to the particular polysaccharides that constitute the capsule of each bacterial type. This research established that polysaccharides play an important part in immunity and led to the development of sensitive diagnostic tests to identify the various types of pneumococcus bacteria.

Banting, Frederick Grant (1891–1941)

Canadian physician who was awarded the Nobel Prize for Physiology or Medicine in 1923 for his discovery, in 1921, of a technique for isolating the hormone insulin. Banting and his colleague Charles Best tied off the ducts of the pancreas to determine the function of the cells known as the islets of Langerhans and thus made possible the treatment of diabetes. John J R Macleod, Banting's mentor, shared the prize, and Banting divided his prize with Best.

Banting was born in Alliston, Ontario, and studied medicine at the University of Toronto, where from 1921 he carried out research into diabetes. It had been suggested that insulin might be concerned in glucose metabolism and that its source might be the islets of Langerhans. Banting reasoned that if the pancreas were destroyed but the islets of Langerhans were retained, the absence of digestive enzymes would allow them to isolate insulin. With Charles Best, one of his undergraduate students, he experimented on dogs. Next, he obtained fetal pancreatic material from an abattoir. Eventually reasonably pure insulin was produced and commercial production of the hormone started. Banting was knighted in 1934.

Beadle, George Wells (1903–1989)

US biologist who was awarded the Nobel Prize for Physiology or Medicine in 1958 with Edward L Tatum and Joshua Lederberg for work in biochemical genetics, forming the 'one-gene–one-enzyme' hypothesis (a single gene codes for a single kind of enzyme).

Beadle was born in Wahoo, Nebraska. In 1931, he went to the California Institute of Technology, where he researched into the genetics of the fruit fly *Drosophila melanogaster*. From 1937 to 1946 he was professor at Stanford University, California, and it was during this period that he collaborated with Tatum.

Earlier, Beadle had shown that the eye colour of *Drosophila* is a result of a series of chemical reactions under genetic control. At Stanford, he used the red bread mould *Neurospora crassa*, which is a simpler organism than *Drosophila*. He subjected colonies of *Neurospora* to X-rays and studied the changes in the nutritional requirements of, and therefore enzymes formed by, the mutant *Neurospora* produced by the irradiation. By repeating the experiment with various mutant strains and culture mediums, Beadle and Tatum deduced that the formation of each individual enzyme is controlled by a single, specific gene. This concept found wide applications in biology and virtually created the science of biochemical genetics.

Berg, Paul (1926–   )

US molecular biologist who in 1972, using gene-splicing techniques developed by others, spliced and combined into a single hybrid the DNA from an animal tumour virus (SV40) and the DNA from a bacterial virus. He shared the Nobel Prize for Chemistry in 1980 for his work on the biochemistry of nucleic acids, especially recombinant DNA.

US biochemist Paul Berg in his laboratory in 1980 just after being awarded the Nobel Prize for Chemistry for his work in genetic engineering, particularly for developing DNA recombinant techniques that enable genes from simple organisms to be inserted into the genetic material of other simple organisms. CORBIS–Bettmann

Berg was born in New York and educated at Pennsylvania State University and Case Western Reserve University. Between 1955 and 1974 he held several positions at Washington University.

In 1956 Berg identified an RNA molecule (later known as a transfer RNA) that is specific to the amino acid methionine. He then perfected a method for making bacteria accept genes from other bacteria. This genetic engineering can be extremely useful for creating strains of bacteria to manufacture specific substances, such as interferon. But there are also dangers: a new, highly virulent pathogenic micro-organism might accidentally be created, for example. Berg has therefore advocated restrictions on genetic engineering research.

Best, Charles Herbert (1899–1978)

Canadian physiologist. Best was one of the team of Canadian scientists including Frederick Banting whose research resulted in 1922 in the discovery of insulin as a treatment for diabetes.

Best also discovered the vitamin choline and the enzyme histaminase, and introduced the use of the anticoagulant heparin.

Best was born in Maine, USA. As one of Banting's undergraduate students at the University of Toronto, he took part in the experiments to isolate insulin. They tied off the pancreatic duct in a group of dogs, which caused atrophy of the pancreas except for the part known as the islets of Langerhans. This eliminated the digestive enzymes normally produced by the pancreas, and left only insulin, produced by the islets of Langerhans. An extract of this was injected into another group of dogs, whose pancreas had been entirely removed so that they had developed diabetes. Gradually, these dogs' condition improved with the injections.

A Banting–Best Department of Medical Research was founded in Toronto, and Best was its director 1941–67.

Bodmer, Walter Fred (1936–   )

German-born English geneticist who was a pioneer of research into the genetics of the HLA histocompatability system, which helps the immune system to distinguish between the body's own cells and foreign, potentially harmful cells, like bacteria, that need to be destroyed and cleared from the body.

The HLA system, which consists of a set of genes and their corresponding antigens presented on the surface of cells, is also important in the way that cells recognize one another and work together during embryonic development. Only when there is overlapping expression of these HLA antigens and genes by two individuals, can transplantation of tissues, organs, or limbs take place between them without rejection by the immune system of the recipient.

Bodmer was born in Frankfurt, Germany just before World War II and studied at Cambridge University in England. After working at Stanford University 1961–70, Bodmer was professor of genetics at Oxford University 1971–79. He was director of research then director general at the Imperial Cancer Research Fund in the UK 1979–95, during which time he was elected a Fellow of the Royal Society and knighted.

Brenner, Sydney (1927–)

South African scientist, one of the pioneers of genetic engineering. Brenner discovered messenger RNA (a link between DNA and the ribosomes in which proteins are synthesized) in 1960.

Brenner became engaged in one of the most elaborate efforts in anatomy ever attempted: investigating the nervous system of nematode worms and comparing the nervous systems of different mutant forms of the animal. About 100 genes are involved in constructing the nervous system of a nematode and most of the mutations that occur affect the overall design of a section of the nervous system.

Brenner was born in Germiston, near Johannesburg, and studied at the University of the Witwatersrand and in the UK at Oxford. From 1957 he researched in the Molecular Biology Laboratory of the Medical Research Council, Cambridge, and in 1980 was appointed its director. In 1996 he became head of the Molecular Sciences Institute, La Jolla, California.

Brenner is also interested in tumour biology and in the use of genetic engineering for purifying proteins, cloning genes, and synthesizing amino acids.

Brown, Michael Stuart (1941–)

US geneticist who was awarded the Nobel Prize for Physiology or Medicine in 1985, together with Joseph Goldstein, for their work on the regulation of cholesterol metabolism. They discovered that individuals with inherited high cholesterol levels have either low levels or deficient forms of the low-density lipoprotein receptor (LDL-receptor) involved in the removal of cholesterol from the blood. The discovery led to the development of new drugs that lower blood cholesterol levels and reduce the risk of heart disease.

Brown and Goldstein studied why some individuals have high levels of cholesterol in their blood and found that this susceptibility to hypercholesterolaemia can be inherited in some families. They showed that cholesterol is normally removed from the blood by the binding of cholesterol-carrying molecules, called low-density lipoproteins (LDLs) to specific receptors (LDL-receptors) on the surface of cells in the body. The resulting LDL-receptor complexes are then absorbed by the cells. They further demonstrated that this uptake inhibits the cells' production of new LDL-receptors, which explains why a diet of high-cholesterol foods can overwhelm the body's natural capacity for removing cholesterol from the blood.

Brown was born in New York in the USA. He received his medical degree from the University of Pennsylvania in 1966 and worked as a junior doctor at the Massachusetts General Hospital in Boston, where he met and became friends with Goldstein. They were reunited and started to work together when Brown was appointed assistant professor at the Southwestern Medical School in Dallas, Texas, in 1971.

Calvin, Melvin (1911–1997)

US chemist who was awarded the Nobel Prize for Chemistry in 1961 for his study of the assimilation of carbon dioxide by plants. Using radioactive carbon-14 as a tracer, he determined the biochemical processes of photosynthesis, in which green plants use chlorophyll to convert carbon dioxide and water into sugar and oxygen.

Calvin was born in St Paul, Minnesota, and studied at Michigan College of Mining and Technology and the University of Minnesota. From 1937 he was on the staff of the University of California, becoming professor in 1947.

Calvin began work on photosynthesis in 1949, studying how carbon dioxide and water combine to form carbohydrates such as sugar and starch in a single-celled green alga, *Chlorella*. He showed that there is in fact a cycle of reactions (now called the Calvin cycle) involving an enzyme as a catalyst.

Carson, Rachel Louise (1907–1964)

US biologist, writer, and conservationist. Her book *Silent Spring* (1962), attacking the indiscriminate use of pesticides, inspired the creation of the modern environmental movement.

Carson was born in Springdale, Philadelphia, and educated at Pennsylvania College for Women and Johns Hopkins University. She worked first at the University of Maryland and the Woods Hole Marine Biological Laboratory in Massachusetts, and then as an aquatic biologist with the US Fish and Wildlife Service 1936–49, becoming its editor-in-chief until 1952.

Her first book, *The Sea Around Us* (1951), was a bestseller and won several literary awards. It was followed by *The Edge of the Sea* (1955), an ecological exploration of the seashore. *Silent Spring* was a powerful

US chemist Melvin Calvin, holding a model of a sucrose molecule, in 1961, the year in which he was awarded the Nobel Prize for Chemistry, for his work on the biochemistry of photosynthesis. Bettmann/CORBIS

denunciation of the effects of pesticides, especially DDT. While writing about broad scientific issues of pollution and ecological exploitation, she also raised important issues about the reckless squandering of natural resources by an industrial world.

Cohen, Stanley (1922–)

US biochemist who was awarded the Nobel Prize for Physiology or Medicine in 1986 jointly with Rita Levi-Montalcini for their work to isolate and characterize growth factors, small proteins that regulate the growth of specific types of cells, such as nerve and epidermal cells.

Cohen helped to purify and characterize nerve growth factor, a small protein produced in the male salivary gland that regulates the growth of small nerves and affects the development of the sensory and sympathetic neurons. He went on to discover another growth factor, called epidermal growth factor, that affects epithelial cell growth, tooth eruption, and eyelid opening. He then laboured to link epidermal growth factor to the regulation of embryonic growth. Subsequent studies by other scientists have shown that this growth factor also plays a crucial part in the exaggerated growth rate of some cancer cells.

Cohen was born in Brooklyn, New York, and studied at Brooklyn College and the universities of Ohio and Michigan. While working at Vanderbilt University in the early 1950s, he became aware of Levi-Montalcini's discovery of the first growth factor, nerve growth factor.

Crick, Francis Harry Compton (1916–)

English molecular biologist who was awarded the Nobel Prize for Physiology or Medicine in 1962, together with Maurice Wilkins and James Watson, for the discovery of the double-helical structure of DNA and of the significance of this structure in the replication and transfer of genetic information.

Using Wilkins's and others' discoveries, Crick and Watson postulated that DNA consists of a double helix consisting of two parallel chains of alternate sugar and phosphate groups linked by pairs of organic bases. They built molecular models which also explained how genetic information could be coded – in the sequence of organic bases. Crick and Watson published their work on the proposed structure of DNA in 1953. Their model is now generally accepted as correct.

Crick was born in Northampton and studied physics at University College, London. During World War II he worked on the development of radar. He then went to do biological research at Cambridge. In 1977 he became a professor at the Salk Institute in San Diego, California.

Later, this time working with South African scientist Sidney Brenner, Crick demonstrated that each group of three adjacent bases (he called a set of three bases a codon) on a single DNA strand codes for one specific amino acid. He also helped to determine codons that code for each of the 20 main amino acids. Furthermore, he formulated the adaptor hypothesis, according to which adaptor molecules mediate between messenger RNA and amino acids. These adaptor molecules are now known as transfer RNAs.

Among his sometimes controversial writings are *Of Molecules and Men* (1966), *Life Itself* (1982), *What Mad Pursuit* (1988), and *The Astonishing Hypothesis* (1994). *See illustration under* **Watson** *on page 85.*

Dawkins, (Clinton) Richard (1941–)

British zoologist whose book *The Selfish Gene* (1976) popularized the theories of sociobiology (social behaviour in humans and animals in the context of evolution). In *The Blind Watchmaker* (1986) he explained the modern theory of evolution.

Dawkins was born in Nairobi, Kenya, and educated at Oxford, where from 1975 he held academic posts.

In *The Selfish Gene* he argued that genes – not individuals, populations, or species – are the driving force of evolution. He suggested an analogous system of cultural transmission in human societies, and proposed the term 'mimeme', abbreviated to 'meme', as the unit of such a scheme. He considered the idea of God to be a meme with a high survival value. His contentions were further developed in *The Extended Phenotype* (1982), primarily an academic work.

Other works include *River Out of Eden* (1995), *Climbing Mount Improbable* (1996), and *Unweaving the Rainbow* (1998), a tribute to the scientific mode of thinking.

Delbrück, Max (1906–1981)

German-born US biologist who was awarded the Nobel Prize for Physiology or Medicine in 1969 with Salvador Luria and Alfred Hershey for their work on the replication mechanism and genetic structure of viruses. He pioneered techniques in molecular biology, studying genetic changes occurring when viruses invade bacteria.

Delbrück was born in Berlin. Initially he pursued studies in astronomy and physics and during 1931–32 he studied with Danish physicist Niels Bohr in Copenhagen and Austrian-born Swiss physicist Wolfgang Pauli in Zurich. Bohr was instrumental in interesting Delbrück in biology. Delbrück left Germany in 1940 because of the rise of the Nazis and went to the United States. In 1947 he became Professor of Biology at California Institure of Technology.

Dobzhansky, Theodosius (1900–1975)

Ukrainian-born (originally Feodosy Grigorevich Dobrzhansky) US geneticist who established evolutionary genetics as an independent discipline. He showed that genetic variability between individuals of the same species is very high and that this diversity is vital to the process of evolution.

His book *Genetics and the Origin of Species* (1937) was the first significant synthesis of Darwinian evolutionary theory and Mendelian genetics. Dobzhansky also proved that there is a period when speciation is only partly complete and during which several races coexist.

Dobzhansky was born in Nemirov and studied at Kiev. After teaching at Kiev and Leningrad universities, he went to the USA in 1927. He was at the California Institute of Technology 1929–40. He became professor of zoology at Columbia University, New York City, 1940; worked at the Rockefeller

Institute (later the Rockefeller University) 1962–71; then he moved to the University of California at Davis.

His book *Mankind Evolving* (1962) had great influence among anthropologists. He wrote on the philosophical aspects of evolution in *The Biological Basis of Human Freedom* (1956) and *The Biology of Ultimate Concern* (1967).

Elion, Gertrude (Belle) (1918–1999)

US biochemist who was awarded the Nobel Prize for Physiology or Medicine in 1988 with her colleague George Herbert Hitchings and James Black for their work on the principles governing the design of new drug treatment, leading to the development of drugs to treat cancer, gout, malaria, and various viral infections.

She was best known for her work to develop new drugs, particularly those which inhibit the synthesis of DNA by diseased cells. Together with her colleague Hitchings she investigated the chemistry and function of two important components of DNA, pyrimidine and purine. From this they developed new drugs to treat leukaemia, malaria, kidney stones, gout, herpes, and AIDS. Elion also helped to develop early forms of immuno-suppressive drugs to enable transplant patients to tolerate the presence of tissues from an unrelated donor.

Elion was born in New York City and graduated from Hunter College in 1937 before obtaining her MSc from New York University. In 1944 she joined the laboratories of Burroughs Wellcome in North Carolina and held the position of research professor of pharmacology and medicine at Duke University from 1983.

Elton, Charles Sutherland (1900–1991)

British ecologist, a pioneer of the study of animal and plant forms in their natural environments, and of animal behaviour as part of the complex pattern of life. He defined the concept of food chains and was an early conservationist. Elton was instrumental in establishing the Nature Conservancy Council (1949), and was much concerned with the impact of introduced species on natural systems.

Elton was born in Liverpool and was educated at Liverpool College and then Oxford University where he graduated in zoology in 1922.

Evans, Alice Catherine (1881–1975)

US microbiologist whose research into the bacterial contamination of milk led to the recognition of the danger of unpasteurized milk. As a result of her research the incidence of brucellosis was greatly reduced when the dairy industry accepted that all milk should be pasteurized.

Evans was born in Neath, Pennsylvania, and studied at Cornell University and the University of Wisconsin, after which she took a research post at the US Department of Agriculture studying the bacteriology of milk and cheese. In 1918 she moved to the Hygienic Laboratories of the United States Public Health Service to research into epidemic meningitis and influenza as well as milk flora.

Brucellosis in humans and cattle had been thought to be two separate diseases until Evans published her findings in 1918. Her results were later confirmed by other scientists, though it was not until the 1930s that the dairy industry accepted that all milk should be pasteurized.

Fisher, Ronald Aylmer (1890–1962)

English statistician and geneticist. He modernized Charles Darwin's theory of evolution, thus securing the key biological concept of genetic change by natural selection. Fisher developed several new statistical techniques and, applying his methods to genetics, published *The Genetical Theory of Natural Selection* (1930).

This classic work established that the discoveries of the geneticist Gregor Mendel could be shown to support Darwin's theory of evolution.

Fisher was born in London and studied at Cambridge. In 1919 he was appointed head of Rothampstead Experimental Station, where he made a statistical analysis of a backlog of experimental data that had built up over more than 60 years.

At Rothamstead, Fisher also bred poultry, mice, snails, and other creatures, and in his papers on genetics contributed to the contemporary understanding of genetic dominance. As a result, in 1933 he was appointed professor of eugenics at University College, London. He was professor of genetics at Cambridge 1943–57.

In statistics, Fisher evolved the rules for decisionmaking that are now used almost automatically, and many other methods that have since been extended to virtually every academic field in which statistical analysis can be applied.

Fleming, Alexander (1881–1955)

Scottish bacteriologist who was awarded the Nobel Prize for Physiology or Medicine in 1945 for his discovery of the bactericidal effect of penicillin in 1928. In 1922 he had discovered lysozyme, an antibacterial enzyme present in saliva, nasal secretions, and tears. While studying this, he found an unusual mould growing on a culture dish, which he isolated and grew into a pure culture. This led to his discovery of penicillin, which came into use in 1941. He shared the award with Howard W Florey and Ernst B Chain, whose research had brought widespread realization of the value of penicillin with its isolation and its development as an antibiotic drug.

Fleming was born in Lochfield, Ayrshire, and studied medicine at St Mary's Hospital, London, where he remained in the bacteriology department for his entire career, becoming professor in 1928.

Fleming discovered the antibacterial properties of penicillin, but its purification and concentration was left to Florey and Chain in Oxford. He identified organisms that cause wound infections and showed how cross-infection by streptococci can occur among patients in hospital wards. He also studied the effects of different antiseptics on various kinds of bacteria and on living cells. His interest in chemotherapy led him to introduce German bacteriologist Paul Ehrlich's Salvarsan into British medical practice. He was knighted in 1944.

Fossey, Dian (1932–1985)

US zoologist. Almost completely untrained, Fossey was sent by Louis Leakey into the African wild. From 1975, she studied mountain gorillas in Rwanda and discovered that they committed infanticide and that females transferred to nearby established groups. Living in close proximity to them, she discovered that they led peaceful family lives.

Fossey was born in San Francisco, California, and began her career as an occupational therapist. She became interested in gorillas in 1963 and began to study mountain gorillas in Zaire (now Democratic Republic of Congo) in 1967. She was murdered by poachers whose snares she had cut, after having spent 18 years living amongst the gorillas and fighting for their conservation.

Franklin, Rosalind Elsie (1920–1958)

English chemist and X-ray crystallographer who was the first to recognize the helical shape of DNA. Her work, without which the discovery of the structure of DNA would not have been possible, was built into James Watson and Francis Crick's Nobel prizewinning description of DNA.

Rosalind Franklin was born in London on 25 July 1920, into a professional family. She was educated at St Paul's School, London, and won an exhibition scholarship in 1938 to study chemistry at Cambridge University. After graduating in 1941 she stayed on to carry out postgraduate study on gas-phase chromatography with Ronald Norrish. From 1942 she studied the physical structure of coal for the British Coal Utilization Research Association, from where she moved to Paris in 1947 to research the graphitization of carbon at high temperatures at the Laboratoire Central des

Services Chimique. She became a skilled X-ray crystallographer, and later applied these techniques to her study of DNA and viruses at King's College and then Birkbeck College, London.

In 1951 Franklin was appointed research associate to John Randall at King's College. Maurice Wilkins and Raymond Gosling at King's had obtained diffraction images of DNA that indicated a high degree of crystallinity and Randall gave Franklin the job of elucidating the structure of DNA.

Working with Gosling, Franklin used her chemical expertise to study the unwieldy DNA molecule and established that DNA exists in two forms – A and B – and that the sugar–phosphate backbone of DNA lies on the outside of the molecule. She also explained the basic helical structure of DNA, and produced X-ray crystallographic studies. However, she was not entirely convinced about the helical structure and was seeking further evidence in support of her theory.

Meanwhile, unknown to Randall, who had presented Franklin's data at a routine seminar, Franklin's work had found its way to her competitors Crick and Watson, at Cambridge University. They incorporated her work with that of others into their description of the double-helical structure of DNA, which was published in 1953 in the same issue of *Nature* that Franklin's X-ray crystallographic studies of DNA were published. Franklin was not bitter about their use of her research material but began writing a corroboration of the Crick–Watson model.

Finding Wilkins difficult to work with, Franklin left King's College and joined John Bernal's laboratory at Birkbeck College to work on the tobacco mosaic virus. She died of cancer on 16 April 1958 at the age of 37, four years before she could be awarded the Nobel Prize for Physiology or Medicine with Watson, Crick, and Wilkins in 1962. The Nobel prize cannot be awarded posthumously.

Frisch, Karl von (1886–1982)

Austrian zoologist who was awarded the Nobel Prize for Physiology or Medicine in 1973 with Konrad Lorenz and Nikolaas Tinbergen for their work on animal behaviour patterns. Karl von Frisch specialized in bees, discovering how they communicate the location of sources of nectar by movements called 'dances'. Frisch was born in Vienna and educated at the universities of Vienna and Munich.

Goodall, Jane (1934–)

English primatologist and conservationist who has studied the chimpanzee community on Lake Tanganyika since 1960, and is a world authority on wild chimpanzees.

English primatologist and conservationist Jane Goodall with a curious chimpanzee, in 1972. She is still active in research in the early 21st century and also tireless in her campaigning for the rights of chimpanzees and other primates in captivity.
Bettmann/CORBIS

Goodall was born in London. She left school at 18 and worked as a secretary and a film production assistant, until she had an opportunity to work for anthropologist Louis Leakey in Africa. She began to study the chimpanzees at the Gombe Stream Game Reserve, on Lake Tanganyika. Goodall observed the lifestyles of chimpanzees in their natural habitats, discovering that they are omnivores, not herbivores as originally thought, and that they have highly developed and elaborate forms of social behaviour. In 1964 she married Hugo van Lawick the Dutch wildlife photographer, and he collaborated with her on several of her books and films. They divorced later. She obtained a PhD from Cambridge University in 1965, despite the fact that she had never been an undergraduate. Her books include *In the Shadow of Man* (1971), *The Chimpanzees of Gombe: Patterns of Behaviour* (1986), and *Through a Window* (1990). In the 1990s most of Goodall's time was devoted to establishing sanctuaries for illegally captured chimpanzees, fundraising, and speaking out against the unnecessary use of animals in research.

Gould, Stephen Jay (1941–   )

US palaeontologist and writer. In 1972 he proposed the theory of punctuated equilibrium, suggesting that the evolution of species did not occur at a steady rate but could suddenly accelerate, with rapid change occurring over a few hundred thousand years. His books include *Ever Since Darwin* (1977), *The Panda's Thumb* (1980), *The Flamingo's Smile* (1985), and *Wonderful Life* (1990).

Gould was born in New York and studied at Antioch College, Ohio, and Columbia University. He became professor of geology at Harvard in 1973 and was later also given posts in the departments of zoology and the history of science.

Gould has written extensively on several aspects of evolutionary science, in both professional and popular books. His *Ontogeny and Phylogeny* (1977) provided a detailed scholarly analysis of his work on the developmental process of recapitulation. In *Wonderful Life* he drew attention to the diversity of the fossil finds in the Burgess Shale Site in Yoho National Park, Canada, which he interprets as evidence of parallel early evolutionary trends extinguished by chance rather than natural selection.

Haldane, J(ohn) B(urdon) S(anderson) (1892–1964)

Anglo-Indian physiologist, geneticist, and author of popular science books. In 1936 he showed the genetic link between haemophilia and colour blindness.

Haldane was born and educated at Oxford. In 1933 he became professor of genetics at University College, London. He emigrated to India in 1957 in protest at the Anglo-French invasion of Suez and was appointed director of the Genetics and Biometry Laboratory in Orissa. He became a naturalized Indian citizen in 1961.

In 1924 Haldane produced the first proof that enzymes obey the laws of thermodynamics.

Haldane carried our research into how the regulation of breathing in humans is affected by the level of carbon dioxide in the bloodstream. During World War II, in 1942, Haldane, who often used his own body in biochemical experiments, spent two days in a submarine to test an air-purifying system.

Haldane was convinced that natural selection and not mutation is the driving force behind evolution. In 1932, he estimated for the first time the rate of mutation of the human gene and worked out the effect of recurrent harmful mutations on a population. He is supposed to have remarked: 'I'd lay down my life for two brothers or eight cousins.'

Hamilton, William D(onald) (1936–2000)

British biologist. By developing the concept of inclusive fitness, he was able to solve the theoretical problem of explaining altruism in animal behaviour in terms of neo-Darwinism.

He was Royal Society Research Professor in the Department of Zoology, at the University of Oxford, England, 1984–2000, and was a fellow of New College, Oxford. Hamilton died of malaria after an expedition to the Congo.

Hershey, Alfred Day (1908–1997)

US biochemist who was awarded the Nobel Prize for Physiology or Medicine in 1969 for his work on the replication mechanism and genetic structure of viruses. He used bacteriophages (viruses that infect bacteria) to demonstrate that DNA, not protein, is the genetic material. His experiments demonstrated that viral DNA is sufficient to transform bacteria.

With Martha Chase he demonstrated that DNA is the genetic material, by studying the T2 bacteriophage, a virus that infects the bacterium *Escherichia coli*. It had been suggested by Roger Herriot in 1951 that a bacteriophage acted like 'a little hypodermic needle full of transforming principles'; the virus as such never enters the cell; only the tail contacts the host and perhaps enzymatically cuts a small hole through the outer membrane and then the nucleic acid of the virus head flows into the cell.

Hershey and Chase tested this hypothesis by labelling the bacteriophage DNA with radioactive phosphorus and the protein with radioactive sulphur. A sample of *E. coli* was infected with the radiolabelled bacteriophage for a short incubation and then the two were separated by centrifugation. The bacteria were found to be full of radioactive phosphorus but practically devoid of radioactive sulphur. The bacteria were also fully competent to produce progeny virus. Hershey and Chase's conclusion was that 'a physical separation of the phage T2 into genetic and nongenetic parts is possible'.

Hershey was born in Owosso, Michigan, USA. He graduated from Michigan State College and for the next 24 years worked at the Carnegie Institution in Washington to provide evidence for the nature of the material in genes.

Hyman, Libbie Henrietta (1888–1969)

US zoologist whose six-volume *The Invertebrates* (1940–68) provided an encyclopedic account of most phyla of invertebrates.

Hyman was born in Des Moines, Iowa, and studied at the University of Chicago, where she remained as a research assistant until 1930. She then travelled to several European laboratories, working for a period at the Stazione Zoologica, Naples, Italy, before returning to New York City to begin to write a comprehensive reference book on the invertebrates, for which she was given office and laboratory space, but no salary, by the American Museum of Natural History.

Initially she worked on flatworms, but soon extended her investigations to a wide spread of invertebrates, especially their taxonomy (classification) and anatomy.

Jacob, François (1920–   )

French biochemist who was awarded the Nobel Prize in Physiology or Medicine in 1965, with Jacques Monod and André Lwoff, for their work on the genetic control of enzyme and virus synthesis. They pioneered research into molecular genetics and showed how the production of proteins from DNA is controlled.

Jacob was born in Nancy and studied at the University of Paris. In 1950 he joined the Pasteur Institute in Paris as a research assistant, becoming head of the Department of Cellular Genetics in 1964 and also professor of cellular genetics at the Collège de France.

Jacob began his work on the control of gene action in 1958, working with Lwoff and Monod. It was known that the types of proteins produced in an organism are controlled by DNA, and Jacob focused his research on how the amount of protein is controlled. He performed a series of experiments in which he cultured the bacterium *Escherichia coli* in various mediums to discover the effect of the medium on enzyme production. He and his team found that there were three types of gene concerned with the production of each specific protein.

Jeffreys, Alec John (1950–   )

British geneticist who discovered the DNA probes necessary for accurate genetic fingerprinting so that a murderer or rapist could be identified by, for example, traces of blood, tissue, or semen.

Jeffreys was born in Oxford. He was educated at Merton College, Oxford, where he graduated in 1972. He was European Molecular Biology Organization Research Fellow at the University of Amsterdam 1975–77. He then moved to the department of genetics at the University of Leicester, where he has remained throughout his career.

Khorana, Har Gobind (1922–   )

Indian-born US biochemist who was awarded the Nobel Prize for Physiology or Medicine in 1968 for his part in the interpretation of genetic code and its function in protein synthesis. In 1976 he led the team that first synthesized a biologically active gene. His work provides much of the basis for gene therapy and biotechnology.

Khorana was born in Raipur in the Punjab, now in Pakistan. He studied at Punjab University; in the UK at Liverpool; and in Switzerland at Zürich; returning to Britain in 1950 to work at Cambridge. He has held academic posts in the USA and Canada, becoming professor at the University of Wisconsin in 1962 and at the Massachusetts Institute of Technology in 1970.

Khorana systematically synthesized every possible combination of the genetic signals from the four nucleotides known to be involved in determining the genetic code. He showed that a pattern of three nucleotides, called a triplet, specifies a particular amino acid (the building blocks of proteins). He further discovered that some of the triplets provided punctuation marks in the code, marking the beginning and end points of protein synthesis.

Khorana has also synthesized the gene for bovine rhodopsin, the pigment in the retina responsible for converting light energy into electrical energy.

Krebs, Hans Adolf (1900–1981)

German-born British biochemist who was awarded the Nobel Prize for Physiology or Medicine in 1953 for his discovery of the citric acid cycle, also known as the *Krebs cycle*, the final pathway by which food molecules are converted into energy in living tissues. He was knighted in 1958.

Krebs first became interested in the process by which the body degrades amino acids. He discovered that nitrogen atoms are the first to be removed (deamination) and are then excreted as urea in the urine. He then investigated the processes involved in the production of urea from the removed nitrogen atoms, and by 1932 he had worked out the basic steps in the urea cycle.

Krebs was born in Hildesheim and studied at the universities of Göttingen, Freiburg, Munich, Berlin, and Hamburg. In 1933, with the rise to power of the Nazis, he moved to the UK, initially to Cambridge and to Sheffield in 1935. He was professor at Sheffield 1945–54, and at Oxford 1954–67.

Leakey, Louis Seymour Bazett (1903–1972)

Kenyan archaeologist, anthropologist, and palaeontologist. With his wife Mary Leakey, he discovered fossils of extinct animals in the Olduvai Gorge in Tanzania, as well as many remains of an early human type. Leakey's conviction that human origins lie in Africa was opposed to contemporary opinion.

Leakey was born in Kabete, Kenya, and studied in the UK at Cambridge. Between 1926 and 1937 he led a series of archaeological research expeditions to East Africa. He was curator of Coryndon Museum, Nairobi, Kenya, 1945–61, and one of the founder trustees of the Kenya National Parks and Reserves. In 1961 he founded the National Museum Centre for Prehistory and Palaeontology.

Leakey began excavations at Olduvai Gorge in 1931. With Mary Leakey, he discovered a site in the Rift Valley of the Acheulian culture, which flourished between 1.5 million and 150,000 years ago. The Leakeys also found the remains of 20-million-year-old apes on an island in Lake Victoria. In 1960 they discovered the remains of *Homo habilis*, 1.7 million years old, and the skull of an Acheulian hand-axe user, *Homo erectus*, which Leakey maintained was on the direct evolutionary line of *Homo sapiens*, the modern human. In 1961 at Fort Ternan, Kenya, he found jawbone fragments of another early primate, believed to be 14 million years old.

His books for a general readership include *Stone Age Africa* (1936) and *White African* (1937).

Leakey, Mary Douglas (1913–1996)

English archaeologist and anthropologist (born Mary Douglas Nicol). In 1948 she discovered, on Rusinga Island, Lake Victoria, East Africa, the prehistoric ape skull known as *Proconsul*, about 20 million years old; and human footprints at Laetoli, to the south, about 3.75 million years old.

Leakey was born in London and became assistant to an archaeologist. Her collaboration with Louis Leakey began when she illustrated a book he was working on. In 1936 Mary Leakey began excavating a Late Stone Age site north of Nairobi, and with her husband discovered the remains of an important Neolithic settlement.

The Leakeys together and separately carried out excavations in Kenya, and accumulated evidence that East Africa was the possible cradle of the human race. By the middle of the 1960s Mary was living almost continuously at the permanent camp they had established at Olduvai Gorge.

She described her work in the book *Olduvai Gorge: My Search for Early Man* (1979).

Lederberg, Joshua (1925–   )

US geneticist who was awarded the Nobel Prize for Physiology or Medicine in 1958 for work on genetic recombination and the organization of bacterial genetic material. He showed that bacteria can reproduce sexually, combining genetic material so that offspring possess characteristics of both parent organisms. He shared the prize with George Beadle and Edward Tatum.

Lederberg is a pioneer of genetic engineering, a science that relies on the possibility of artificially shuffling genes from cell to cell. He realized in 1952 that bacteriophages, viruses which invade bacteria, can transfer genes from one bacterium to another, a discovery that led to the deliberate insertion by scientists of foreign genes into bacterial cells.

Lederberg was born in New Jersey and studied at Columbia and at Yale, where he worked with Tatum. He was at the University of Wisconsin

US geneticist Joshua Lederberg in 1958, the year he was awarded the Nobel Prize for Physiology or Medicine with fellow Americans George Beadle and Edward Tatum for their pioneering work in the field of biochemical genetics. Hulton-Deutsch Collection/CORBIS

1947–59, rising to professor, and moved in 1959 to Stanford University, California, becoming director of the Kennedy Laboratories of Molecular Medicine in 1962.

Lewontin, Richard C(harles) (1929–)

US geneticist. A prolific writer and a former editor of scientific journals, he made a major contribution to the study of population genetics, evolution, and philosophical and social aspects of human behaviour. He is also known as a controversial critic of his professional colleagues and a commentator on the applications of biological knowledge to broader issues. Lewontin was born in New York City. He was a biometrician at Columbia University 1953–54, an assistant professor at North Carolina State College 1954–58, and a professor at the universities of Rochester 1958–64, Chicago 1964–73, and Harvard from 1973.

Lorenz, Konrad Zacharias (1903–1989)

Austrian ethologist who was awarded the Nobel Prize for Physiology or Medicine in 1973 with Nikolaas Tinbergen and Karl von Frisch for their work on animal behaviour patterns. He studied the relationship between instinct and behaviour, particularly in birds, and described the phenomenon of imprinting in 1935. His books include *King Solomon's Ring* (1952) (on animal behaviour) and *On Aggression* (1966) (on human behaviour).

Lorenz was born in Vienna and studied medicine there and in the USA at Columbia University. In 1940 he was appointed professor of general psychology at the Albertus University in Königsberg, Germany. Lorenz sympathized with Nazi views on eugenics, and in 1938 applied to join the Nazi party. From 1942 to 1944 he was a physician in the German army, and then spent four years in the USSR as a prisoner of war. Returning to Austria, he successively headed various research institutes.

Together, Lorenz and Tinbergen discovered how birds of prey are recognized by other birds. All birds of prey have short necks, and the sight of any bird – or even a dummy bird – with a short neck causes other birds to fly away.

Luria, Salvador Edward (1912–1991)

Italian-born US physician who was awarded the Nobel Prize for Physiology or Medicine in 1969 for his work on the replication mechanism and genetic structure of viruses. Luria was a pacifist and was identified with efforts to keep science humanistic.

Luria was born in Turin. He left fascist Italy in 1938, going first to France, where he became a research fellow at the Institut du Radium in Paris, and then to the USA in 1940. From 1943 he taught at a number of universities and in 1959 became a professor at the Massachusetts Institute of Technology (MIT). He founded the MIT Center for Cancer Research, which he directed in the period 1972–85. For some time he taught a course in world literature to graduate students at MIT and at Harvard Medical School to ensure their involvement in the arts.

Lysenko, Trofim Denisovich (1898–1976)

Soviet biologist who believed in the inheritance of acquired characteristics (changes acquired in an individual's lifetime) and used his position under Joseph Stalin officially to exclude Gregor Mendel's theory of inheritance. He was removed from office after the fall of Nikita Khrushchev in 1964.

As leader of the Soviet scientific world, Lysenko encouraged the defence of mechanistic views about the nature of heredity and speciation. This created an environment conducive to the spread of unverified facts and theories, such as the doctrine of the noncellular 'living' substance and the transformation of viruses into bacteria. Research in several areas of biology came to a halt.

Lysenko was born in Karlovka in the Russian Ukraine, and educated at the Uman School of Horticulture and the Kiev Agricultural Institute. From 1929 to 1938 he held senior positions at the Ukrainian All-Union Institute of Selection and Genetics in Odessa, becoming director of the Institute of Genetics of the USSR Academy of Sciences in 1940. In 1965 he was removed from his post and stripped of all authority.

By advocating vernalization (a method of making seeds germinate quickly in the spring), Lysenko achieved considerable increases in crop yields, and this was the basis of his political support. As his influence increased, he enlarged the scope of his theories, using his authority to remove any opposition.

Margulis, Lynn Alexander (1938–)

US cell biologist who made a major contribution to the study of the origin, morphogenesis, cytoplasmic genetics, and the evolution of slime moulds and other protists. She is a proponent of the controversial Gaia hypothesis, which views planet Earth as a homeostatic physicochemical system whose surface is actively influenced by the actions of all living organisms. Margulis was born in Chicago, Illinois. She taught and performed research at Boston University 1966–88, and became a Distinguished University Professor at the University of Massachusetts, Amherst, from 1988.

Maynard Smith, John (1920–)

English geneticist and evolutionary biologist who applied game theory to animal behaviour and developed the concept of the evolutionary stable strategy as a mathematical technique for studying the evolution of behaviour.

Maynard Smith was born in London and educated at Eton and Cambridge. He graduated as an aeronautical engineer in 1941 and received a degree in zoology from University College, London in 1951. He taught at University College, London 1951–65, and was appointed professor of biology at the University of Sussex in 1965.

His works include *Mathematical Ideas in Biology* (1968), *Models in Ecology* (1974), *Evolution of Sex* (1978) and *Evolution and the Theory of Games* (1983). His popular book *The Theory of Evolution* (1958), was widely influential.

Mayr, Ernst Walter (1904–)

German-born US zoologist who was influential in the development of modern evolutionary theories. He led a two-year expedition to New Guinea and the Solomon Islands where he studied the effects of founder populations and speciation on the evolution of the indigenous birds and animals. This research caused him to support neo-Darwinism, a synthesis of the ideas of Darwin and Mendel, being developed at that time.

Mayr was born in Kempten, Germany. He studied medicine at Greifswald University 1923–25 and graduated with a PhD from the University of Berlin in 1926, where he continued to work until 1930. He carried out taxonomic research at the American Museum of Natural History in New York 1931–53 where he was responsible for avian taxonomy. He published more than 100 papers in this area, including *Birds of the Southwest Pacific* (1945). In 1937 he contributed to Dobzhansky's *Genetics and the Origin of Species*, which outlined the neo-Darwininist synthesis of evolution and Mendelian genetics and was crucial in the widespread acceptance of the theory of evolution.

In 1950 he proposed an alternative classification for fossils, which included the hominid fossils and was widely accepted. He was appointed Alexander Agassiz professor of zoology at Harvard University in 1953, and from 1961 until his retirement in 1970, held the post of director of the Museum of Comparative Zoology. He has written and edited a number of books, including several upon the development of evolutionary thought, which are standard texts on university courses to this day.

Milstein, César (1927–)

Argentine-born British molecular biologist who was awarded the Nobel Prize for Physiology or Medicine in 1984 for his work on immunity and the discovery of a technique for producing highly specific, monoclonal antibodies, which give immunity against specific diseases. He shared the prize with Georges Köhler and Niels Jerne.

Monoclonal antibodies are cloned cells that can be duplicated in limitless quantities and, when introduced into the body, can be targeted to seek out sites of disease. Milstein and his colleagues had thus devised a means of accessing the immune system for the purposes of research, diagnosis, and treatment.

Milstein was born in Bahía Blanca and studied at Buenos Aires. From 1963 he worked in the UK at the Laboratory of Molecular Biology, Cambridge, and later became joint head of its Protein Chemistry Division.

Milstein and his colleagues were among the first to determine the complete sequence of the short, low-molecular-weight part of the immunoglobulin molecule (known as the light chain). He then determined the nucleotide sequence of a large portion of the messenger RNA for the light chain. His findings led him to the technique for preparing monoclonal antibodies.

Monod, Jacques Lucien (1910–1976)

French biochemist who was awarded the Nobel Prize for Physiology or Medicine in 1965 with his co-workers André Lwoff and François Jacob for research into the genetic control of enzyme and virus synthesis.

Monod was born and educated in Paris. From 1945 he worked at the Pasteur Institute, where he collaborated with Lwoff and Jacob. In 1953, Monod became director of the Department of Cellular Biochemistry at the Pasteur Institute and also a professor at the University of Paris. In 1971, he was appointed director of the entire Pasteur Institute.

Working on the way in which genes control intracellular metabolism in micro-organisms, Monod and his colleagues postulated the existence of a class of genes (which they called operons) that regulate the activities of the genes that actually control the synthesis of enzymes within the cell. They further hypothesized that the operons suppress the activities of the enzyme-synthesizing genes by affecting the synthesis of messenger RNA.

In his book *Chance and Necessity* (1971), Monod summoned contemporary biochemical discoveries to support the idea that all forms of life result from random mutation (chance) and Darwinian selection (necessity).

Montagnier, Luc (1932–   )

French molecular biologist who first identified the human immunodeficiency virus (HIV) in 1983, the single-stranded RNA retrovirus that causes AIDS. Patients with the disease die from rare infections because their immune systems are crippled by the virus.

Montagnier was educated in Paris and held a number of research posts before being appointed to run the Viral Oncology Unit in 1985 and the Department of AIDS and Retroviruses in 1990 at the Pasteur Institute in Paris.

Morgan, Thomas Hunt (1866–1945)

US geneticist who was awarded the Nobel Prize for Physiology or Medicine in 1933 for his work on the role of chromosomes in heredity. He helped establish that genes are located on the chromosomes, discovered sex chromosomes, and invented the techniques of genetic mapping. He was the first to work on the fruit fly *Drosophila*, which has since become a major subject of genetic studies.

Morgan was born in Lexington, Kentucky, and studied at Johns Hopkins University. He was professor of experimental zoology at Columbia University in the period 1904–28, when he was appointed director of the Laboratory of Biological Sciences at the California Institute of Technology.

Following the rediscovery of Austrian scientist Gregor Mendel's work, Morgan's interest turned from embryology to the mechanisms involved in heredity, and in 1908 he began his research on the genetics of *Drosophila*. From his findings he postulated that certain characteristics are sex-linked, that the X-chromosome carries several discrete hereditary units (genes), and that the genes are linearly arranged on chromosomes. He also demonstrated that sex-linked characters are not invariably inherited together, from which he developed the concept of crossing-over and the associated idea that the extent of crossing-over is a measure of the spatial separation of genes on chromosomes.

Morgan published a summary of his work in *The Mechanism of Mendelian Heredity* (1915).

Mullis, Kary Banks (1944–)

US molecular biologist who was awarded the Nobel Prize for Chemistry in 1993 for the invention of the polymerase chain reaction (PCR) technique, which allows specific regions of DNA to be copied many times from a tiny sample, thus amplifying it to a large enough quantity to be analysed. This technique signalled an end to the laborious method of producing DNA fragments in vivo. He shared the Nobel prize with Michael Smith.

In PCR, a small sample of DNA (for example, from a blood sample) is cut into segments and denatured (broken down) into single strands. Short oligonucleotide probes complementary to the DNA are prepared, and added in large amounts to the denatured DNA, and then incubated at 50–60°C. The probe joins to its correct site on the DNA, and acts as a starting point for synthesis of a new DNA chain. After the synthesis has finished the mixture is heated to 95°C to melt the newly formed DNA duplexes. The cycle can be repeated in order to amplify the desired sequence, and in just a few hours more than 100 billion copies can be made. These can then be used for analysis. The technique is now commonly used worldwide and is particularly important for disease diagnosis, for example, in the test for HIV.

Mullis was born in Lenoir, North Carolina, and educated at the Georgia Institute of Technology and the University of California, Berkeley, where he obtained his PhD in 1973. After conducting research at the University of Kansas Medical School and at the San Francisco campus of the University of California, Mullis joined the Cetus Corporation of Emeryville, California, in 1979.

Nüsslein-Volhard, Christiane (1942–)

German geneticist who was awarded the Nobel Prize for Physiology or Medicine in 1995 with Edward Lewis and Eric Wieschaus for their discovery of genes that control the early stages of the body's development. Nüsslein-Volhard did much research on the embryonic development of the fruit fly *Drosophila melanogaster*. She examined 40,000 random gene mutations for their effect on the fly's development and identified 150 genes. She has since cloned several of those genes and worked out their interactions.

Nüsslein-Volhard performed her experiments to identify all of the genes involved in the development of the fruit fly at the European Laboratory for Molecular Biology at Heidelberg. The mutant strains of flies she created have since been worked on by many other developmental biologists.

She was inspired in the late 1970s by the pioneering work of Edward Lewis, who had identified the transformations in the fruit fly that cause substitution of one segment of the body for another. These transformations were found to be the result of mutations in a gene family called the bithorax complex. Genes at the beginning of the complex were found to control anterior body segments, while genes further down the genetic map controlled more posterior body segments. This work was shown to be of particular importance when it was demonstrated that the gene ordering of this complex is conserved in humans.

Since 1986 she has been director of the genetics division of the Max Planck Institute for Developmental Biology, Tübingen.

In the 1990s Nüsslein-Volhard embarked on a large-scale project using zebrafish instead of fruit flies to generate and classify genetic variations. In 2000 Nüsslein-Volhard's team joined with Artemis Pharmaceuticals in Cologne, on the Tübingen 2000 screen of some 17 million zebrafish. Zebrafish sperm will be exposed to chemical mutagens, and the subsequent mutations will be studied in an effort to discover the mutations of every developmental gene.

Rothschild, Miriam (1908–)

English zoologist and entomologist who studied fleas and was the first to work out the flea jumping mechanism. She also studied fleas' reproductive cycles and linked this, in rabbits, to the hormonal changes within the host. She has written around 350 papers on entomology, zoology, neurophysiology, and chemistry.

She had no formal education until she was 17. She began degrees in zoology and English before settling upon marine biology. She studied snail-borne parasites for seven years till her laboratory was bombed in 1940. During the war she made a food for chickens from seaweed and worked decoding German communications.

English zoologist and entomologist Miriam Rothschild relaxing at home. At the beginning of the 21st century she is still active in conservation, despite being in her nineties.
Michael Freeman/Corbis

She studied woodpigeons and was the first to realize that they carry bovine TB. After the war she wrote her first book *Fleas, Flukes and Cuckoos*. She spent 20 years studying fleas and also catalogued her father's extensive flea collection. She also studied butterflies.

Still active in her nineties, she worked on plants and studied the telepathic relationship between people and their pets. Her interest in animal consciousness has led her to press for reform in the treatment of animals in agriculture.

Sanger, Frederick (1918–   )

English biochemist who was awarded the Nobel Prize for Chemistry in 1958 for determining the structure of insulin, and again in 1980 for work on the chemical structure of genes. He was the first person to be awarded the chemistry prize twice.

Sanger's second Nobel prize was shared with two US scientists, Paul Berg and Walter Gilbert, for establishing methods of determining the sequence of nucleotides strung together along strands of RNA and DNA. He also worked out the structures of various enzymes and other proteins.

Sanger was born in Gloucestershire and studied at Cambridge, where he spent his whole career. In 1961 he became head of the Protein Chemistry Division of the Medical Research Council's Molecular Biology Laboratory.

Between 1943 and 1953, Sanger and his co-workers determined the sequence of 51 amino acids in the insulin molecule. By 1945 he had discovered a compound, Sanger's reagent (2,4-dinitrofluorobenzene), which attaches itself to amino acids, and this enabled him to break the protein chain into smaller pieces and analyse them using paper chromatography.

From the late 1950s, Sanger worked on genetic material, and in 1977 he and his co-workers announced that they had established the sequence of the more than 5,000 nucleotides along a strand of RNA from a bacterial virus called R17. They later worked out the order for mitochondrial DNA, which has approximately 17,000 nucleotides.

Schaller, George B(eals) (1933–   )

German-born US mammalogist. Schaller became a research zoologist at the New York Zoological Society in 1966. He wrote highly acclaimed books on African and Asian mammals based on his own pioneering studies. In 1980 he was awarded the World Wildlife Fund Gold Medal for his contributions to the understanding and conservation of endangered species. Schaller was born in Berlin.

Sturtevant, Alfred Henry (1891–1970)

US geneticist who was the first, in 1911, to map the position of genes on a chromosome. He worked with US biologist Thomas Morgan.

In 1903, Sturtevant began his seminal experiments on the genetics of the fruit fly *Drosophila melanogaster*. In May 1910, Sturtevant and Morgan discovered a mutated *Drosophila* with a white eye, instead of the normal red. Sturtevant's first breeding experiments were with white-eyed and red-eyed flies. He also developed other mutations using genotoxic agents such as X-rays.

Using these variant flies, Sturtevant developed methods for mapping gene positions on chromosomes. In 1911, he produced the first gene map ever derived, showing the positioning of five genes on a *Drosophila* X chromosome: white-eyed, vermilion-eyed, rudimentary wings, small wings, and yellow body.

Sturtevant and Morgan determined the gene order along the chromosome by working out the recombination frequencies between the linked genes. During meiosis (cell division that produces reproductive cells with half the number of chromosomes) in a heterozygous, phenotypically normal female, an X chromosome carrying the mutations and a normal X chromosome will rearrange or 'crossover'. Males derived from these females will carry a combination of mutations. Those mutations that are closest together on the chromosome will be seen with the greatest frequency in the phenotypes (traits) of the male flies.

Inheritance of these mutations in flies was not strictly according to Mendel's rules since female flies had to inherit two mutated X chromosomes to demonstrate the phenotype, whereas males only had to acquire a single mutated X chromosome. This made the discovery that the five genes were on the same chromosome striking.

Tatum, Edward Lawrie (1909–1975)

US microbiologist who was awarded the Nobel Prize for Physiology or Medicine in 1958 for discovery that genes regulate precise chemical effects. He shared the prize with his co-workers George Beadle and Joshua Lederberg.

Tatum was born in Boulder, Colorado, and studied at the University of Wisconsin. He worked with Beadle at Stanford in 1937–41 and with Lederberg at Yale, where he became professor in 1946. He ended his career at the Rockefeller Institute for Medical Research from 1957.

Beadle and Tatum used X-rays to cause mutations in bread mould, studying particularly the changes in the enzymes of the various mutant strains. This led them to conclude that for each enzyme there is a corresponding gene. From 1945, with Lederberg, Tatum applied the same technique to bacteria and showed that genetic information can be passed from one bacterium to another. The discovery that a form of sexual reproduction can occur in bacteria led to extensive use of these organisms in genetic research.

Tinbergen, Niko(laas) (1907–1988)

Dutch-born British zoologist who was awarded the Nobel Prize for Physiology or Medicine in 1973 for his work in animal behaviour patterns. He specialized in the study of instinctive behaviour in animals, and was one of the founders of ethology, the scientific study of animal behaviour in natural surroundings. He shared the prize with Konrad Lorenz (with whom he worked on several projects) and Karl von Frisch.

Tinbergen investigated other aspects of animal behaviour, such as learning, and also studied human behaviour, particularly aggression, which he believed to be an inherited instinct that developed when humans changed from being predominantly herbivorous to being hunting carnivores.

Tinbergen was born in The Hague and educated at Leiden, where he became professor in 1947. From 1949 he was in Oxford, and established a school of animal-behaviour studies there.

In *The Study of Instinct* (1951), Tinbergen showed that the aggressive behaviour of the male three-spined stickleback is stimulated by the red coloration on the underside of other males (which develops during the mating season). He also demonstrated that the courtship dance of the male is stimulated by the sight of the swollen belly of a female that is ready to lay her eggs.

In *The Herring Gull's World* (1953), he described the social behaviour of gulls, emphasizing the importance of stimulus–response processes in territorial behaviour.

Watson, David Meredith Seares (1886–1973)

English embryologist and palaeobiologist who provided the first evidence that mammals evolved from reptiles. From the fossilized remains of primitive reptiles and mammals collected on trips to South Africa and Australia 1911–14, he pieced together the evolutionary line linking reptiles to early mammals.

Watson was born in Higher Broughton, Lancashire. He graduated from Manchester University in chemistry and geology, but began publishing papers on palaeobiology while he was still an undergraduate.

With the outbreak of World War I, he returned to England to join the RAF. From 1921 until his retirement in 1965 he was based at University College, London. In 1952 he was Alexander Agassiz visiting professor at Harvard. He was elected to the Royal Society in 1922, and was awarded the Darwin medal in 1942 and the Linnaeus medal in 1949.

Watson, James Dewey (1928–   )

US biologist who was awarded the Nobel Prize for Physiology or Medicine in 1962 for the discovery of the double-helical structure of DNA and determining the significance of this structure in the replication and transfer of genetic information. He shared the prize with his co-worker Francis Crick.

Crick and Watson published their work on the proposed structure of DNA in 1953, and explained how genetic information could be coded.

Watson was born in Chicago and studied there and at Indiana. He initially specialized in viruses but shifted to molecular biology and in 1951 he went to the Cavendish Laboratory at Cambridge, England, where he performed the work on DNA with Crick. In 1953 Watson returned to the USA. He became professor at Harvard in 1961 and director of the Cold Spring Harbor Laboratory of Quantitative Biology in 1968, and was head of the US government's Human Genome Project 1989–92.

Crick and Watson envisaged DNA replication occurring by a parting of the two strands of the double helix, each organic base thus exposed linking

James Watson (left) and Francis Crick in 1953, the year in which they determined the double helix structure of DNA. Bettmann/CORBIS

with a nucleotide (from the free nucleotides within a cell) bearing the complementary base. Thus two complete DNA molecules would eventually be formed by this step-by-step linking of nucleotides, with each of the new DNA molecules comprising one strand from the original DNA and one new strand.

Whipple, George Hoyt (1878–1976)

US physiologist who was awarded the Nobel Prize for Physiology or Medicine in 1934 for work on the treatment of pernicious anaemia by increasing the amount of liver in the diet. His research interest concerned the formation of haemoglobin in the blood. He showed that anaemic dogs, kept under restricted diets, responded well to a liver regime, and that their haemoglobin quickly regenerated. This work led to a cure for pernicious anaemia. He shared the prize with George Minot and William Murphy.

Whipple was born in Ashland, New Hampshire, and was educated at Yale and Johns Hopkins before becoming a professor at the University of California, where he concentrated on his anaemia research.

Wilkins, Maurice Hugh Frederick (1916–)

New Zealand-born British molecular biologist who was awarded the Nobel Prize for Physiology or Medicine in 1962 with Francis Crick and James Watson for the discovery of the double-helical structure of DNA and of the significance of this structure in the replication and transfer of genetic information.

Wilkins began his career as a physicist working on luminescence and phosphorescence, radar, and the separation of uranium isotopes, and worked in the USA during World War II on the development of the atomic bomb. After the war he turned his attention from nuclear physics to molecular biology, and studied the genetic effects of ultrasonic waves, nucleic acids, and viruses by using ultraviolet light.

Wilkins was born in Pongaroa and studied in the UK at Cambridge. He became professor of biophysics at London in 1970.

Studying the X-ray diffraction pattern of DNA, he discovered that the molecule has a double helical structure and passed on his findings to Crick and Watson.

Wilson, Edward Osborne (1929–)

US biologist and a leading authority on ants. Osborne is a pioneer of biodiversity and sociobiology, the study of the social behaviour of all animals including humans. Through his books he has become a great popularizer of science and he has won several awards including two Pulitzer prizes.

Wilson was born in Birmingham, Alabama, on 10 June 1929 and graduated in biology from the University of Alabama in 1949, obtaining a PhD from Harvard in 1955. In the same year he completed a taxonomic analysis of the ant genus *Lasius*. He was appointed to the Harvard faculty in 1956, after which he made a number of important discoveries about ants, including the fact that they communicate through chemical substances called pheromones. He developed the concept of the taxon cycle in which he links speciation and species dispersal with the habitats encountered by organisms in the process of expanding their populations.

With Canadian ecologist Robert MacArthur, Wilson developed a theory of the equilibrium of island populations, which they published in *Theory of Island Biogeography* (1967). He subsequently conducted experiments with Daniel Simberloff in mangrove clumps in the Florida Keys to confirm their hypothesis that a 'dynamic equilibrium number of species exists in any island'. To do this, they enumerated the species of insect in each island population, then eliminated all of them by fumigation, finding in the succeeding months that the same number of species returned to recolonize the islands.

Wilson's book *The Insect Societies* (1971) was a comprehensive survey of his entomological work and revealed in detail the complicated relationships and behaviour patterns of ants and other social insects in their own environments. His second book, *Sociobiology: The New Synthesis* (1975), caused controversy among certain groups of scientists who saw one chapter in particular as politically inflammatory. In this chapter he elucidated his theory on the biological basis of human society. He proposed that human social behaviour followed the same basic biological principles as the behaviour of groups of animals, attributing 90% of human behaviour to environment and only 10% to genetic factors. In 1979 with his exploration of the implications of sociobiology for human aggression, morality, and sexuality, *On Human Nature*, Wilson won a Pulitzer prize. In another controversial theory, he showed how apparently altruistic behaviour in insects, birds, and mammals is actually genetically and biologically programmed and may have evolved through natural selection. In this theory the individual can be sacrificed to preserve the genes of closely related individuals.

Among his other books, *The Ants* (1990) is a summary of all that is known about ants, *In Search of Nature* is an introduction to all Wilson's ideas, and *Consilience The Unity of Knowledge* (1998) draws on the physical sciences, biology, anthropology, psychology, religion, and philosophy to show how human intellectual mastery of the truths of the universe has its roots in the ancient Greek philosophy of the intrinsic orderliness governing the cosmos – an idea that flourished in the Enlightenment. He explains why the original goals of the Enlightenment are reappearing in science and the humanities. *Consilience* was a candidate for the first Samuel Johnson Prize for Non-fiction in 1999.

Wilson was professor of zoology at Harvard from 1964, becoming F B Baird Professor of Science in 1976, and has been curator of entomology at the Museum of Comparative Zoology at Harvard since 1972.

Wright, Sewall (1889–1988)

US geneticist and statistician. During the 1920s he helped modernize Charles Darwin's theory of evolution, using statistics to model the behaviour of populations of genes.

Wright's work on genetic drift centred on a phenomenon occurring in small isolated colonies where the chance disappearance of some types of gene leads to evolution without the influence of natural selection.

Wright was born in Melrose, Massachusetts, and educated at the University of Illinois and Harvard. He taught at the University of Chicago for 28 years, before becoming professor of genetics at the University of Wisconsin 1955–60.

Part Two

4 Directory of Organizations and Institutions

Anatomical Society of Great Britain and Ireland

Scientific organization, founded in 1887, for the promotion and development of the anatomical and related sciences, serving principally anatomists in the UK and the Republic of Ireland, but also has members worldwide. The *Journal of Anatomy*, covering all aspects of normal human and comparative anatomy, is published on behalf of the Society by Cambridge University Press.

Address

The Anatomical Society of Great Britain and Ireland
Department of Human Anatomy
University of Oxford
South Parks Road
Oxford OX1 3QX, UK
phone: +44 (01865) 272165
fax: +44 (01865) 272420
e-mail: @human-anatomy.oxford.ac.uk
Web site: http://www.sm.ic.ac.uk/

Australian Society for Microbiology

Professional, non-profitmaking organization, founded in 1959 to further the science of microbiology in Australia. The ASM has branches in each state and the Australian Capital Territory, and each branch organizes lectures, workshops, and other scientific activities. ASM publications include its official journal *Microbiology Australia*, published five times a year, and the annual volume *Recent Advances in Microbiology*. A Federation of Asia Pacific Microbiology Societies has been formed under the auspices of the ASM for the further dissemination of relevant microbiology issues, especially the identification, treatment, eradication, and management of infectious diseases.

Address

Australian Society for Microbiology
Unit 23, 20 Commercial Road

Melbourne, Victoria 3004, Australia
phone: +61 (3) 9867 8699
fax: +61 (3) 9867 8722
e-mail: TheASM@asm.auz.com
Web site: http://home.vicnet.net.au/~asm/welcom2.htm

Biochemical Society

A UK-based organization that promotes the study of biochemistry by providing on-line news and information on current research and meetings. The Society is also committed to helping to improve the public's understanding of scientific issues and to assisting science teachers through a network of Regional Sections. It publishes its own scientific journal *The Biochemist* and also produces resource materials for schools, provides careers advice, and organizes lectures on scientific and professional themes.

Address
The Biochemical Society
59 Portland Place
London W1B 1QW, UK
phone: +44 (020) 7580 5530
fax: +44 (020) 7637 3626
e-mail: genadmin@biochemistry.org
Web site: http://www.demon.co.uk/bes/

British Ecological Society

Founded in 1913, the British Ecological Society (BES) is the oldest of its kind in the world. It is an independent organization, receiving no outside funding, whose aims are to promote the science of ecology through research, publications, and conferences and to use the findings of such research for public education and to influence policy decisions which involve ecological matters. Thus the society is committed to using ecology as a basis for nature conservation, sound environmental management, and sustainable development. The BES has a worldwide membership base including teachers, local authority, ecologists, research scientists, conservationists, environmental consultants, and many others with an active interest in natural history and the environment.

Address
British Ecological Society
26 Blades Court, Deodar Road
Putney, London SW15 2NU, UK
phone: +44 (020) 8871 9797
fax: +44 (020) 8871 9779

e-mail: general@ecology.demon.co.uk
Web site: http://demon.co.uk/bes/

Convention on International Trade in Endangered Species of Wild Fauna and Flora (CITES)

This international convention was formed in 1975. CITES maintains detailed information and databases on the status of many endangered and threatened species. The CITES Web site is written in English, Spanish, and French, and provides much archived information as well as current news and details of its members and forthcoming events.

Address
CITES Secretariat
International Environment House
15 Chemin des Anémones
CH+1219 Châtelaine-Geneva, Switzerland
phone: +41 (22) 917 8139/40
fax: +41 (22) 797 3417
e-mail: cites@unep.ch
Web site: http:// www.wcmc.org.uk:80/CITES/index.shtml

Council for Responsible Genetics (CRG)

Established in 1983, the CGR is a national non-profit organization based in the US. The CRG encourages informed public debate about the social, ethical, and environmental implications of new genetic research, both in human genetics and commercial biotechnology and the environment, and advocates the responsible employment of new genetic technology. It is also actively involved in tracking biotech developments, writing position papers, creating model legislation, providing public education, and alerting the public to a variety of genetically-related issues. In addition, CRG publishes a bi-monthly newsletter, *GeneWatch*, which is the only US newsletter that continually monitors the ethical, social, and ecological impacts of biotechnology.

Address
5 Upland Road, Suite 3
Cambridge, MA 02140, USA
phone: +1 (617) 868 0870
fax: +1 (617) 491 53446
e-mail: crg@gene-watch.org
Web site: http://www.gene-watch.org

European Molecular Biology Organization (EMBO)

International body for the promotion of molecular biology studies in Europe. It is funded by contributions from its 23 member states, which together form the European Molecular Biology Conference (EMBC). EMBO produces the scientific journal of molecular biology *EMBO Journal*, published twice monthly by the Oxford University Press.

Address

Postfach 1022.40

D-69012 Heidelberg, Germany

phone: +49 (6221) 383031

fax: +49 (6221) 384879

e-mail: EMBO@EMBL-Heidelberg.de

Web site: http://www.embo.org/

European Molecular Biology Laboratory (EMBL)

Scientific institution for research into molecular and cell biology. It was established in 1974 and consists of a main laboratory in Heidelberg, Germany, and three outstations: Hamburg, Germany; Grenoble, France; and Hinxton, near Cambridge, UK. The Hinxton outstation specializes in bioinformatics research, while Hamburg and Grenoble have highly intensive X-rays and neutron radiation for structural studies; EMBL is also a teaching and training centre for molecular biology, and is supported by 14 European countries and Israel.

Address

Postfach 10.2209

69012 Heidelberg

Federal Repuplic of Germany

phone: +49 (6221) 3870 (sic)

fax: +49 (6221) 387306

e-mail: @EMBL-Heidelberg.de

Web site: http://www.embl-heidelberg.de/

Federation of European Microbiological Societies

International scientific organization for the promotion of microbiology in Europe. Linking some 38 microbiological societies thoughout Europe, the Federation encourages joint activities, facilitating communication among microbiologists. It supports meetings and laboratory courses, provides fellowships and grants for young scientists, and publishes journals and books in related fields.

Address
FEMS Central Office
Poortlandplein 6, 2628 BM Delft
The Netherlands
phone: +31 (15) 278 5604
fax: +31 (15) 278 5696
e-mail: fems@tudelft.nl
Web site: http://www.elsevier.nl:80/inca/homepage/sah/fems/menu.htm

Genetical Society

A UK-based registered charity that organizes a wide-ranging programme
of scientific meetings covering all areas of genetical research. It manages
and co-owns two leading academic journals in the field, *Genes and Development* and *Heredity*. The Genetical Society has a worldwide membership.

Address
Genetical Society
Roslin Institute
Roslin, Midlothian EH25 9PS, UK
phone: +44 (0131) 527 4472
fax: +44 (0131) 440 0434
e-mail: gensoc.memsec@bbsrc.ac.uk
Web site: http://www.genetics.org.uk/

Institute for Human Gene Therapy

A newly-formed campus-based research institute that seeks to provide a
foundation for the basic research that is necessary to assure the success of
human gene therapy. The IHGT is heavily involved in the training and
education of scientists who desire careers in gene therapy.

Address
Institute for Human Gene Therapy
Rm 204, Wistar Institute
University of Pennsylvania
University of Pennsylvania Health System
3601 Spruce Street, Philadelphia
PA 19104 4268, USA
fax: +1 (215) 898 6588
Web site: http://www.med.upenn.edu/ihgt/

Institute of Biology

Chartered professional body for UK biologists; founded in 1950 to promote
biology as a science and to develop applications of biology. It has more
than 70 affiliated societies and 16,500 members.

Address
Institute of Biology
20–22 Queensberry Place
London SW7 2ZY, UK
phone: +44 (0171) 581 8333
fax: +44 (0171) 823 9409
e-mail: info@iob.primex.co.uk
Web site: http://www.iob.org/

Institute of Biomedical Science
British professional body for biomedical scientists. Its aim is to promote and develop biomedical science and its practioners. It was founded in 1912 and changed its name from the Institute of Medical Laboratory Sciences in 1994; it has branches in Hong Kong, Cyprus, and Gibraltar.

Address
The Institute of Biomedical Science
12 Coldbath Square, London EC1R 5HL, UK
phone: +44 (0171) 713 0214
fax: +44 (0171) 436 4946
e-mail: mail@ibms.org
Web site: http://www.ibms.org/

International Federation for Medical and Biological Engineering
International scientific organization for the research and development of medical and biological engineering. It was founded in 1959 as the International Federation for Medical Electronics and Biological Engineering, and now has 43 affiliated organizations.

Address
IFMBE Secretariat
Department of Biomedical Engineering
Huddinge University Hospital
SE-141 86 Huddinge, Sweden
phone: +46 (8) 585 80852
fax: +46 (8) 585 86290
Web site: http://www.iupesm.org/ifmbe.html

International Union of Biological Sciences
Non-profitmaking scientific organization for study and research in biological sciences. It was established in 1919 and is a founding member of the International Council of Scientific Unions (ICSU). The Union has close relationships with the United Nations Educational, Scientific and Cultural

Organization (UNESCO), the European Commission, and other organizations, in the development of joint collaborative research and training programmes related to biological sciences.

Address
IUBS, 51 Boulevard de Montmorency
75016 Paris, France
phone: +33 (1) 4525 0009
fax: +33 (1) 4525 2029
e-mail: iubs@paris7.jussieu.fr
Web site: http://www.iubs.org/

National Centre for Biotechnology Education (NCBE)

Independent British organization for the provision of information, training, and resources for schools and colleges, industry, professional organizations, and the general public. The NCBE was founded in 1985 to support the teaching of biotechnology in schools and colleges, and was the first of its type in Europe; it is part of the Department of Microbiology at the University of Reading. Initially funded via a UK government grant, the Centre is now self-funded by charging for its services.

Address
NCBE
School of Animal and Microbiological Sciences
The University of Reading, Whiteknights
PO Box 228, Reading RG6 6AJ, UK
phone: +44 (0)118 9873743
fax: +44 (0)118 9750140
Web site: http://www.ncbe.reading.ac.uk/

Natural History Museum

The Natural History Museum has a long history that can be traced back to the middle of the 18th century. It is the national museum of natural history in the UK, and a centre of scientific excellence in the fields of taxonomy and biodiversity. The Museum aims to maintain and develop its collections, whilst employing them to promote the discovery, understanding, responsible use, and enjoyment of the natural world. In addition to purely academic research the Natural History Museum provides a wealth of resources for schools and colleges.

Address
The Natural History Museum
Cromwell Road, London, SW7 5BD, UK
tel: +44 (020) 7942 5011
Web site: http://www.nhm.ac.uk/

Roslin Institute

International centre for research on molecular and quantative genetics of farm animals and poultry science. Its major research programmes include the biology of reproduction, developmental biology and growth, and animal welfare and behaviour. It is an independent non-profit organization, sponsored by the Biotechnology and Biological Sciences Research Council (BBSRC).

Address

Roslin Institute, Roslin
Midlothian, EH25 9PS, UK
phone: +44 (0131) 527 4200
fax: +44 (0131) 440 0434
e-mail: roslin.library@bbsrc.ac.uk
Web site: http://www2.ri.bbsrc.ac.uk/

Sanger Centre

Named after a pioneer in the field of DNA sequencing English biochemist Frederick Sanger, the Sanger Centre is a genome research centre founded by the Wellcome Trust and the Medical Research Council. Its purpose is to further the knowledge of the whole DNA sequences of organisms, particularly through large-scale sequencing and data analysis. This institute is actively involved in the Human Genome Project, and is also determining the genetic code of other model organisms. The data obtained from this institute should underpin research on human biology and disease in the 21st century and beyond.

Address

The Sanger Centre
Wellcome Trust Genome Campus
Hinxton, Cambridge, CB10 1SA, UK
phone: +44 (01223) 834244
fax: +44 (01223) 494919
Web site: http://www.sanger.ac.uk/

Society for Experimental Biology

British non-profitmaking scientific organization for the promotion of all aspects of experimental biology. Its three main sections include animal, cell, and plant biology. The Society holds an annual symposium on a specialized topic, the proceedings of which are published; it also sponsors the monthly *Journal of Experimental Biology*, which publishes research papers in the plant sciences.

Address
The Society for Experimental Biology
Burlington House, Piccadilly
London W1V 0LQ, UK
phone: +44 (0171) 439 8732
fax: +44 (0171) 287 4786
e-mail: v.wragg@sebiol.demon.co.uk
Web site: http://www.demon.co.uk/SEB/

Society for General Microbiology

British scientific organization for the advancement of the science of microbiology. It was founded in 1945, holding its first scientific meeting in
Cambridge the same year; Sir Alexander Fleming was elected as its first
president. The SGM supports microbiology worldwide through its various
grant schemes, prize lectures, and awards. The Society's publications
include the *Journal of General Microbiology*, first published in 1947, and
the *Journal of General Virology*, founded in 1966.

Address
Society for General Microbiology
Marlborough House, Basingstoke Road
Spencer's Wood, Reading RG7 1AE, UK
phone: +44 (0118) 988 1800
fax: +44 (0118) 988 5656
e-mail: web.admin@socgenmicrobiol.org.uk
Web site: http://www.socgenmicrobiol.org.uk/

The Institute for Genomic Research (TIGR)

TIGR is a non-profit-seeking organization based in the US that has interests in the structure and function of the DNA of a whole spectrum of
organisms, from viruses and bacteria to plants and animals – including
humans. This institute maintains DNA and protein databases that may be
accessed and used for scientific research.

Address
The Institute for Genomic Research
9712 Medical Center Drive
Rockville, MD 20850, USA
phone: +1 (301) 838 0200
fax: +1 (301) 838 0208
Web site: http://www.tigr.org/

World Conservation Union

The World Conservation Union, or IUCN (International Union for the Conservation of Nature), was created in 1948 and is the world's largest conservation-related organization. Its mission is to influence, encourage and assist societies throughout the world to conserve the integrity and diversity of nature and to ensure that any use of natural resources is both equitable and ecologically sustainable.

Address
IUCN – The World Conservation Union
Rue Mauverney 28
CH-1196 Gland, Switzerland
Web site: http://www.iucn.org/

Worldwide Fund for Nature (WWF)

International organization to protect biological resources and preserve endangered plant and animal species. It is funded largely through membership dues, corporate subscriptions, legacies, foundation grants, and governments and aid agencies.

Address
Avenue du Mont-Blanc
Ch-1196 Gland, Switzerland
phone: +41 (22) 364 9111
fax: +41 (22) 364 5358
Web site: http://www.panda.org

5   Selected Works for Further Reading

Attenborough, David *Life on Earth*, 1979

One of the best written introductions to the variety of life on Earth – and beautifully illustrated too. Based on his award-winning TV series of the same name, Attenborough takes you through the whole 'story of evolution', beginning with the primeval soup and ending up with us.

Attenborough, David *The Private Life of Plants*, 1995

Beautifully illustrated account of the lives of plants, combined with detailed text and the traditional Attenborough enthusiasm.

Austin, C R, and Short, R V (eds) *Reproduction in Mammals*, 1982

A scholarly, comprehensive, and authoritative reference series justly famous for its clear and interesting presentation of up-to-date data and theory. Early volumes cover germ cells and fertilization, hormones in reproduction, embryonic and fetal development, reproductive patterns, and the manipulation of reproduction.

Baker, Robin *Sperm Wars*, 1996

Since the 1970s, biologists have been fascinated by the biological and evolutionary implications of sperm from different males competing for fertilization of the egg in the female reproductive tract. This is the first popular book on the phenomenon in humans. It summarizes an immense amount of information, all carefully documented. Iconoclastic and provocative.

Bonner, John Tyler *Life Cycles*, 1993

An evolutionary biologist who has devoted his life to the study of slime moulds. Writing with clarity and humour, he sets reproduction in the context of the life cycle – a linkage of evolution, development, and the complex activities of adult organisms. Filled with wonderful insights and interesting examples.

Calvino, Italo *The Growth of Biological Thought*, 1967

Short stories inspired by science. Several of the stories spring from the wonders of cell division, and have their own kind of truth.

Clark, David and Russell, Lonnie *Molecular Biology Made Simple*, 1997

Aimed at students, but with a lively writing style that gives it appeal to a wider audience.

Cohen, Jack *Reproduction*, 1977

A standard, well-illustrated introduction that collects together information on all aspects of biological reproduction.

Colinvaux, Paul *Why Big Fierce Animals Are Rare*, 1980

A good introduction to the science of ecology. Each chapter looks at a feature of the complex and fascinating set of relations that exist between plants, animals, and environment. If you want to read about how animals and plants get on with their normal day-to-day life, undisturbed by people and pollution, this book would be a good start.

Conway-Morris, Simon *The Crucible of Creation: The Burgess Shale and the Rise of Animals*, 1999

Written by the authority on the Burgess Shale deposits, in western Canada, which is renowned for its unique fossils, this is an account of the Burgess Shale fauna and the scientists involved in its history. Like Stephen Jay Gould's *Wondeful Life*, Conway-Morris also provides his own speculation about how the Burgess Shale fits into the story of human evolution.

Cooper, David, and Lanza, Robert *Xeno*, Oxford, 2000

The medical, ethical, and economical dangers and challenges of xeno-transplantation are analysed in this useful introduction to the subject.

Dawkins, Richard *The Blind Watchmaker*, 1986

Argues that Darwinian natural selection is the only known theory that could, in principle, explain adaptive complexity.

de Waal, Frans *Peacemaking Among Primates*, 1989

The author draws on his own detailed observations and those of other leading experts to describe primate reproductive behaviour in captivity and in the wild. A stimulating tale of relationships, rivalries, and reconciliations.

Edey, Maitland A, and Johanson, Donald C *Blueprints*, 1989

A brilliantly written and exciting account that shows just how much has been achieved by the geneticists. The history of science made vivid.

Eldredge, Niles *Reinventing Darwin: the Great Evolutionary Debate*, 1995

Whilst evolution by natural selection is widely accepted, the modern interpretations of evolution vary widely. An overview of the arguments supporting the two main theories in evolutionary biology that have developed since Darwin.

Ford, Norman D *When Did I Begin?*, 1991

In-depth analysis of an important ethical problem: when, exactly, does a human embryo become an individual?

Fortey, Richard A *Life: An Unauthorized Biography*, 1997

Concerns both biological and artificial life.

Goodall, D W, (ed) *Ecosystems of the World*, 1977–

Monumental, multi-volume compendium series with extensive bibliographies.

Gould, Stephen Jay *The Panda's Thumb*, 1980

A collection of essays by a master science writer able to breathe life into facts both general and particular. Here, Gould reflects on the evolution of the panda, investigates Charles Darwin, and wonders whether 'dinosaurs were dumb'. Fine bedtime reading.

Jones, Steve *Darwin's Ghost: The Origin of Species Updated*, 2000

Whilst virtually everybody had heard of *The Origin of Species*, very few people have actually read the book. Here, Steve Jones has attempted to make Darwin's arguments more accessible to a wider audience by rewriting the famous book with current knowledge but still maintaining the original chapter headings and ideas.

Jones, Stephen (ed) *The Cambridge Encyclopedia of Human Evolution*, 1992

Edited by a team led by Steve Jones, the well known geneticist, a comprehensive and up-to-date survey of all aspects of human evolution, with some fascinating information.

Jones, Steve *The Language of the Genes*, 1993

Entertaining yet restrained, the celebrated geneticist gives a reliable account of what we do and don't know about our genes.

Kimbrell, Andrew *The Human Body Shop*, 1993

The author reviews the technological and commercial controls of human reproduction, arguing that our current legal and technical framework is inadequate to deal with advances in biotechnology.

King, Barry (ed) *Time and the Hunter*, 1986

Different contributors give their account of some of the most interesting aspects of cell biology, including evolution, motility, and protein synthesis.

Kolata, Gina *CLONE: The Road to Dolly and the Path Ahead*, 1998

Describes the events leading to the birth of Dolly the sheep, the world's first clone using non-reproductive cells. Kolata also discusses the implications and ethics of what this advance in genetic technology means to humans.

Lear, Linda *Rachel Carson: Witness for Nature*, 1997

The first full biography, it describes both Carson's life and career, and also her influence on the environmental movement.

Lewontin, Richard C *The Triple Helix: Gene, Organism, and Environment*, 2000

Lewontin explains the themes, controversies, and debates in biology over the quarter century since his classic *The Genetic Basis of Evolutionary Change* appeared. He emphasizes the reciprocal relationship of the three factors in the course of evolution, and warns against reducing evolution to a sequence of events predetermined by genetic programming.

Lewontin, Richard *The Red Queen Hypothesis*, 1991

Lectures originally given on Canadian radio. A sustained attack on the idea that DNA controls people – or even cells.

Margulis, Lynne, Sagan, Dorion, and Eldredge, Niles *What Is Life?*, 2000

The question 'what is life?' has dominated biological and philosophical thinking for centuries. These authors delve into the topic using illustrations, science, philosophy, history and poetry to provide a captivating overview of the history of life, its essences and future.

Margulis, Lynn, and Schwartz, Karlene *Five Kingdoms : An Illustrated Guide to the Phyla of Life on Earth*, 1999

An excellent work on classification with an updated molecular analysis for the third edition.

Maynard Smith, Joan *Shaping Life: Genes, Embryos and Evolution*, 1998

A discussion that brings together two influential branches of biology that have traditionally been separate fields: adaptation, or why bodies are the way they are, and a major question in embryology – how genes control development and build bodies that way.

Maynard Smith, Joan and Szathmáry, Eörs *The Origins of Life: From the Birth of Life to the Origins of Language*, 1999

The authors present an original picture of evolution. Central to the book is a discussion of the way in which information is passed through generations, starting from the appearance of the first replicating molecules, through the evolution of cooperating animal societies, and finishing with the development of language in humans.

Mayr, Enst *One Long Argument: Charles Darwin and the Genesis of Modern Evolutionary Thought*, 1993

Ernst Mayr provides a very good introduction to the complex history of the development of evolutionary theory. Darwin's five main theories are described and defended against the major critical arguments.

Milgrom, Lionel R *The Colours of Life*, 1998

A very readable, though detailed, look at the chemistry of colour in living things that will tell you just why grass is green.

Paul, William (ed) *Immunology*, 1991

Authoritative papers from the *Scientific American*, covering the fascinating science of immunology. Difficult in parts but a wonderful book for conveying how clever cells can be.

Proctor, Michael, and Yeo, Peter *The Pollination of Plants*, 1973

A rich source of information on the many and varied ways plants have found of getting pollen from one to another.

Rabinow, Paul *Making PCR: A Story of Biotechnology*, 1996

An original account by an anthropologist of the Biotech company Cetus which developed the PCR procedure that has revolutionized genetic research during the last few decades. This book documents the benefits of the commercial approach to science and the conflicts caused by financial and prestige considerations.

Ridley, Matt *Genome: The Autobiography of a Species in 23 Chapters*, 2000

This book devotes one chapter to the role of a gene in human development and adult life for each of the 23 human chromosomes. Ridley also discusses the world-changing implications that genetic research, and in particular the Human Genome Project, will bring to our lives and also our attitudes to such research.

Ridley, Mark *The Problems of Evolution*, 1986

Witty and cultivated essays on particular topics of controversy; or of lively discussion in the field of evolution.

Ridley, Matt *Cell Biology*, 1993

Highly readable account of the way the genes inside our cells have organized life in favour of sex.

Ritvo, Harriet *The Platypus and the Mermaid and other Figments of the Classifying Imagination*, 1997

A wide-ranging look at classification at its broadest. It is both authoritative and compelling.

Rose, Steven *The Chemistry of Life*, 1991

This is an up-to-date and authoritative survey of the chemical goings-on inside a cell. Rose is a professor at the Open University and here makes a technical subject pretty approachable.

Rose, Steven, Kamin, Leon, and Lewontin, Richard *Not in our Genes*, 1984

Political as well as biological, these essays are an argument against the so-called reductionist ideas that suggest genes are in charge.

Schrödinger, Erwin *What is Life?*, 1944

This is one of the great science classics of the 20th century, elegantly written by an eminent physicist. His theoretical approach to the question of life involved an analysis of how genes must work, an analysis which set the agenda for the new post-war study of molecular biology.

Singer, Peter *A Darwinian Left: Politics, Evolution and Cooperation*, 1999

A brief account of how Darwinian theory has been used in politics, especially by the right wing. Singer, a philosopher, also provides moral insights into how modern evolutionary theory may be used by left-wing thinkers in the future.

Smith, J L B *Old Four Legs: The Story of the Coelacanth*, 1956

A historical account of the original discovery of the coelacanth off South Africa and the race to find the source population by one of the original people involved in bringing this remarkable 'living fossil' to science.

Thomson, Keith *Living Fossil: The Story of the Coelacanth*, 1991

Provides a history of the discovery of the coelacanth by M Courtney-Latimer and Professor J L B Smith. Thomson also provides an account of what scientific research has discovered about the physiology, behaviour, and ecology of the coelacanth and also its importance to evolutionary biology.

The coelacanth is the sole survivor of an ancient group of fishes. It is a heavy-bodied fish with fleshy fin lobes and small scales. It grows to a weight of 90 kg/200 lb and is dark brown to blue in colour.

Tudge, Colin *The Engineer in the Garden*

Sometimes disturbing account of how animals and plants may grow up to be different – thanks to genetic engineering.

Vroon, Piet *Smell: The Secret Seducer*, 1998

The biology of the olfactory system and its importance in human affairs.

Watson, James D *The Double Helix*, 1968

A terrific read about arguably the greatest scientific breakthrough of our age – the discovery of the structure of DNA by the two young Cambridge scholars James Watson and Francis Crick. If you think that scientists are remote and cold, this book will quickly change your mind.

Wilkie, Tom *Perilous Knowledge*, 1993

Useful account of the Human Genome Project – the mapping and decoding of each and every one of our genes. Wilkie is a science journalist and so well placed to understand and express public concerns over the moral consequences of molecular biology.

Wolpert, Lewis *The Triumph of the Embryo*, 1994

A straightforward and informative account of the development of the vertebrate embryo. This is Wolpert's own research field, and he writes with verve.

6   Web Sites

Access Excellence

http://www.accessexcellence.org

US-based site for biology teachers sponsored by a biotechnology company, this site has plenty to interest the casual browser as well – particularly its 'What's new?' section, with weekly science reports and interviews with scientists making the news, and 'About biotech', an in-depth look at the field of biotechnology.

AIDS Virtual Library

http://www.planetq.com/aidsvl/index.html

This site is maintained by volunteers and deals with the social, political, and medical aspects of AIDS, HIV, and other related issues. The organizers welcome suggestions for new topics for the AIDS virtual library.

Amino Acids

http://www.chemie.fu-berlin.de/chemistry/bio/amino-acids_en.html

Small but interesting site giving the names and chemical structures of all the amino acids. The information is available in both English and German.

Anatomy and Physiology

http://www.msms.doe.k12.ms.us/biology/anatomy/apmain.html

Anatomy and physiology page for secondary-school students. Click on one of several images of body parts such as the heart or digestive system, to get to a helpful description of its functions, with an annotated diagram and hypertext links to further details on various aspects.

Animal Diversity Web

http://animaldiversity.ummz.umich.edu/

Impressive database on animal diversity, from the Museum of Zoology at the University of Michigan. Click on a group of animals, then go to an individual animal to receive information on its taxonomy, habitat, and behaviour.

Animal Info – Information on Rare, Threatened, and Endangered Animals

http://www.animalinfo.org/

Fascinating, text-only profiles of the world's rarest mammals, some of whose populations, such as that of the northern hairy-nosed wombat, have fallen below three figures. Find information on specific animals in the individual species index or browse the species group index.

ARKive

http://www.arkive.org.uk

A growing database of zoomable photographs and video clips of the world's endangered plants, animals, and habitats form the core of this visually stunning Web site. In an effort to harness the power of cyberspace in the interests of global biodiversity, the ARKive project provides well-researched biological and taxonomic information on each species, an impassioned page on the importance of conserving rare species, and a wealth of educational and fun resources for children and teachers.

Atlas of the Body: the Endocrine System

http://www.ama-assn.org/insight/gen_hlth/atlas/newatlas/endo.htm

Basic guide to the human endocrine system, with a diagram showing the location of various glands in the body. A simple table explains the functions of the glands and the hormones they produce.

Bacteria in Sickness and in Health

http://microbios1.mds.qmw.ac.uk/underground/bactsick/bactsick.html

Guide to the goodies of the microbial world, the bacteria that form the healthy flora of the human body. The site looks at various parts of the body, such as the gut, mouth, nose, and throat, and the bacteria that they normally contain, and explains how to tell when a bacteria is acting as a pathogen.

Bacterial Evolution: Score one for Punk Eek

http://www.sciam.com/explorations/072196explorations.html

Part of a larger site maintained by *Scientific American*, this page reports on research conducted at Michigan State University in which scientists sped up the evolution of bacteria in order to study the theory of 'punctuated equilibrium', which seeks to explain why evolutionary changes sometimes take place with relative suddenness after aeons of general stasis. The text includes hypertext links to further information, and there is also a list of links to critical analysis of punctuated equilibrium and related sites on the Web.

Bad Bug Book – Salmonella
http://vm.cfsan.fda.gov/~mow/chap1.html

Fact sheet with basic information about salmonella. It offers details on the nature and the diagnostic procedures of the disease, susceptible groups, and the potential complications following the disease, as well as guidelines for cooking eggs, the food mainly associated with salmonella.

Beginners' Guide to Molecular Biology
http://www.iacr.bbsrc.ac.uk/notebook/courses/guide/

Excellent introductory material aimed at GCSE- and A-level molecular biologists. Part of the Molecular Biology Online site, this page provides a thematic overview of the topic, with detailed information on many aspects of the cell.

Biodiversity: Introduction
http://kaos.erin.gov.au/life/general_info/op1.html#foreword

Introduction to a wider site on Australian biodiversity, which does an excellent job of explaining the global importance of maximum species' diversity. The page includes a discussion of the use of plants for medicinal purposes.

'Biodiversity Loss Threatens New Treatments'
http://www.bmj.com/cgi/content/full/316/7140/1261/l

Part of a collection of articles maintained by the *British Medical Journal*, this page features the full text of a news article originally published on 25 April 1998 that reports on how the loss of biodiversity will adversely affect the future of human health. You can also search the collections under which this article appears, search other articles written by the author of this article, and submit or read responses to this article.

Bioenergy Information Network
http://bioenergy.ornl.gov/

US government site about the possibilities and research into producing energy from rapidly replaced trees and grasses. There are sections on 'Biopower basics', 'The biopower industry', and a library of photos and video stills.

Biological Control
http://www.nysaes.cornell.edu:80/ent/biocontrol/

University-based site on the various methods of biological control used by farmers in the USA. This includes sections on parasitoids, predators, pathogens, and weed feeders. Each section contains images and sections on 'Relative effectiveness' and 'Pesticide susceptibility'.

111

Biology for Children

http://www.kapili.com/biology4kids/index.html

Fun, interactive introduction to biology. You can take a quiz to test your knowledge of the basics, take a tour around the site, or search for specific information.

Biology Project

http://www.biology.arizona.edu/

A large, educational Web site set up by the University of Arizona that deals with many aspects of biology, including cell biology, developmental biology, human health, genetics, and molecular biology.

Biology Timeline

http://www.zoologie.biologie.de/history.html

Chronology of important developments in the biological sciences. It includes items from the mentioning of hand pollination of date palms in 1800 BC to the Nobel prize award for the discovery of site-directed mutagenesis in 1993. The site also includes a list of sources.

Biomass

http://www.nrel.gov/research/industrial_tech/biomass.html

Information on biomass from the US Department of Energy. A graph supports the textual explanation of the fact that the world is only using 7% of annual biomass production. There is a clear explanation of the chemical composition of biomass and development of technologies to transform it into usable fuel sources.

BodyQuest: the Nervous System

http://library.thinkquest.org/10348/find/content/nervous.html

This page on the nervous system contains an overview of the way in which the brain sends, receives, and processes the nerve impulses that control everything we do. Part of a much larger site on the human body, it discusses the roles played by the central, peripheral, and autonomic nervous systems, and provides experiments to answer such questions as 'How do we balance?' and 'Why do we have two eyes?'

Body Systems and Homeostasis

http://www.mhhe.com/biosci/genbio/maderbiology/supp/homeo.html

Thorough, text-only description of the way in which the systems of the body act to preserve homeostasis (constancy of the body's internal environment irrespective of external factors). The page – a supplement to a textbook written by Sylvia Mader, includes a table of the major endocrine glands and the hormones they produce.

Bugs in the News!

http://falcon.cc.ukans.edu/~jbrown/bugs.html

Lively articles fill you in not just on the micro-organisms in the news, but also on immunity, antibiotics, and molecular-biology issues in the 'real' world.

Carnivorous Plant Frequently Asked Questions

http://www.sarracenia.com/faq.html

A great site for anyone who wants to know anything about carnivorous plants – or just to see some pictures. There is extensive detailed information, but the site is presented in a relaxed and entertaining manner, making it a pleasure to read. There are also plenty of photos, and a particularly large section reserved for the notorious Venus fly trap.

Cell Membrane Transport

http://mindquest.net/biology/cell-biology/outlines/ec4guide.html

Study guide to cell membrane transport, part of a larger site devoted to cellular biology. The well-written text covers important concepts such as diffusion, osmosis, active transport, symport, and facilitated diffusion. Take the online exam when you have finished studying.

Cells Alive

http://www.cellsalive.com/

Lively and attractive collection of microscopic and computer-generated images of living cells and micro-organisms. It includes sections on HIV infection, penicillin, and how antibodies are made.

Cells: Diffusion

http://www.dcn.davis.ca.us/~carl/diffuse.htm

Concise description of cell diffusion, the means by which materials travel in and out of a cell. With the help of clear diagrams, the page explains the related concepts of osmosis, facilitated diffusion, and active transport.

Cell Structure and Function

http://www.mindquest.net/biology/cell-biology/outlines/
ec3guide.html

Good, basic guide to the properties of cells. Part of a larger cellular biology resource, this page follows an easy-to-follow introduction with illustrated explanations of prokaryotic and eukaryotic cells.

Cellular Organization
http://gened.emc.maricopa.edu/bio/bio181/BIOBK/BioBookCELL2.
html#Table of Contents

Thorough introduction to cellular biology. This academic Web site covers
the size, shape, and constituent parts of various cells, with the clear text
illustrated with diagrams and slides.

Center for Biodiversity: Study of Plants and Animals
http://www.inhs.uiuc.edu/cbd/main/generalinfo.html

If you've ever wondered about the mysteries of astacology, this site will
provide the answers, as well as introducing other, less obscure, branches
of taxonomic biology such as herpetology, mammology, and botany.
Linked to the Illinois Natural History Survey's vast collection of photographs, this is an excellent resource for anyone wanting to explore the
vast diversity of life on Earth.

Circulatory System: Online Learning
http://library.thinkquest.org/25896/

Wide-ranging guide to the circulatory system. This attractive Web site
contains pages on blood, arteries, veins, and capillaries, the heart, and
diseases of the circulatory system. Accessible text and clear, attractive
diagrams make this an excellent secondary-school resource.

Classification of Living Things
http://daphne.palomar.edu/animal/default.htm

Well-written introduction to the principles of Linnaean classification.
This Web site explains the general principles of taxonomy, with lavish
use of photography, diagrams, and hypertext links. It follows this with a
number of tables illustrating taxonomic relationships, such as the five
kingdoms of life. A table of human classification shows how people fit
into the scheme.

Crick, Francis Harry Compton
http://kroeber.anthro.mankato.msus.edu/information/biography/
abcde/crick_francis.htmlm

Profile of the life and achievements of the pioneer molecular biologist.
It traces his upbringing and education and how he brought his knowledge of X-ray diffraction to his work with James Watson in unravelling
the structure of DNA. There is a photo, a listing of Crick's major books
and articles, and a bibliography.

Cytogenetics Gallery

http://www.pathology.washington.edu/Cytogallery

Online gallery of chromosomes from the Pathology Department of the University of Washington, Seattle. This in-depth look at the chromosome contains a concise definition of the subject as well as a collection of images used to show how scientists pin-point chromosomal abnormalities.

Dawkins, Richard

http://www.world-of-dawkins.com/

Biographical information about Richard Dawkins, plus quotes, interviews, papers, articles, and excerpts from his books. This is an unofficial site gathering together a whole host of regularly updated information from a wide variety of sources.

Dennis Kunkel's Microscopy

http://www.pbrc.hawaii.edu/~kunkel/

This site is a photomicographer's dream – full of pictures taken with both light and electron microscopes. As well as several differing galleries of images, there is also information about microscopy and how the pictures were taken.

Desert Plant Survival

http://www.desertusa.com/du_plantsurv.html

Attractive and readable page on the mechanisms plants use to survive in the hostile environment of the desert. Part of a larger site on desert survival, this page describes the main features of the xerophytes – plants such as cacti which have altered their physical structure for the sake of survival – and the phreatophytes, which adapt to their arid habitat by growing roots long enough to reach the water table.

Designer Genes

http://library.thinkquest.org/18258/index2.htm

A very colourful Web site produced by a collaboration of high-school students from around the world. It provides plenty of easy-to-understand information about genetics and bioengineering, and, should you wish, you can even test your genetic knowledge with a quiz!

Dinofish.com

http://www.dinofish.com/

Contains much historical information about the discovery, study, and conservation of the coelacanth, a 400-million-year-old species of fish, as well as recent news and listings of scientific articles. Also on the site is a virtual swimming coelacanth, some on-line videos, and a shop for coelacananth enthusiasts!

DNA From The Beginning
http://vector.cshl.org/dnaftb/index.html

A very informative, fun site, with lots of animation and multimedia resources, for those who which to learn something about the 'stuff of life'.

Dobzhansky, Theodosius
http://kroeber.anthro.mankato.msus.edu/information/biography/abcde/dobzhansky_theodosius.html

Profile of the pioneering geneticist. It traces his childhood interest in insects, the frustration of his ambitions in the Soviet Union, and his subsequent research in the USA. There are photos of Dobzhansky and a bibliography.

Dr Frankenstein, I presume?
http://www.salonmagazine.com/feb97/news/news2970224.html

Interview with the man who made the first cloned mammal using adult cells, Dolly. Embryologist Dr Ian Wilmut speaks to Andrew Ross about his worries and his future projects, about the distinction between science fiction and human cloning, and about what could go wrong with researching this delicate area.

Dr James D Watson Profile
http://www.achievement.org/autodoc/page/wat0pro-1

Description of the life and works of the discoverer of the structure of the DNA molecule, Dr James Watson. Watson won the Nobel prize for his most famous discovery (made with Francis Crick) in 1962. The Web site contains not only a profile and biographical information, but also holds a lengthy interview with Watson from 1991 accompanied by a large number of photographs, video sequences, and audio clips.

Dr NAD's Mini-Course
http://www.geocities.com/CapeCanaveral/5229/n_1.htm

Dr NAD's step-by-step mini-course uses helpful graphics and readable text to guide you through the basics of plant structure and reproduction. It provides a clear explanation of the differences between plant and animal cells.

Endangered Species
http://eelink.net/EndSpp/

Good facts and pictures on species under threat from extinction. Also contains some information about the nature of historical extinctions, as well as news and links to conservation organizations around the globe.

Endangered Species Home Page
http://www.fws.gov/r9endspp/endspp.html

US Fish and Wildlife site with full details of its ongoing conservation programmes. The site also contains a 'Kids' Corner', a gallery of images, and a link to the latest edition of its *Endangered Species Bulletin*.

Environmental Organization Web Directory
http://www.webdirectory.com

A site that contains thousands of links, Web sites and contact addresses from over 100 countries. This is the largest exclusively environmental directory for those interested in environmental issues and information.

Evolutionist, The
http://cpnss.lse.ac.uk/darwin/evo/

Online magazine devoted to evolutionary ideas which includes features, interviews, and comment. It currently includes an article on the recent political interest in Darwinism and a column on the limits of evolutionary theory.

Evolution: Theory and History
http://www.ucmp.berkeley.edu/history/evolution.html

Dedicated to the study of the history and theories associated with evolution, this site explores topics on classification, taxonomy, and dinosaur discoveries, and then looks at the key figures in the field and reviews their contributions.

Eye
http://retina.anatomy.upenn.edu/~lance/eye/eye.html

Thorough information on the physical structures of the eye, from the University of Pennsylvania, USA. The page is divided into sections covering the main parts of the eye, such as the retina, cornea, iris, pupil, and lens.

From Reactor to Refrigerator
http://whyfiles.news.wisc.edu/054irradfood/index.html

Part of the Why Files project, published by the National Institute for Science Education (NISE) and funded by the National Science

Foundation, this page explains the how, why, and what of food irradiation. The highly readable text, laid out over five pages, includes information about other techniques being offered as means to protect food. Numerous images and diagrams enhance the text throughout. You will also find a comprehensive bibliography of sources for further research.

Fungi

http://www.herb.lsa.umich.edu/kidpage/factindx.htm

University-run network of hyperlinked pages on fungi, from their earliest fossil records to their current ecology and life cycles, from how they are classified systematically to how they are studied. Although this page is not shy of technical terms, there are clear explanations and pictures to help the uninitiated.

Fungus 2000

http://194.131.255.3/bmspages/Fungus2000/Fungus2000.htm

As a challenge to the British Mycological Society to record at least 2000 species of fungus in the year 2000, this site was set up to display information about the fungi inhabiting the British Isles. It allows the reader to search the database and also provides maps of UK fungal distribution.

GCSE Biology

http://www.purchon.co.uk/science/biology.html

Attractive and easy-to-use Web site covering all the main elements of the GCSE topic 'Life Processes and Living Things'. It is broken down into sections, such as 'Animal and plant cells', 'Blood', 'Vitamins', and so on. Each topic page contains hypertext links to further information where needed.

GCSE Bitesize Revision – Biology

http://www.bbc.co.uk/education/gcsebitesize/science_biology/
index.shtml

Handy revision guide for GCSE Biology, from the BBC's 'Bitesize' revision Web site. Work your way through 'Revision bites' on key areas of the syllabus, then move on to the 'Test bites' on each subject when you are feeling more confident of your level of knowledge.

Gene CRC

http://www.genecrc.org/

A very well laid out site that was developed for those who wish to keep up with accurate and up-to-date information on genetical research. As well as providing 'hot news' and discussion about ethical issues, it also contains a glossary, educational resources, and fun pages for children.

Gene School 99
http://library.thinkquest.org/28599/

Designed for school students and teachers, this is a comprehensive online exploration of the discoveries and innovations of modern gene science. A useful page on the fundamentals of genetics is accompanied by links to news stories on genes and genetics. The brave new world of cloning is explained in another section, while an interactive page contains genetics-based games, quizzes, and experiments.

Genetic Technology
http://whyfiles.news.wisc.edu/075genome/

Wry and thought-provoking look at genetic science. Starting with a dig at the morals of a past US president, who was posthumously exposed by developments in gene mapping, this Web site continues with an intelligent consideration of the potential offered by the human genome project, and the limitations of genetics.

Gertrude B Elion Profile
http://www.achievement.org/autodoc/page/eli0pro-1

Description of the life and work of the winner of the Nobel Prize for Medicine or Physiology Gertrude Elion. The Web site contains not only a profile and biographical information, but also holds a lengthy interview with Elion from 1991 accompanied by a large number of photographs, video sequences, and audio clips.

Hello Dolly
http://whyfiles.news.wisc.edu/034clone/

Imaginative and humorous look at the issue of cloning, presented by the *Why Files*, an online magazine on the science behind the news. Genes, chromosomes, DNA, ethical considerations, and the 'lucky lamb' itself are all covered here. The magazine also features a series of interviews with specialists on genetics, bioethics, and other fields related to the experiment.

Hidden Killers
http://library.thinkquest.org/23054/gather/index.shtml

Viruses are exposed in all their 'villainy' in this sophisticated and dramatic Web site. An excellent and detailed guide to the basic facts on viruses is presented alongside further pages explaining the lethal potential of these micro-organisms and the dangers of their use as weapons.

Homeostasis

http://biology.colchsfc.ac.uk/brian/homeost.html

Text-only, but thorough, explanation of homeostasis. This page, part of a larger site covering many anatomical topics, covers glucoregulation, osmoregulation, the function of a nephron, and thermoregulation.

Hopkins, Sir Frederick Gowland

http://web.calstatela.edu/faculty/nthomas/hopkins.htm

Maintained by Nigel Thomas, PhD, at California State University, Los Angeles, this page is devoted to the life and scientific work of Frederick Hopkins. Biographical information includes text and a timeline of important moments in Hopkins' life. You will also find a bibliography of books by and about Hopkins. A special 'science section' provides information on essential amino acids and vitamins. There is also a bibliography of texts about vitamins.

Human Anatomy

http://library.thinkquest.org/28297/body.html

Quick guide to human anatomy. The Web site is divided into three sections, on the skeleton, the digestive system and the respiratory system. Each gives a breakdown of the constituent parts and their functions.

Human Anatomy Online

http://www.innerbody.com/htm/body.html

Fun, interactive, and educational site on the human body. The site is divided into many informative sections, including hundreds of images, and animations for Java-enabled browsers.

Human Genetic Disease: A Layman's Approach

http://mcrcr2.med.nyu.edu/murphp01/lysosome/hgd.htm

Comprehensive manual of cell biology for the family. It includes discussions of cell structure, DNA, chromosomes, and the detection of genetic defects. It also outlines the main goals of state-of-the-art genetic research.

Human Genome Project Information

http://www.ornl.gov/TechResources/Human_Genome/home.html

US-based site devoted to this mammoth project – with news, progress reports, a molecular genetics primer, and links to other relevant sites.

Immunology

http://www.nutramed.com/immunology/index.htm

Excellent and easy-to-understand introduction to the science of immunology. The clearly written text describes how the immune system works, the function of antibodies. The site also explains what happens when the immune system fails to work, or works too well, and the problems of allergies and hypersensitivity.

Integration and Control: How Nervous Systems Work

http://research.umbc.edu/~farabaug/nerve3.html

Page on the nervous system from the University of Maryland. The page describes concepts such as the reflex arc, and explains the main differences between the nervous systems of vertebrate and invertebrate species.

Interactive Mitosis Tutorial

http://www.sci.sdsu.edu/multimedia/mitosis/

Shockwave-enhanced explanation of mitosis, the process of cell division in non-reproductive eukaryotic cells. All terms are clearly explained. The site also provides animated GIFs for those whose connections are slow.

Interactive Respiratory Physiology Encyclopedia

http://omie.med.jhmi.edu/res_phys/Encyclopedia/Menu.HTML

Virtual encyclopedia of the human respiratory system, from Johns Hopkins School of Medicine. Click on a topic from 'Air flow' to 'Surfactant', to find a well-illustrated and authoritative entry. Designed with trainee doctors in mind, this is clear enough to be useful to students at a less advanced level.

International Federation of Organic Farming Movements

http://ecoweb.dk/ifoam/

Site of an international organization working to promote sustainable organic agriculture. There are a clear summary of the organization's goals, reports of international campaigns on food and farming issues, press releases, contacts for the hundreds of affiliated organizations, and details of related publications.

Introduction to Chromosomes

http://gslc.genetics.utah.edu/basic/concepts/chromosomes.html

Introduction to chromosomes that is part of a much larger site on genetic science based in Utah. A 'clickable' diagram of two chromosomes is used to show how geneticists tell chromosomes apart. The page also contains links to information on DNA and proteins.

Introduction to Evolutionary Biology
http://www.talkorigins.org/faqs/faq-intro-to-biology.html

Intelligent and readable explanation of the theory of evolution, the cornerstone of modern biology. Author Chris Colby presents the main aspects of evolutionary biology, and robustly confronts the 'evolution versus creation' debate. An interesting section dispels common misconceptions about evolution, and demonstrates how changes to the environment can affect the way in which a species evolves.

Introduction to Photosynthesis and its Applications
http://photoscience.la.asu.edu/photosyn/education/photointro.html

Good general introduction to photosynthesis, written by a professor at Arizona State University, USA. A discussion of the basics – illustrated with photographs and diagrams, is followed by an explanation of photosynthetic electron transfer, carbon fixation, and the effects of increasing exposure to carbon dioxide.

Introduction to Proteins
http://biotech.icmb.utexas.edu/pages/science/protein_intro.html

Introduction to the world of proteins with discussions of their structures and sequences, as well as descriptions of some major kinds of proteins. The site also includes a useful glossary and offers a variety of photographic shots.

Journey into Phylogenetic Systematics
http://www.ucmp.berkeley.edu/clad/clad4.html

Online exhibition about evolutionary theory with a specific emphasis on phylogenetic systematics: the way that biologists reconstruct the pattern of events that has led to the distribution and diversity of life. The site provides an introduction to the philosophy, methodology, and implication of cladistic analysis, with a separate section on the need for cladistics. Many of the scientific terms are included in an illuminating glossary.

Kingdom Monera: the Prokaryotes
http://fig.cox.miami.edu/Faculty/Dana/monera.html

Clearly written guide to the Kingdom Monera, otherwise known as bacteria and the most numerous organisms on Earth. The site describes the basic types of bacteria: archaebacteria, eubacteria, and the mycoplasms, and shows how to identify them. It also covers bacterial reproduction and movement, and the economic importance of these micro-organisms.

Life in Extreme Environments
http://www.reston.com/astro/extreme.html

Fully searchable database of information on the scientific research into plants and animals living in extreme conditions. The site includes sections on organisms that can survive extremes of darkness, cold, radiation, and heat.

Live A Life Page
http://alife.fusebox.com/

Fascinating page that brings together interactive programs to simulate ecological and evolutionary processes. Included is an adaptation of Richard Dawkins's Biomorphs program, described in *The Blind Watchmaker*, which enables the user to select 'morphs' for certain qualities and watch as their offspring evolve.

Lucy Test
http://www.geocities.com/CapeCanaveral/Lab/8853

Was the extinct primate known as Lucy really our evolutionary ancestor? Evaluate the fossil evidence for yourself by taking this intriguing test, which asks you to review a series of three skeleton photographs and decide which belongs to *Australopithecus afarensis* ('Lucy'). One is genuine, one belongs to a modern human, and one to a chimp. This site provides thought-provoking material on the evolution debate, but also gives a taste of real scientific inquiry.

Major Biomes of the World
http://www.runet.edu/~swoodwar/CLASSES/GEOG235/biomes/main.html

Site providing information on the distribution and nature of the world's major biomes. It looks at the structure, growth patterns, and taxonomy of the vegetation, in the context of soil types and climate variations. The site contains supporting materials for students including an online glossary and study hints.

Microbe Zoo
http://commtechlab.msu.edu/sites/dlc-me/zoo/

Colourful and interactive zoo of some of the microbes that surround us. It includes sections on the 'domestic' microbes, the vampire ones that suck the life from other bacteria, the killers which destroy stone buildings, those in aquatic environments, and those that are to be found in beer, bread, chocolate, wine, and other food.

Microbial Underground
http://www.ch.ic.ac.uk/medbact/microbio.html

Extensive site of resources for the microbiologist that includes a news section, links to culture collections, a newsgroup, and courses. This root page also contains images and an audio clip.

Mitosis and Meiosis
http://buglady.clc.uc.edu/biology/bio104/meiosis.htm

Clear and detailed description of meiosis, the process of division in reproductive cells. The text is linked to a companion page on mitosis, and there is an animated comparison between the two processes.

Molecular Expressions: The Amino Acid Collection
http://micro.magnet.fsu.edu/aminoacids/index.html

Fascinating collection of images showing what all the known amino acids look like when photographed through a microscope. There is also a detailed article about the different amino acids.

Molecular Expressions: The DNA Collection
http://micro.magnet.fsu.edu/micro/gallery/dna/dna4.html

Spectacular gallery of DNA photographic representations in the laboratory as well as *in vivo*. This site also has links to several other sites offering photographs through a microscope of various substances, including computer chips and various pharmaceutical substances.

Molecular Expressions: The Vitamin Collection
http://micro.magnet.fsu.edu/vitamins/index.html

Fascinating collection of images showing what all the known vitamins look like when recrystallized and photographed through a microscope. There is also a brief article about vitamins.

Mystery of Smell
http://www.hhmi.org/senses/d/d110.htm

As part of a much larger site called 'Seeing, Hearing, and Smelling the World', here is a page examining the way our sense of smell works. It is divided into four sections called 'The vivid world of odours', 'Finding the odourant receptors', 'How rats and mice – and probably humans – recognize odours', and 'The memory of smells'. This site makes good use of images and animations to help with the explanations, so it is best viewed with an up-to-date browser.

Myxo Web

http://www.wvonline.com/myxo/

All there is to know about myxomycetes. For the general reader there is a good description of these extraordinary organisms and how to identify, collect, and cultivate fungi. There are large numbers of dramatic photographs of fruiting specimens. For professional myxomycologists this site also includes links to international myxo sites.

Natural History of Genetics

http://gslc.genetics.utah.edu/

Through a combination of scientific experts and teachers, this site offers an accessible and well designed introduction to genetics. It includes several guided projects with experiments and explanations aimed initially at young teenage children. However, this site also includes 'Intermediate' and 'Expert' sections allowing this page to be used by a wide variety of ages and levels of expertise. In addition to the experiments, the site also includes sections on such topics as 'Core genetics', 'Teacher workshops', and 'Fun stuff'.

Natural History of Genes

http://gslc.genetics.utah.edu/

A very well-developed site developed as a joint project between the University of Utah Eccles Institute of Human Genetics, Museum of Natural History, and School of Medicine. It is designed for teachers, students, and families, and provides a diverse array of material, from how to extract DNA to information on genetic disorders, current topics, and much more.

Nature

http://www.nature.com/

Nature's site features recent and archive news articles from this well-established science magazine. Although there is a strong encouragement to subscribe to the magazine, there are several full articles freely available online, as well as a full sample issue of the magazine, and regularly updated 'Breaking news' and 'Nature science update' sections.

Nervous System

http://www.ama-assn.org/insight/gen_hlth/atlas/newatlas/nerve2.htm

Clear diagram of the nervous system, labelling the main nerves of the human body.

Odyssey of Life

http://www.pbs.org/wgbh/nova/odyssey/

Companion to the US Public Broadcasting Service (PBS) television programme *Nova*, this page examines the formation of embryos. It includes time-lapse video sequences of growing embryos. Two leading spokespersons of the evolution/creation debate state their opposing viewpoints regarding the age-old question 'How did we get here'? Their debate is carried out online through a series of letters in which they reply to the other's position and expand on their own. There is also an interview with the photographer of the programme in which he discusses the tricky techniques and technology required to film living embryos inside the womb.

Outbreak: Emerging Diseases

http://www.outbreak.org/cgi-unreg/dynaserve.exe/emergence.html

Comprehensive Web site that includes details of online information services addressing emerging diseases around the world.

Plants and their Structure

http://gened.emc.maricopa.edu/bio/bio181/BIOBK/
BioBookPLANTANAT.html

Informative guide to the structure of plants. The page begins with a hypertext exploration of the general organization of plant species, then moves on to a discussion of plant cells and tissue types. Diagrams and microscopic images accompany the text.

Question of Genes: Inherited Risks

http://www.pbs.org/gene/

Companion to a US Public Broadcasting Service (PBS) television programme, this page explores the controversial subject of genetic testing, emphasizing its social, ethical, and emotional consequences. It includes summaries of the seven case studies featured on the television programme, including video clips. There is also a section on the basics of genetic testing, which features the transcript of an interview with a genetic counsellor. You will also find a list of resources for further research and a forum for discussion.

Rachel Carson Homestead

http://www.rachelcarson.org/

Information on the life and legacy of the pioneering ecologist from the trust preserving Carson's childhood home. There is a biography of Carson, details of books by and about Carson, and full details of the work of the conservation organizations continuing her work.

'Recent Advances: Diabetes'

http://www.bmj.com/cgi/content/full/316/7139/1221

Part of a collection of articles maintained by the *British Medical Journal*, this page features the full text of an 18 April 1998 clinical review regarding the alarming rise in the number of patients with diabetes around the world. The text includes diagrams, and there is a list of references. In addition to the clinical review, you will find a list of related articles from the extensive PubMed collection. You can also search the collections under which this article appears, search other articles written by the author of this article, and submit or read responses to this article. There is a list of references at the bottom of the article.

Reference Guide for Vitamins

http://www.realtime.net/anr/vitamins.html

Quick reference guide to vitamins. After an overview of vitamins in general, the page describes the functions of common and obscure vitamins, and explains what happens when the body doesn't get enough of them.

Secret Sense in the Human Nose?

http://www.hhmi.org/senses/d/d210.htm

As part of a much larger site called 'Seeing, Hearing, and Smelling the World', here is a page examining the way our sense of smell detects odours we are not aware of. It is divided into three sections called 'Sniffing out social and sexual signals', 'Triggers of innate behaviour', and 'Pheromones and mammals'. This site makes good use of images and animations to help with the explanations, so it is best viewed with an up-to-date browser.

State of the Environment

http://www.environment-agency.gov.uk/state_of_enviro/index3+.html

Britain's Environment Agency's page on the environment, with access to data collected and studied by the Agency on the topics of 'Bathing water quality', 'River habitats', and 'River gauging stations'. There is also more general information on the current 'Stresses and strains' on the environment.

Structure of the Human Respiratory System

http://www.stemnet.nf.ca/~dpower/resp/struct~1.htm

Short guide to the human respiratory system. This page describes the functions of the major structures such as the nose, and explains what happens to their effectiveness when they are exposed to tobacco smoke.

Talksaver Cell Biology

http://www.talksaver.com/cell_biology/01_nutshell.htm

Excellent and well-written guide to the basics of cellular biology. The site contains chapters on DNA and the storage of information within a cell, the way in which cells acquire and process energy, and the applications of cellular biology to all branches of medical and life science.

The Interactive Fly

http://sdb.bio.purdue.edu/fly/aimain/laahome.htm/

The classic model organism in genetical research and developmental biology is now at your fingertips with this interactive site. It provides a cyberspace guide to how genes regulate the development of a fruit fly.

Tree of Life

http://phylogeny.arizona.edu/tree/phylogeny.html

Project designed to present information about the phylogenetic relationships and characteristics of organisms, illustrating the diversity and unity of living organisms.

Virtual Body

http://www.medtropolis.com/vbody/

If ever something was worth taking the time to download the Shockwave plug-in for, this is it. Authoritative and interactive anatomical animations complete with voice-overs guide you round the whole body, with sections on the brain, digestive system, heart, and skeleton.

Virtual Cell

http://www.life.uiuc.edu/plantbio/cell//

The Virtual Cell site provides you with a variety of options that allow you to explore the microscopic structures inside cells using only your mouse; this site also includes real electron micrographs of these tiny structures and provides some information on their function.

Virtual Galápagos

http://www.terraquest.com/galapagos/

Visually stunning site following a 1996 voyage to the Galápagos Islands, the 'Living laboratory of evolution'. Follow the progress of the expedition by reading the crew's daily dispatches, or click on a number of links for information on the fabulously varied wildlife of the islands and the factors that threaten this unique habitat.

Visible Embryo

http://www.visembryo.com/

Learn about the first four weeks of human development.

Visible Human Project

http://www.nlm.nih.gov/research/visible/visible_gallery.html

Sample images from a long-term US project to collect a complete set of anatomically detailed, three-dimensional representations of the human body.

What the Heck is an E. coli?

http://falcon.cc.ukans.edu/~jbrown/ecoli.html

Explains the basics behind this bacterium which can cause food poisoning, including information on the dangerous strain of the bacterium and how it developed. It contains guidelines to reduce the risk of infection. There are a number of links throughout the article to sites expanding on issues raised.

Willow Biomass for Energy

http://www.esf.edu/pubprog/brochure/willow/willow.htm

Description of the environment friendly use of willow biomass as an energy source. The site goes on to discuss the possibilities of wood energy plantations which could be producing 'green' energy in the near future.

Your Genes, Your Choices: Exploring the Issues Raised by Genetic Research

http://www.ornl.gov/hgmis/publicat/genechoice/index.html

Illustrated, electronic book that describes the science of genetic research, as well as the ethical, legal, and social issues that it raises. Detailed and informative in itself, the site also contains an extensive bibliography.

7 Glossary

abiotic factor

non-living variable within the ecosystem, affecting the life of organisms. Examples include temperature, light, and water. Abiotic factors can be harmful to the environment, as when sulphur dioxide emissions from power stations produce acid rain.

abzyme

in biotechnology, an artificially created antibody that can be used like an enzyme to accelerate reactions.

acclimation or acclimatization

physiological changes induced in an organism by exposure to new environmental conditions. When humans move to higher altitudes, for example, the number of red blood cells rises to increase the oxygen-carrying capacity of the blood in order to compensate for the lower levels of oxygen in the air.

In evolutionary terms, the ability to acclimate is an important adaptation as it allows the organism to cope with the environmental changes occurring during its lifetime.

acetyl coenzyme A (acetyl CoA)

compound active in processes of metabolism. It is a heat-stable coenzyme with an acetyl group ($-COCH_3$) attached by sulphur linkage. This linkage is a high-energy bond and the acetyl group can easily be donated to other compounds. Acetyl groups donated in this way play an important part in glucose breakdown as well as in fatty acid and steroid synthesis. It is involved in the Krebs cycle, the cyclical pathway involved in the intracellular metabolism of foodstuffs.

acid rain

acidic precipitation thought to be caused principally by the release into the atmosphere of sulphur dioxide (SO_2) and oxides of nitrogen, which dissolve in pure rainwater making it acidic. Sulphur dioxide is formed by the burning of fossil fuels, such as coal, that contain high quantities of sulphur; nitrogen oxides are contributed from various industrial activities and from car exhaust fumes. Acidity is measured on the pH scale, where the value of 0 represents liquids and solids that are completely acidic and 14 represents those that are highly alkaline. Distilled water is neutral and has a pH of 7. Normal rain has a value of 5.6. It is slightly acidic due to the presence of carbonic acid formed by the mixture of carbon dioxide (CO_2) and rainwater. Acid rain has values of 5.6 or less on the pH scale.

acquired character

feature of the body that develops during the lifetime of an individual, usually as a result of repeated use or disuse, such as the enlarged muscles of a weight-lifter.

French naturalist Jean Baptiste Lamarck's theory of evolution assumed that acquired characters were passed from parent to offspring. Modern evolutionary theory does not recognize the inheritance of acquired characters because there is no reliable scientific evidence that it occurs, and because no mechanism is known whereby bodily changes can influence the genetic material. The belief that this does not occur is known as central dogma.

adaptation

any change in the structure or function of an organism that allows it to survive and reproduce more effectively in its environment. In evolution, adaptation is thought to occur as a result of random variation in the genetic make-up of organisms coupled with natural selection. Species become extinct when they are no longer adapted to their environment.

adaptive radiation

in evolution, the formation of several species, with adaptations to different ways of life, from a single ancestral type. Adaptive radiation is likely to occur whenever members of a species migrate to a new habitat with unoccupied ecological niches. It is thought that the lack of competition in such niches allows sections of the migrant population to develop new adaptations, and eventually to become new species.

The colonization of newly formed volcanic islands has led to the development of many unique species. The 13 species of Darwin's finch on the Galápagos Islands, for example, are probably descended from a single species from the South American mainland. The parent stock evolved into different species that now occupy a range of diverse niches.

adenosine triphosphate

compound present in cells. See ATP.

ADP

abbreviation for adenosine diphosphate, the chemical product formed in cells when ATP breaks down to release energy.

adrenal gland or suprarenal gland

triangular endocrine gland situated on top of the kidney. The adrenals are soft and yellow, and consist of two parts: the cortex and medulla. The *cortex* (outer part) secretes various steroid hormones and other hormones that control salt and water metabolism and regulate the use of carbohydrates, proteins, and fats. The *medulla* (inner part) secretes the hormones adrenaline and noradrenaline which, during times of stress, cause the heart to beat faster and harder, increase blood flow to the heart and muscle cells, and dilate airways in the lungs, thereby delivering more oxygen to cells throughout the body and in general preparing the body for 'fight or flight'.

adrenaline or epinephrine

hormone secreted by the medulla of the adrenal glands. Adrenaline is synthesized from a closely related substance, noradrenaline, and the two hormones are released into the bloodstream in situations of fear or stress.

Adrenaline's action on the liver raises blood-sugar levels by stimulating glucose production and its action on adipose tissue raises blood fatty-acid levels; it also increases the heart rate, increases blood flow to muscles, reduces blood flow to the skin with the production of sweat, widens the smaller breathing tubes (bronchioles) in the lungs, and dilates the pupils of the eyes.

aerobic

term used to describe those organisms that require oxygen (usually dissolved in water) for the efficient release of energy contained in food molecules, such as glucose. They include almost all organisms (plants as well as animals) with the exception of certain bacteria, yeasts, and internal parasites. Aerobic reactions occur inside every cell and lead to the formation of energy-rich ATP, subsequently used by the cell for driving its metabolic processes. Oxygen is used to convert glucose to carbon dioxide and water, thereby releasing energy.

Most aerobic organisms die in the absence of oxygen, but certain organisms and cells, such as those found in muscle tissue, can function for short periods anaerobically (without oxygen). Anaerobic organisms can survive without oxygen.

aestivation

state of inactivity and reduced metabolic activity, similar to hibernation, that occurs during the dry season in species such as lungfish and snails. In botany, the term is used to describe the way in which flower petals and sepals are folded in the buds. It is an important feature in plant classification.

aggression

behaviour used to intimidate or injure another organism (of the same or of a different species), usually for the purposes of gaining territory, a mate, or food. Aggression often involves an escalating series of threats aimed at intimidating an opponent without having to engage in potentially dangerous physical contact. Aggressive signals include roaring by red deer, snarling by dogs, the fluffing-up of feathers by birds, and the raising of fins by some species of fish.

agonist

muscle that contracts and causes a movement. Contraction of an agonist is complemented by relaxation of its antagonist. For example, the biceps (in the front of the upper arm) bends the elbow whilst the triceps (lying behind the biceps) straightens the arm.

allele

one of two or more alternative forms of a gene at a given position (locus) on a chromosome, caused by a difference in the sequence of DNA. Blue and brown eyes in humans are determined by different alleles of the gene for eye colour. Organisms with two sets of chromosomes (diploids) will have two copies of each gene. If the two alleles are identical the individual is said to be homozygous at that locus; if different, the individual is heterozygous at that locus. Some alleles show dominance over others.

allometry

regular relationship between a given feature (for example, the size of an organ) and the size of the body as a whole, when this relationship is not a simple proportion of body size. Thus, an organ may increase in size proportionately faster, or slower, than body size does. For example, a human baby's head is much larger in relation to its body than is an adult's.

alloparental care

in animal behaviour, the care of another animal's offspring. 'Fostering' is common in some birds, such as pigeons, and social mammals, such as meerkats. Usually both the adoptive parent and the young benefit.

altruism

helping another individual of the same species to reproduce more effectively, as a direct result of which the altruist may leave fewer offspring itself. Female honey bees (workers) behave altruistically by rearing sisters in order to help their mother, the queen bee, reproduce, and forgo any possibility of reproducing themselves.

amino acid

water-soluble organic molecule, mainly composed of carbon, oxygen, hydrogen, and nitrogen, containing both a basic amino group (NH_2) and an acidic carboxyl (COOH) group. They are small molecules able to pass through membranes. When two or more amino acids are joined together, they are known as peptides; proteins are made up of peptide chains folded or twisted in characteristic shapes.

Many different proteins are found in the cells of living organisms, but they are all made up of the same 20 amino acids, joined together in varying combinations (although other types of amino acid do occur infrequently in nature). Eight of these, the *essential amino acids*, cannot be synthesized by humans and must be obtained from the diet. Children need a further two amino acids that are not essential for adults. Other animals also need some preformed amino acids in their diet, but green plants can manufacture all the amino acids

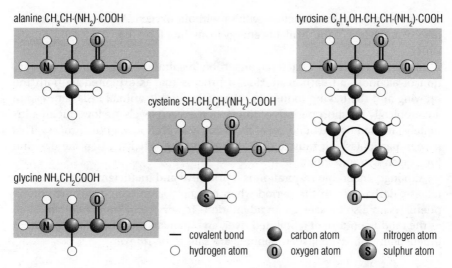

alanine CH$_3$CH·(NH$_2$)·COOH

tyrosine C$_6$H$_4$OH·CH$_2$CH·(NH$_2$)·COOH

cysteine SH·CH$_2$CH·(NH$_2$)·COOH

glycine NH$_2$CH$_2$COOH

— covalent bond   ● carbon atom   Ⓝ nitrogen atom
○ hydrogen atom   Ⓞ oxygen atom   Ⓢ sulphur atom

Amino acids are natural organic compounds that make up proteins and can thus be considered the basic molecules of life. There are 20 different common amino acids. They consist mainly of carbon, oxygen, hydrogen, and nitrogen. Each amino acid has a common core structure (consisting of two carbon atoms, two oxygen atoms, a nitrogen atom, and four hydrogen atoms) to which is attached a variable group, known as the R group. In glycine, the R group is a single hydrogen atom; in alanine, the R group consists of a carbon and three hydrogen atoms.

they need from simpler molecules, relying on energy from the Sun and minerals (including nitrates) from the soil.

amylase
one of a group of enzymes that break down starches into their component molecules (sugars) for use in the body. It occurs widely in both plants and animals. In humans, it is found in saliva and in pancreatic juices.

Human amylase has an optimum pH of 7.2–7.4. Like most enzymes amylase is denatured by temperatures above 60°C.

anabolism
process of building up body tissue, promoted by the influence of certain hormones. It is the constructive side of metabolism, as opposed to catabolism.

anaerobic
not requiring oxygen for the release of energy from food molecules such as glucose. Anaerobic organisms include many bacteria, yeasts, and internal parasites. Anaerobic respiration in humans is less efficient than aerobic respiration at releasing energy, but releases energy faster: see respiration.

Obligate anaerobes, such as certain primitive bacteria, cannot function in the presence of oxygen; but *facultative anaerobes*, like the fermenting yeasts and most bacteria, can function with or without oxygen. Anaerobic organisms release much less of the available energy from their food than do aerobic organisms.

In plants, yeasts, and bacteria, anaerobic respiration results in the production of alcohol and carbon dioxide, a process that is exploited by both the brewing and the baking industries. Normally aerobic animal cells can respire anaerobically for short periods of time when oxygen levels are low, but are ultimately fatigued by the build-up of the lactic acid produced in the process. This is seen particularly in muscle cells during intense activity, when the demand for oxygen can outstrip.

Although anaerobic respiration is a primitive and inefficient form of energy release, deriving from the period when oxygen was missing from the atmosphere, it can also be seen as an adaptation. To survive in some habitats, such as the muddy bottom of a polluted river, an organism must be to a large extent independent of oxygen; such habitats are said to be *anoxic*.

analogous

term describing a structure that has a similar function to a structure in another organism, but not a similar evolutionary path. For example, the wings of bees and of birds have the same purpose – to give powered flight – but have different origins.

Compare homologous.

animal or metazoan

member of the kingdom Animalia, one of the major categories of living things, the science of which is *zoology*. Animals are all multicellular heterotrophs (they obtain their energy from organic substances produced by other organisms); they have eukaryotic cells (the genetic material is contained within a distinct nucleus) which are bounded by a thin cell membrane rather than the thick cell wall of plants. Most animals are capable of moving around for at least part of their life cycle.

animal behaviour

scientific study of the behaviour of animals, either by comparative psychologists (with an interest mainly in the psychological processes involved in the control of behaviour) or by ethologists (with an interest in the biological context and relevance of behaviour; see ethology).

anoxia or hypoxia

deprivation of oxygen, a condition that rapidly leads to collapse or death, unless immediately reversed.

antagonist

muscle that relaxes in response to the contraction of its agonist muscle. The biceps, in the front of the upper arm, bends the elbow whilst the triceps, lying behind the biceps, straightens the arm.

antenna

appendage ('feeler') on the head. Insects, centipedes, and millipedes each have one pair of antennae but there are two pairs in crustaceans, such as shrimps. In insects, the antennae are involved with the senses of smell and touch; they are frequently complex structures with large surface areas that increase the ability to detect scents.

anterior

front of an organism, usually the part that goes forward first when the animal is moving. In higher organisms the anterior end of the nervous system, over the course of evolution, has developed into a brain with associated receptor organs able to detect stimuli including light and chemicals.

antibody

protein molecule produced in the blood by lymphocytes in response to the presence of foreign or invading substances (antigens); such substances include the proteins carried on the surface of infecting micro-organisms. Antibody production is only one aspect of immunity in vertebrates.

Each antibody acts against only one kind of antigen and combines with it to form a 'complex'. This action may render antigens harmless, or it may destroy micro-organisms by setting off chemical changes that cause them to self-destruct.

antigen

any substance that causes the production of antibodies by the body's immune system. Common antigens include the proteins carried on the surface of bacteria, viruses, and pollen grains. The proteins of incompatible blood groups or tissues also act as antigens, which has to be taken into account in medical procedures such as blood transfusions and organ transplants.

apoptosis or cell suicide

self-destruction of a cell. All cells contain genes that cause them to self-destruct if damaged, diseased, or as part of the regulation of cell numbers during the organism's normal development. Many cancer cells have mutations in genes controlling apoptosis, so understanding apoptosis may lead to new cancer treatments where malfunctioning cells can be instructed to destroy themselves.

During apoptosis, a cell first produces the enzymes needed for self-destruction before shrinking to a characteristic spherical shape with balloon-like bumps on its outer surface. The enzymes break down its contents into small fragments which are easily digestible by surrounding cells.

aposematic coloration

warning coloration markings that make a dangerous, poisonous, or foul-tasting animal particularly conspicuous and recognizable to a predator. Examples include the yellow and black stripes of bees and wasps, and the bright red or yellow colours of many poisonous frogs and snakes. See also mimicry.

Archaea

group of micro-organisms that are without a nucleus and have a single chromosome. Some taxonomists put these bacteria in their own kingdom, separate from other bacteria. All are strict anaerobes, that is, they are killed by oxygen. This is thought to be a primitive condition and to indicate that Archaea are related to the earliest life forms, which appeared about 4 billion years ago, when there was little oxygen in the Earth's atmosphere. They are found in undersea vents, hot springs, the Dead Sea, and salt pans, and have even adapted to refuse tips.

Archaea was originally classified as bacterial, but in 1996 when the genome of *Methanococcus jannaschii* (an archaeaon that lives in undersea vents at temperatures around 100°C/212°) was sequenced, US geneticists found that 56% of its genes were unlike those of any other organism, making Archaea unique.

arthropod

member of the phylum Arthropoda; an invertebrate animal with jointed legs and a segmented body with a horny or chitinous casing (exoskeleton), which is shed periodically and replaced as the animal grows. Included are arachnids such as spiders and mites, as well as crustaceans, millipedes, centipedes, and insects.

artificial selection

selective breeding of individuals that exhibit the particular characteristics that a plant or animal breeder wishes to develop. In plants, desirable features might include resistance to disease, high yield (in crop plants), or attractive appearance. In animal breeding, selection has led to the development of particular breeds of cattle for improved meat production (such as the Aberdeen Angus) or milk production (such as Jersey cows).

Artificial selection was practised by the Sumerians at least 5,500 years ago and carried on through the succeeding ages, with the result that all common vegetables, fruit, and livestock are long modified by selective breeding. Artificial selection, particularly of pigeons, was studied by the English evolutionist Charles Darwin who saw a similarity between this phenomenon and the processes of natural selection.

ascorbic acid ($C_6H_8O_6$ or vitamin C)

relatively simple organic acid found in citrus fruits and vegetables. It is soluble in water and destroyed by prolonged boiling, so soaking or overcooking of vegetables reduces their vitamin C content. Lack of ascorbic acid results in scurvy.

In the human body, ascorbic acid is necessary for the correct synthesis of collagen. Lack of vitamin C causes skin sores or ulcers, tooth and gum problems, and burst capillaries (scurvy symptoms) owing to an abnormal type of collagen replacing the normal type in these tissues.

The Australian billygoat plum, *Terminalia ferdiandiana*, is the richest natural source of vitamin C, containing 100 times the concentration found in oranges.

asexual reproduction

reproduction that does not involve the manufacture and fusion of sex cells (gametes). The process carries a clear advantage in that there is no need to search for a mate nor to develop complex pollinating mechanisms; every asexual organism can reproduce on its own. Asexual reproduction can therefore lead to a rapid population build-up. However, there is little genetic variation because the progeny are identical to the parent.

assimilation

in animals, the process by which absorbed food molecules, circulating in the blood, pass into the cells and are used for growth, tissue repair, and other metabolic activities. The actual destiny of each food molecule depends not only on its type, but also on the body requirements at that time.

assortative mating

in population genetics, selective mating in a population between individuals that are genetically related or have similar characteristics. If sufficiently consistent, assortative mating can theoretically result in the evolution of new species without geographical isolation (see speciation).

ATP or adenosine triphosphate

abbreviation for a nucleotide molecule found in all cells. It can yield large amounts of energy, and is used to drive the thousands of biological processes needed to sustain life, growth, movement, and reproduction. Green plants use light energy to manufacture ATP as part of the process of photosynthesis. In animals, ATP is formed by the breakdown of glucose molecules, usually obtained from the carbohydrate component of a diet, in a series of reactions termed respiration. It is the driving force behind muscle contraction and the synthesis of complex molecules needed by individual cells.

autolysis

destruction of a cell after its death by the action of its own enzymes, which break down its structural molecules.

autoradiography

technique for following the movement of molecules within an organism, especially a plant, by labelling with a radioactive isotope that can be traced on photographs. It is commonly used to study photosynthesis, where the pathway of radioactive carbon dioxide can be traced as it moves through the various chemical stages.

autosome

any chromosome in the cell other than a sex chromosome. Autosomes are of the same number and kind in both males and females of a given species.

autotroph

any living organism that synthesizes organic substances from inorganic molecules by using light or chemical energy. Autotrophs are the *primary producers* in all food chains since the materials they synthesize and store are the energy sources of all other organisms. All green plants and many planktonic organisms are autotrophs, using sunlight to convert carbon dioxide and water into sugars by photosynthesis.

auxin

plant hormone that promotes stem and root growth in plants. Auxins influence many aspects of plant growth and development, including cell enlargement, inhibition of development of axillary buds, tropisms, and the initiation of roots. *Synthetic auxins* are used in rooting powders for cuttings, and in some weed-killers, where high auxin concentrations cause such rapid growth that the plants die. They are also used to prevent premature fruitdrop in orchards. The most common naturally occurring auxin is known as indoleacetic acid, or IAA. It is produced in the shoot apex and transported to other parts of the plant.

bacillus

genus of rod-shaped bacteria that occur everywhere in the soil and air. Some are responsible for diseases such as anthrax or for causing food spoilage.

backcross

cross between an offspring and one of its parents, or an individual that is genetically identical to one of its parents. It is a breeding technique used to determine the genetic makeup of an individual organism.

bacteria singular bacterium

microscopic single-celled organisms lacking a nucleus. Its DNA is formed as a circular loop. Bacteria are widespread, present in soil, air, and water, and as parasites on and in other living things. Some parasitic bacteria cause disease by producing toxins, but others are harmless and may even benefit their hosts. Bacteria usually reproduce by binary fission (dividing into two equal parts), and this may occur approximately every 20 minutes. Only 4,000 species of bacteria are known; bacteriologists believe that around 3 million species may actually exist.

Classification

Bacteria are now classified biochemically, but their varying shapes provide a rough classification; for example, *cocci* are round or oval, *bacilli* are rodlike, *spirilla* are spiral, and *vibrios* are shaped like commas. Exceptionally, one bacterium has been found, *Gemmata obscuriglobus*, that does have a nucleus. Unlike viruses, bacteria do not necessarily need contact with a live cell to become active.

Bacteria can be classified into two broad classes (called Gram positive and negative) according to their reactions to certain stains, or dyes, used in microscopy. The staining technique, called the Gram test after Danish bacteriologist Hans Gram, allows doctors to identify many bacteria quickly.

Bacteria have a large loop of DNA, sometimes called a bacterial chromosome. In addition there are often small, circular pieces of DNA known as plasmids that carry spare genetic information. These plasmids can readily move from one bacterium to another, even though the bacteria may be of different species. In a sense, they are parasites within the bacterial cell, but they survive by coding characteristics that promote the survival of their hosts. For example, some plasmids confer antibiotic resistance on the bacteria they inhabit. The rapid and problematic spread of antibiotic resistance among bacteria is due to plasmids, but they are also useful to humans in genetic engineering. There are ten times more bacterial cells than human cells in the human body.

bacteriophage
virus that attacks bacteria, commonly called a phage. Such viruses are useful vectors in genetic engineering for introducing modified DNA.

balance of nature
idea that there is an inherent equilibrium in most ecosystems, with plants and animals interacting so as to produce a stable, continuing system of life on Earth. The activities of human beings can, and frequently do, disrupt the balance of nature.

Organisms in the ecosystem are adapted to each other – for example, waste products produced by one species are used by another and resources used by some are replenished by others; the oxygen needed by animals is produced by plants while the waste product of animal respiration, carbon dioxide, is used by plants as a raw material in photosynthesis. The nitrogen cycle, the water cycle, and the control of animal populations by natural predators are other examples.

base pair
in biochemistry, the linkage of two base (purine or pyrimidine) molecules that join the complementary strands of DNA. Adenine forms a base pair with thymine (or uracil in RNA) and cytosine pairs with guanine in a double stranded nucleic acid molecule.

One base lies on one strand of the DNA double helix and one on the other, so that the base pairs link the two strands like the rungs of a ladder. In DNA, there are four bases: adenine and guanine (purines) and cytosine and thymine (pyrimidines). Adenine always pairs with thymine and cytosine with guanine.

B cell or B lymphocyte
type of lymphocyte that develops in the bone marrow and aids the immune system by producing antibodies. Each B cell produces just one type of antibody, specific to a single antigen.

bicarbonate indicator

pH indicator sensitive enough to show a colour change as the concentration of the gas carbon dioxide increases. The indicator is used in photosynthesis and respiration experiments to find out whether carbon dioxide is being liberated. The initial red colour changes to yellow as the pH becomes more acidic. Carbon dioxide, even in the concentrations found in exhaled air, will dissolve in the indicator to form a weak solution of carbonic acid, which will lower the pH and therefore give the characteristic colour change.

binary fission

form of asexual reproduction, whereby a single-celled organism, such as a bacterium or amoeba, divides into two smaller 'daughter' cells.

binomial system of nomenclature

system in which all organisms are identified by a two-part Latinized name. Devised by the biologist Linnaeus, it is also known as the Linnaean system. The first name is capitalized and identifies the genus; the second identifies the species within that genus, for example within the bear genus *Ursus* there is *Ursus arctos*, the grizzly bear, and *Ursus maritimus*, the polar bear.

biochemical oxygen demand (BOD)

amount of dissolved oxygen taken up by micro-organisms in a sample of water. Since these micro-organisms live by decomposing organic matter, and the amount of oxygen used is proportional to their number and metabolic rate, BOD can be used as a measure of the extent to which the water is polluted with organic compounds.

biochemistry

science concerned with the chemistry of living organisms: the structure and reactions of proteins (such as enzymes), nucleic acids, carbohydrates, and lipids.

Its study has led to an increased understanding of life processes, such as those by which organisms synthesize essential chemicals from food materials, store and generate energy, and pass on their characteristics through their genetic material. A great deal of medical research is concerned with the ways in which these processes are disrupted. Biochemistry also has applications in agriculture and in the food industry (for instance, in the use of enzymes).

biodegradable

capable of being broken down by living organisms, principally bacteria and fungi. In biodegradable substances, such as food and sewage, the natural processes of decay lead to compaction and liquefaction, and to the release of nutrients that are then recycled by the ecosystem.

This process can have some disadvantageous side effects, such as the release of methane, an explosive greenhouse gas. However, the technology now exists for waste tips to collect methane in underground pipes, drawing it off and using it as a cheap source of energy. Nonbiodegradable substances, such as glass, heavy metals, and most types of plastic, present serious problems of disposal.

biodiversity
measure of the variety of the Earth's animal, plant, and microbial species, of genetic differences within species, and of the ecosystems that support those species. Its maintenance is important for ecological stability and as a resource for research into, for example, discovering new drugs and crops.

Estimates of the number of species vary widely because many species-rich ecosystems, such as tropical forests, contain unexplored and unstudied habitats. Especially among small organisms, many are unknown; for instance, it is thought that only 1–10% of the world's bacterial species have been identified. The most significant threat to biodiversity comes from the destruction of rainforests and other habitats in the southern hemisphere. It is estimated that 7% of the Earth's surface hosts 50–75% of the world's biological diversity. Costa Rica, for example, has an area less than 10% of the size of France but possesses three times as many vertebrate species.

bioengineering
application of engineering to biology and medicine. Common applications include the design and use of artificial limbs, joints, and organs, including hip joints and heart valves.

biogenesis
biological term coined in 1870 by English scientist Thomas Henry Huxley to express the hypothesis that living matter always arises out of other similar forms of living matter. It superseded the opposite idea of spontaneous generation or abiogenesis (that is, that living things may arise out of nonliving matter).

biogeography
study of how and why plants and animals are distributed around the world, in the past as well as in the present; more specifically, a theory describing the geographical distribution of species developed by Robert MacArthur and US zoologist Edward O Wilson. The theory argues that, for many species, ecological specializations mean that suitable habitats are patchy in their occurrence. For example, for a dragonfly, ponds in which to breed are separated by large tracts of land, and for edelweiss adapted to alpine peaks the deep valleys between cannot be colonized.

biological clock
regular internal rhythm of activity, produced by unknown mechanisms, and not dependent on external time signals. Such clocks are known to exist in almost all animals, and also in many plants, fungi, and unicellular organisms; the first biological clock gene in plants was isolated in 1995 by a US team of

researchers. In higher organisms, there appears to be a series of clocks of graded importance. For example, although body temperature and activity cycles in human beings are normally 'set' to 24 hours, the two cycles may vary independently, showing that two clock mechanisms are involved.

biological control

control of pests such as insects and fungi through biological means, rather than the use of chemicals. This can include breeding resistant crop strains; inducing sterility in the pest; infecting the pest species with disease organisms; or introducing the pest's natural predator. Biological control tends to be naturally self-regulating, but as ecosystems are so complex, it is difficult to predict all the consequences of introducing a biological controlling agent.

Ladybirds are sometimes used to control aphids as both adults and larvae feed on them. In 1998, French researchers patented a method of selective breeding to produce hardy flightless ladybirds for use in biological control, as captive populations are far more effective than mobile ones.

The introduction of the cane toad to Australia 50 years ago to eradicate a beetle that was destroying sugar beet provides an example of the unpredictability of biological control. Since the cane toad is poisonous it has few Australian predators and it is now a pest, spreading throughout eastern and northern Australia at a rate of 35 km/22 mi a year.

biology

science of life. Biology includes all the life sciences – for example, anatomy and physiology (the study of the structure of living things), cytology (the study of cells), zoology (the study of animals), botany (the study of plants), ecology (the study of habitats and the interaction of living species), animal behaviour, embryology, and taxonomy (classification), and plant breeding. Increasingly in the 20th century biologists have concentrated on molecular structures: biochemistry, biophysics, and genetics (the study of inheritance and variation).

biology, applied

practical application of biological knowledge. Applied biology is directed towards the manipulation and control of living organisms and the environment in the light of biological knowledge, since many of the world's most urgent problems, such as overpopulation and disease, food production, environmental pollution, and waste disposal, are born of or fostered by biological ignorance. It covers a vast spectrum of subjects including forestry and fisheries, pest and weed control, pollution control, human and animal nutrition, microbiology, and immunology.

bioluminescence

production of light by living organisms. It is a feature of many deep-sea fishes, crustaceans, and other marine animals. On land, bioluminescence is seen in some nocturnal insects such as glow-worms and fireflies, and in certain bacteria and fungi. Light is usually produced by the oxidation of luciferin, a reaction catalysed by the enzyme luciferase. This reaction is unique, being the only known biological oxidation that does not produce heat. Animal luminescence is involved in communication, camouflage, or the luring of prey, but its function in some organisms is unclear.

biomass

total mass of living organisms present in a given area. It may be specified for a particular species (such as earthworm biomass) or for a general category (such as herbivore biomass). Estimates also exist for the entire global plant biomass. Measurements of biomass can be used to study interactions between organisms, the stability of those interactions, and variations in population numbers. Where dry biomass is measured, the material is dried to remove all water before weighing.

biome

broad natural assemblage of plants and animals shaped by common patterns of vegetation and climate. Examples include the tundra biome and the desert biome.

biometry

literally, the measurement of living things, but generally used to mean the application of mathematics to biology. The term is now largely obsolete, since mathematical or statistical work is an integral part of most biological disciplines.

biophysics

application of physical laws to the properties of living organisms. Examples include using the principles of mechanics to calculate the strength of bones and muscles, and thermodynamics to study plant and animal energetics.

biorhythm

rhythmic change, mediated by hormones, in the physical state and activity patterns of certain plants and animals that have seasonal activities. Examples include winter hibernation, spring flowering or breeding, and periodic migration. The hormonal changes themselves are often a response to changes in day length (photoperiodism); they signal the time of year to the animal or plant. Other biorhythms are innate and continue even if external stimuli such as day length are removed. These include a 24-hour or circadian rhythm, a 28-day or circalunar rhythm (corresponding to the phases of the Moon), and even a year-long rhythm in some organisms.

Such innate biorhythms are linked to an internal or biological clock, whose mechanism is still poorly understood.

biosensor

device based on microelectronic circuits that can directly measure medically significant variables for the purpose of diagnosis or monitoring treatment. One such device measures the blood sugar level of diabetics using a single drop of blood, and shows the result on a liquid crystal display within a few minutes.

biosphere

narrow zone that supports life on our planet. It is limited to the waters of the Earth, a fraction of its crust, and the lower regions of the atmosphere. The biosphere is made up of all the Earth's ecosystems. It is affected by external forces such as the Sun's rays, which provide energy, the gravitational effects of the Sun and Moon, and cosmic radiations.

biosynthesis

synthesis of organic chemicals from simple inorganic ones by living cells – for example, the conversion of carbon dioxide and water to glucose by plants during photosynthesis. Other biosynthetic reactions produce cell constituents including proteins and fats.

Biosynthesis requires energy; in the initial stages of photosynthesis this is obtained from sunlight, but more often it is supplied by the ATP molecule. The term is also used in connection with biotechnology processes.

Biosynthesis requires energy; in the initial or light-dependent stages of photosynthesis this is obtained from sunlight, but in all other instances, it is supplied chemically by ATP and NADPH. The term is also used in connection with the products achieved through biotechnology processes.

biotechnology

industrial use of living organisms to manufacture food, drugs, or other products. The brewing and baking industries have long relied on the yeast micro-organism for fermentation purposes, while the dairy industry employs a range of bacteria and fungi to convert milk into cheeses and yoghurts. Enzymes, whether extracted from cells or produced artificially, are central to most biotechnological applications.

Recent advances include genetic engineering, in which single-celled organisms with modified DNA are used to produce insulin and other drugs.

biotic factor

organic variable affecting an ecosystem – for example, the changing population of elephants and its effect on the African savannah.

bivalent

name given to the pair of homologous chromosomes during reduction division (meiosis).

blastomere

cell formed in the first stages of embryonic development, after the splitting of the fertilized ovum, but before the formation of the blastula or blastocyst.

blastula

early stage in the development of a fertilized egg, when the egg changes from a solid mass of cells (the morula) to a hollow ball of cells (the blastula), containing a fluid-filled cavity (the blastocoel).

blood

fluid circulating in the arteries, veins, and capillaries of vertebrate animals; the term also refers to the corresponding fluid in those invertebrates that possess a closed circulatory system. Blood carries nutrients and oxygen to each body cell and removes waste products, such as carbon dioxide. It is also important in the immune response and, in many animals, in the distribution of heat throughout the body.

In humans blood makes up 5% of the body weight, occupying a volume of 5.5 l/10 pt in the average adult. It is composed of a fluid called plasma, in which are suspended microscopic cells of three main varieties:

Red cells (erythrocytes) form nearly half the volume of the blood, with about 6 million red cells in every millilitre of an adult's blood. They transport oxygen around the body. Their red colour is caused by haemoglobin.

White cells (leucocytes) are of various kinds. Some (phagocytes) ingest invading bacteria and so protect the body from disease; these also help to repair injured tissues. Others (lymphocytes) produce antibodies, which help provide immunity.

Blood *platelets* (thrombocytes) assist in the clotting of blood.

Blood cells constantly wear out and die and are replaced from the bone marrow. Red blood cells die at the rate of 200 billion per day but the body produces new cells at an average rate of 9,000 million per hour.

blood group

any of the types into which blood is classified according to the presence or otherwise of certain antigens on the surface of its red cells. Red blood cells of one individual may carry molecules on their surface that act as antigens in another individual whose red blood cells lack these molecules. The two main antigens are designated A and B. These give rise to four blood groups: having A only (A), having B only (B), having both (AB), and having neither (O). Each of these groups may or may not contain the rhesus factor. Correct typing of blood groups is vital in transfusion, since incompatible types of donor and recipient blood will result in coagulation, with possible death of the recipient. The ABO system was first described by Austrian scientist Karl Landsteiner in 1902. Subsequent research revealed at least 14 main types of blood group systems, 11 of which are involved with induced antibody production. Blood typing is also of importance in forensic medicine, cases of disputed paternity, and in anthropological studies.

In the UK, 44% of people are blood group O, 45% blood group A, 8% group B, and 3% group AB.

botany

study of living and fossil plants, including form, function, interaction with the environment, and classification. Botany is subdivided into a number of specialized studies, such as the identification and classification of plants (taxonomy), their external formation (plant morphology), their internal arrangement (plant anatomy), their microscopic examination (plant histology), their functioning and life history (plant physiology), and their distribution over the Earth's surface in relation to their surroundings (plant ecology). Palaeobotany concerns the study of fossil plants, while economic botany deals with the utility of plants.

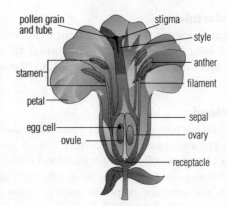

Cross section of a typical flower showing its basic components: sepals, petals, stamens (anthers and filaments), and carpel (ovary and stigma). Flowers vary greatly in the size, shape, colour, and arrangement of these components.

brain

in higher animals, a mass of interconnected nerve cells forming the anterior part of the central nervous system, whose activities it coordinates and controls. In vertebrates, the brain is contained by the skull. At the base of the brainstem, the *medulla oblongata* contains centres for the control of respiration, heartbeat rate and strength, and blood pressure. Overlying this is the *cerebellum*, which is concerned with coordinating complex muscular processes such as maintaining posture and moving limbs.

The cerebral hemispheres (*cerebrum*) are paired outgrowths of the front end of the forebrain, in early vertebrates mainly concerned with the senses, but in higher vertebrates greatly developed and involved in the integration of all sensory input and motor output, and in thought, emotions, memory, and behaviour.

breeding

crossing and selection of animals and plants to change the characteristics of an existing breed or cultivar (variety), or to produce a new one.

Cattle may be bred for increased meat or milk yield, sheep for thicker or finer wool, and horses for speed or stamina. Plants, such as wheat or maize, may be bred for disease resistance, heavier and more rapid cropping, and hardiness to adverse weather.

calyx

collective term for the sepals of a flower, forming the outermost whorl of the perianth. It surrounds the other flower parts and protects them while in bud. In some flowers, for example, the campions *Silene*, the sepals are fused along their sides, forming a tubular calyx.

carbon cycle

sequence by which carbon circulates and is recycled through the natural world. Carbon dioxide is released into the atmosphere by living things as a result of respiration. The CO_2 is taken up and converted into carbohydrates during photosynthesis by plants and by organisms such as diatoms and dinoflagellates in the oceanic plankton; the oxygen component is released back into the atmosphere. The carbon they accumulate is later released back into circulation in various ways. The simplest occurs when an animal eats a plant and carbon is transferred from, say, a leaf cell to the animal body. Carbon is also released through the decomposition of decaying plant matter, and the burning of fossil fuels such as coal (fossilized plants). The oceans absorb 25–40% of all carbon dioxide released into the atmosphere.

Today, the carbon cycle is in danger of being disrupted by the increased consumption and burning of fossil fuels, and the burning of large tracts of tropical forests, as a result of which levels of carbon dioxide are building up in the atmosphere and probably contributing to the greenhouse effect.

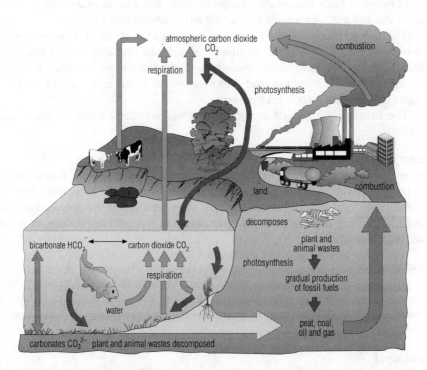

The carbon cycle is necessary for the continuation of life. Since there is only a limited amount of carbon in the Earth and its atmosphere, carbon must be continuously recycled if life is to continue. Other chemicals necessary for life – nitrogen, sulphur, and phosphorus, for example – also circulate in natural cycles.

carbon dioxide (CO_2)

colourless, odourless gas, slightly soluble in water and denser than air. It is formed by the complete oxidation of carbon.

Carbon dioxide is produced by living things during the processes of respiration and the decay of organic matter, and plays a vital role in the carbon cycle. It is used as a coolant in its solid form (known as 'dry ice'), and in the chemical industry. Its increasing density contributes to the greenhouse effect and global warming.

carcinogen

any agent that increases the chance of a cell becoming cancerous, including various chemical compounds, some viruses, X-rays, and other forms of ionizing radiation. The term is often used more narrowly to mean chemical carcinogens only.

carnivore

organism that eats other animals. In zoology, mammal of the order Carnivora. Although its name describes the flesh-eating ancestry of the order, it includes pandas, which are herbivorous, and civet cats, which eat fruit.

Carnivores have the greatest range of body size of any mammalian order, from the 100 g/3.5 oz weasel to the 800 kg/1,764 lb polar bear.

The characteristics of the Carnivora are sharp teeth, small incisors, a well-developed brain, a simple stomach, a reduced or absent caecum, and incomplete or absent clavicles (collarbones); there are never less than four toes on each foot; the scaphoid and lunar bones are fused in the hand; and the claws are generally sharp and powerful.

The mammalian order Carnivora includes cats, dogs, bears, badgers, and weasels.

carrying capacity

in ecology, the maximum number of animals of a given species that a particular habitat can support. When the carrying capacity is exceeded, there is insufficient food (or other resources) for the members of the population. The population may then be reduced by emigration, reproductive failure, or death through starvation.

catabolism

destructive part of metabolism where living tissue is changed into energy and waste products. It is the opposite of anabolism. It occurs continuously in the body, but is accelerated during many disease processes, such as fever, and in starvation.

catalyst

substance that alters the speed of, or makes possible, a chemical or biochemical reaction but remains unchanged at the end of the reaction. Enzymes are natural biochemical catalysts. In practice most catalysts are used to speed up reactions.

cell

basic structural unit of life. It is the smallest unit capable of independent existence, which can reproduce itself exactly. All living organisms – with the exception of viruses – are composed of one or more cells. Single cell organisms such as bacteria, protozoa, and other micro-organisms are termed *unicellular*, while plants and animals which contain many cells are termed *multicellular* organisms. Highly complex organisms such as human beings consist of billions of cells, all of which are adapted to carry out specific functions – for instance, groups of these specialized cells are organized into tissues and organs. Although these cells may differ widely in size, appearance, and function, their essential features are similar.

Cells divide by mitosis, or by meiosis when gametes are being formed.

The cytoplasm of all cells contains ribosomes, which carry out protein synthesis, and DNA, the coded instructions for the behaviour and reproduction of the cell and the chemical machinery for the translation of these instructions into the manufacture of proteins. Viruses lack this translation machinery and so have to parasitize cells in order to reproduce themselves.

Eukaryote cells

In eukaryote cells, found in protozoa, fungi, and higher animals and plants, DNA is organized into chromosomes and is contained within a nucleus. Each eukaryote has a surrounding membrane, which is a thin layer of protein and

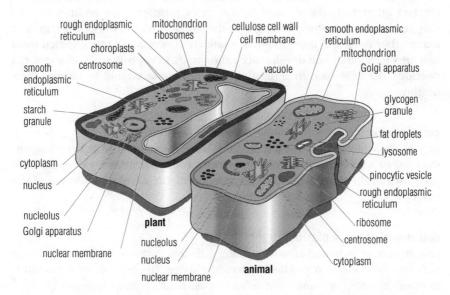

Typical plant and animal cell. Plant and animal cells share many structures, such as ribosomes, mitochondria, and chromosomes, but they also have notable differences: plant cells have chloroplasts, a large vacuole, and a cellulose cell wall. Animal cells do not have a rigid cell wall but have an outside cell membrane only.

fat that restricts the flow of substances in and out of the cell and encloses the cytoplasm, a jellylike material containing the nucleus and other structures (organelles) such as mitochondria. The nuclei of some cells contain a dense spherical structure called the nucleolus, which contains ribonucleic acid (RNA) for the synthesis of ribosomes. The only cells of the human body which have no nucleus are the red blood cells.

In general, plant cells differ from animal cells in that the membrane is surrounded by a cell wall made of cellulose. They also have larger vacuoles (fluid-filled pouches), and contain chloroplasts that convert light energy to chemical energy for the synthesis of glucose.

Prokaryote cells
In prokaryote cells, found in bacteria and cyanobacteria, the DNA forms a simple loop and there is no nucleus. The prokaryotic cell also lacks organelles such as mitochondria, chloroplasts, endoplasmic reticulum, Golgi apparatus, and centrioles, which perform specialized tasks in eukaryotic cells.

cell differentiation
in developing embryos, the process by which cells acquire their specialization, such as heart cells, muscle cells, skin cells, and brain cells. The seven-day-old human pre-embryo consists of thousands of individual cells, each of which is destined to assist in the formation of individual organs in the body.

Research has shown that the eventual function of a cell, in for example, a chicken embryo, is determined by the cell's position. The embryo can be mapped into areas corresponding with the spinal cord, the wings, the legs, and many other tissues. If the embryo is relatively young, a cell transplanted from one area to another will develop according to its new position. As the embryo develops the cells lose their flexibility and become unable to change their destiny.

cell division
process by which a cell divides, either meiosis, associated with sexual reproduction, or mitosis, associated with growth, cell replacement, or repair. Both processes of division involve the duplication of DNA and the splitting of the nucleus.

cell membrane or plasma membrane
thin layer of protein and fat surrounding cells that controls substances passing between the cytoplasm and the intercellular space. The cell membrane is semipermeable, allowing some substances to pass through and some not.

Generally, small molecules such as water, glucose, and amino acids can penetrate the membrane, while large molecules, such as starch, cannot. Membranes also play a part in active transport, hormonal response, and cell metabolism.

central dogma

in genetics and evolution, the fundamental belief that genes can affect the nature of the physical body, but that changes in the body (acquired character, for example, through use or accident) cannot be translated into changes in the genes.

central nervous system (CNS)

brain and spinal cord, as distinct from other components of the nervous system. The CNS integrates all nervous function.

In invertebrates it consists of a paired ventral nerve cord with concentrations of nerve-cell bodies, known as *ganglia* in each segment, and a small brain in the head. Some simple invertebrates, such as sponges and jellyfishes, have no CNS but a simple network of nerve cells called a *nerve net*.

centriole

structure found in the cells of animals that plays a role in the processes of meiosis and mitosis (cell division).

centromere

part of the chromosome where there are no genes. Under the microscope, it usually appears as a constriction in the strand of the chromosome, and is the point at which the spindle fibres are attached during meiosis and mitosis (cell division).

centrosome

cell body that contains the centrioles. During cell division the centrosomes organize the microtubules to form the spindle that divides the chromosomes into daughter cells. Centrosomes were first described in 1887, independently by German biologist Theodor Boveri (1862–1915) and Belgian biologist Edouard van Beneden.

chemosynthesis

method of making protoplasm (contents of a cell) using the energy from chemical reactions, in contrast to the use of light energy employed for the same purpose in photosynthesis. The process is used by certain bacteria, which can synthesize organic compounds from carbon dioxide and water using the energy from special methods of respiration.

Nitrifying bacteria are a group of chemosynthetic organisms that change free nitrogen into a form that can be taken up by plants; nitrobacteria, for example, oxidize nitrites to nitrates. This is a vital part of the nitrogen cycle. As chemosynthetic bacteria can survive without light energy, they can live in dark and inhospitable regions, including the hydrothermal vents of the Pacific ocean. Around these vents, where temperatures reach up to 350°C/662°F, the chemosynthetic bacteria are the basis of a food web supporting fishes and other marine life.

chemotaxis

property that certain cells have of attracting or repelling other cells. For example, white blood cells are attracted to the site of infection by the release of substances during certain types of immune response.

chemotropism

movement by part of a plant in response to a chemical stimulus. The response by the plant is termed 'positive' if the growth is towards the stimulus or 'negative' if the growth is away from the stimulus.

Fertilization of flowers by pollen is achieved because the ovary releases chemicals that produce a positive chemotropic response from the developing pollen tube.

chimera or chimaera

organism composed of tissues that are genetically different. Chimeras can develop naturally if a mutation occurs in a cell of a developing embryo, but are more commonly produced artificially by implanting cells from one organism into the embryo of another.

chlorophyll

group of pigments including chlorophyll a and chlorophyll b, the green pigments in plants; it is responsible for the absorption of light energy during photosynthesis.

The pigment absorbs the red and blue-violet parts of sunlight but reflects the green, thus giving plants their characteristic colour.

Other chlorophylls include chlorophyll c (in brown algae) and chlorophyll d (found in red algae).

Chlorophyll is found within chloroplasts, present in large numbers in leaves. Cyanobacteria (blue-green algae) and other photosynthetic bacteria also have chlorophyll, though of a slightly different type. Chlorophyll is similar in structure to haemoglobin, but with magnesium instead of iron as the reactive part of the molecule.

chordate

animal belonging to the phylum Chordata, which includes vertebrates, sea squirts, amphioxi, and others. All these animals, at some stage of their lives, have a supporting rod of tissue (notochord or backbone) running down their bodies.

Chordates are divided into three major groups: tunicates, cephalochordates, and craniates (including all vertebrates).

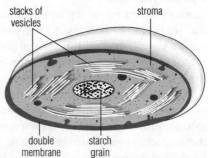

Chlorophyll molecules on the membranes of the vesicle stacks capture light energy to produce food by photosynthesis.

chromosome

structure in a cell nucleus that carries the genes. Each chromosome consists of one very long strand of DNA, coiled and folded to produce a compact body. The point on a chromosome where a particular gene occurs is known as its locus. Most higher organisms have two copies of each chromosome, together known as a *homologous pair* (they are diploid) but some have only one (they are haploid). There are 46 chromosomes in a normal human cell. See also mitosis and meiosis.

Chromosomes are only visible during cell division; at other times they exist in a less dense form called chromatin.

The first artificial human chromosome was built by US geneticists in 1997. They constructed telomeres, centromeres, and DNA containing genetic information, which they removed from white blood cells, and inserted them into human cancer cells. The cells assembled the material into chromosomes. The artificial chromosome was successfully passed onto all daughter cells.

cilia singular cilium

small hairlike organs on the surface of some cells, particularly the cells lining the upper respiratory tract. Their wavelike movements waft particles of dust and debris towards the exterior. Some single-celled organisms move by means of cilia. In multicellular animals, they keep lubricated surfaces clear of debris. They also move food in the digestive tracts of some invertebrates.

circulatory system

system of vessels in an animal's body that transports essential substances (blood or other circulatory fluid) to and from the different parts of the body. It was first discovered and described by English physician, William Harvey. All mammals except for the simplest kinds – such as sponges, jellyfish, sea anemones, and corals – have some type of circulatory system. Some invertebrates (animals without a backbone), such as insects, spiders, and most shellfish, have an 'open' circulatory system which consists of a simple network of tubes and hollow spaces. Other invertebrates have pumplike structures that send blood through a system of blood vessels. All vertebrates (animals with a backbone), including human beings, have a 'closed' circulatory system which principally consists of a pumping organ – the heart – and a network of blood vessels.

cistron

in genetics, the segment of DNA that is required to synthesize a complete polypeptide chain. It is the molecular equivalent of a gene.

CITES (Convention on International Trade in Endangered Species)

international agreement under the auspices of the IUCN with the aim of regulating trade in endangered species of animals and plants. The agreement came into force in 1975 and by 1997 had been signed by 138 states. It prohibits any trade in a category of 8,000 highly endangered species and controls trade in a further 30,000 species.

Animals and plants listed in Appendix 1 of CITES are classified endangered, and all trade in that species is banned; those listed in Appendix 2 are classified vulnerable, and trade in the species is controlled without a complete ban; those listed in Appendix 3 are subject to domestic controls while national governments request help in controlling international trade.

cladistics

method of biological classification that uses a formal step-by-step procedure for objectively assessing the extent to which organisms share particular characteristics, and for assigning them to taxonomic groups called *clades*. Clades comprise all the species descended from a known or inferred common ancestor plus the ancestor itself, and may be large – consisting of a hierarchy of other clades.

class

used in biological classification, it is a subdivision of phylum and forms a group of related orders. For example, all mammals belong to the class Mammalia and all birds to the class Aves. Among plants, all class names end in 'idae' (such as Asteridae) and among fungi in 'mycetes'; there are no equivalent conventions among animals. Related classes are grouped together in a phylum.

classification

arrangement of organisms into a hierarchy of groups on the basis of their similarities. The basic grouping is a species, several of which may constitute a genus, which in turn are grouped into families, and so on up through orders, classes, phyla (in plants, sometimes called divisions), and finally to kingdoms.

The oldest method of classification, called *phenetic classification*, aims to classify organisms on the basis of as many as possible of their observable characteristics: their morphology, anatomy, physiology, and so on. Greek philosopher Theophrastus adopted this method in the 4th century BC, when he classified plants into trees, shrubs, undershrubs, and herbs.

Awareness of evolutionary theory, however, led to the development of *phylogenetic classification*, which aims to classify organisms in a way that mirrors their evolutionary and genetic relationship. Species are grouped according to shared characteristics believed to be derived from common ancestors (care being taken to exclude shared characteristics known to be due to convergent evolution – such as the wings of bats and birds). In practice, most present-day systems of classification compromise between the phenetic and the phylogenetic approaches.

Cladistics is a recent phylogenetic method that applies a strict, objective procedure, often assisted by computer analysis, to classify species according to characteristics derived from a common ancestor.

climax community

assemblage of plants and animals that is relatively stable in its environment. It is brought about by ecological succession and represents the point at which succession ceases to occur.

In temperate or tropical conditions, a typical climax community comprises woodland or forest and its associated fauna (for example, an oak wood in the UK). In essence, most land management is a series of interferences with the process of succession.

The theory, created by Frederic Clement in 1916, has been criticized for not explaining 'retrogressive' succession, when some areas revert naturally to pre-climax vegetation.

clone

any one of a group of genetically identical cells or organisms. An identical twin is a clone; so, too, are bacteria living in the same colony. 'Clone' also describes genetically engineered replicas of DNA sequences.

coccus plural cocci

member of a group of globular bacteria, some of which are harmful to humans. The cocci contain the subgroups *streptococci*, where the bacteria associate in straight chains, and *staphylococci*, where the bacteria associate in branched chains.

codominance

failure of a pair of alleles, controlling a particular characteristic, to show the classic recessive-dominant relationship. Instead, aspects of both alleles may show in the phenotype. For example, the human blood group AB shows the phenotype effect of both A and B codominant genes.

The snapdragon shows codominance in respect to colour. Two alleles, one for red petals and the other for white, will produce a pink colour if the alleles occur together as a heterozygous form.

codon (also coding triplet)

in genetics, a triplet of bases in a molecule of DNA or RNA that directs the placement of a particular amino acid during the process of protein (polypeptide) synthesis. There are 64 codons in the genetic code.

coefficient of relationship

probability that any two individuals share a given gene by virtue of being descended from a common ancestor. In sexual reproduction of diploid species, an individual shares half its genes with each parent, with its offspring, and (on average) with each sibling; but only a quarter (on average) with its grandchildren or its siblings' offspring; an eighth with its great-grandchildren, and so on. In certain species of insects (for example honey bees), females have only one set of chromosomes (inherited from the mother), so that sisters are identical in genetic make-up; this produces a different set of coefficients. These coefficients are important in calculations of inclusive fitness.

coenzyme

small organic nonprotein compound that attaches to an enzyme and is necessary for its correct functioning. Tightly bound coenzymes are known as prosthetic groups; more loosely bound ones are called cofactors. The coenzyme itself is not usually changed during a reaction. If it is, it is usually converted rapidly back to its original form. Well known coenzymes include NAD, ATP, and coenzyme A.

coevolution

evolution of those structures and behaviours within a species that can best be understood in relation to another species. For example, some insects and flowering plants have evolved together: insects have produced mouthparts suitable for collecting pollen or drinking nectar, and plants have developed chemicals and flowers that will attract insects to them. Parasites often evolve and speciate with their hosts.

Coevolution occurs because both groups of organisms, over millions of years, benefit from a continuing association, and will evolve structures and behaviours that maintain this association.

cold-blooded

of animals, dependent on the surrounding temperature; see *poikilothermy*.

colonization

in ecology, the spread of species into a new habitat, such as a freshly cleared field, a new motorway verge, or a recently flooded valley. The first species to move in are called *pioneers*, and may establish conditions that allow other animals and plants to move in (for example, by improving the condition of the soil or by providing shade). Over time a range of species arrives and the habitat matures; early colonizers will probably be replaced, so that the variety of animal and plant life present changes. This is known as succession.

commensalism

relationship between two species whereby one (the commensal) benefits from the association, whereas the other neither benefits nor suffers. For example, certain species of millipede and silverfish inhabit the nests of army ants and live by scavenging on the refuse of their hosts, but without affecting the ants.

communication

signalling of information by one organism to another, usually with the intention of altering the recipient's behaviour. Signals used in communication may be *visual* (such as the human smile or the display of colourful plumage in birds), *auditory* (for example, the whines or barks of a dog), *olfactory* (such as the odours released by the scent glands of a deer), *electrical* (as in the pulses emitted by electric fish), or *tactile* (for example, the nuzzling of male and female elephants).

community

in ecology, an assemblage of plants, animals, and other organisms living within a circumscribed area. Communities are usually named by reference to a dominant feature such as characteristic plant species (for example, an oak-hickory community), or a prominent physical feature (for example, a freshwater-pond community).

compensation point

point at which there is just enough light for a plant to survive. At this point all the food produced by photosynthesis is used up by respiration. For aquatic plants, the compensation point is the depth of water at which there is just enough light to sustain life (deeper water = less light = less photosynthesis).

competition

in ecology, the interaction between two or more organisms, or groups of organisms (for example, species), that use a common resource which is in short supply. Competition invariably results in a reduction in the numbers of one or both competitors, and in evolution contributes both to the decline of certain species and to the evolution of adaptations.

Thus plants may compete with each other for sunlight, or nutrients from the soil, while animals may compete amongst themselves for food, water, or refuge.

complementation

in genetics, the interaction that can occur between two different mutant alleles of a gene in a diploid organism, to make up for each other's deficiencies and allow the organism to function normally.

congenital disease

disease that is present at birth. It is not necessarily genetic in origin; for example, congenital herpes may be acquired by the baby as it passes through the mother's birth canal.

conjugation

temporary union of two single cells (or hyphae in fungi) with at least one of them receiving genetic material from the other: the bacterial equivalent of sexual reproduction. A fragment of the DNA from one bacterium is passed along a thin tube, the pilus, into another bacterium.

conservation

action taken to protect and preserve the natural world, usually from pollution, overexploitation, and other harmful features of human activity. The late 1980s saw a great increase in public concern for the environment, with membership of conservation groups, such as Friends of the Earth, Greenpeace, and the US Sierra Club, rising sharply. Globally the most important issues include the depletion of atmospheric ozone by the action of chlorofluorocarbons (CFCs), the build-up of carbon dioxide in the atmosphere (thought to contribute to an intensification of the greenhouse effect), and deforestation.

continuous variation (also quantitative variation)

slight difference of an individual characteristic, such as height, across a sample of the population. Although there are very tall and very short humans, there are also many people with an intermediate height. The same applies to weight. Continuous variation can be due to the influence of many genes rather than a single one, or from the influence of individuals' environments.

contractile vacuole

tiny organelle found in many single-celled freshwater organisms. It slowly fills with water, and then contracts, expelling the water from the cell.

Freshwater protozoa such as *Amoeba* absorb water by the process of osmosis, and this excess must be eliminated. The rate of vacuole contraction slows as the external salinity is increased, because the osmotic effect weakens; marine protozoa do not have a contractile vacuole.

control

process by which a tissue, an organism, a population, or an ecosystem maintains itself in a balanced, stable state. Blood sugar must be kept at a stable level if the brain is to function properly, and this steady-state is maintained by an interaction between the liver, the hormone insulin, and a detector system in the pancreas.

In the ecosystem, the activities of the human race are endangering the balancing mechanisms associated with the atmosphere in general and the greenhouse effect in particular.

control experiment

essential part of a scientifically valid experiment, designed to show that the factor being tested is actually responsible for the effect observed. In the control experiment all factors, apart from the one under test, are exactly the same as in the test experiments, and all the same measurements are carried out. In drug trials, a placebo (a harmless substance) is given alongside the substance being tested in order to compare effects.

convergent evolution or convergence

independent evolution of similar structures in species (or other taxonomic groups) that are not closely related, as a result of living in a similar way. Thus, birds and bees have wings, not because they are descended from a common winged ancestor, but because their respective ancestors independently evolved flight.

corticotrophin-releasing hormone (CRH)

hormone produced by the hypothalamus that stimulates the adrenal glands to produce the steroid cortisol, essential for normal metabolism. CRH is also produced by the placenta and a surge in CRH may trigger the beginning of labour.

cortisol

hormone produced by the adrenal glands. It plays a role in helping the body combat stress and is at its highest level in the blood at dawn.

cosmid

fragment of DNA, for example from the human genome, inserted into a bacterial cell. The bacterium replicates the fragment along with its own DNA. In this way the fragments are copied for a gene library. Cosmids are characteristically 40,000 base pairs in length. The most commonly used bacterium is *Escherichia coli*. A yeast artificial chromosome (YAC) works in the same way.

courtship

behaviour exhibited by animals as a prelude to mating. The behaviour patterns vary considerably from one species to another, but are often ritualized forms of behaviour not obviously related to courtship or mating (for example, courtship feeding in birds).

Courtship ensures that copulation occurs with a member of the opposite sex of the right species. It also synchronizes the partners' readiness to mate and allows each partner to assess the suitability of the other.

crossing over

process that occurs during meiosis. While homologous chromosomes are lying alongside each other in pairs, each partner may twist around the other and exchange corresponding chromosomal segments. It is a form of genetic recombination, which increases variation and thus allows offspring to vary from their parents.

culture

growing of living cells and tissues in laboratory conditions.

cyanobacteria singular cyanobacterium

alternative name for blue-green algae. These organisms are actually not algae but bacteria. The ancestors of modern cyanobacteria generated the oxygen that caused a transformation some 2 billion years ago of the Earth's atmosphere.

cyclodextrin

ring-shaped glucose molecule chain created in 1993 at Osaka University, Japan. Cyclodextrins are commonly used in food additives, and can also be used as capsules to deliver drugs, as cutters to separate ions and molecules, and as catalysts for chemical reactions.

They generally consist of 6–8 glucose molecules linked together in a ring, leaving a central hole of 0.45–0.8 nanometres, which can hold a small molecule such as benzene. They can be joined together to form tubes even smaller than DNA, the length and width of which can be controlled. They could hypothetically be used in the production of large scale integrated computer systems.

cytochrome

protein responsible for part of the process of respiration by which food molecules are broken down in aerobic organisms. Cytochromes are part of the electron transport chain, which uses energized electrons to reduce molecular oxygen (O_2) to oxygen ions (O^{2-}). These combine with hydrogen ions (H^+) to form water (H_2O), the end product of aerobic respiration. As electrons are passed from one cytochrome to another, energy is released and used to make ATP.

cytology

study of the structure of cells and their functions. Major advances have been made possible in this field by the development of electron microscopes.

cytoplasm

part of the cell outside the nucleus. Strictly speaking, this includes all the organelles (mitochondria, chloroplasts, and so on), but often cytoplasm refers to the jellylike matter in which the organelles are embedded (correctly termed the cytosol). The cytoplasm is the site of protein synthesis.

In many cells, the cytoplasm is made up of two parts: the *ectoplasm* (or plasmagel), a dense gelatinous outer layer concerned with cell movement, and the *endoplasm* (or plasmasol), a more fluid inner part where most of the organelles are found.

cytoskeleton

in a living cell, a matrix of protein filaments and tubules that occurs within the cytosol (the liquid part of the cytoplasm). It gives the cell a definite shape, transports vital substances around the cell, and may also be involved in cell movement.

DDT (dichloro-diphenyl-trichloroethane) $(C1C_6H_5)_2CHC(HC1_2)$

insecticide discovered in 1939 by Swiss chemist Paul Müller. It is useful in the control of insects that spread malaria, but resistant strains develop. DDT is highly toxic and persists in the environment and in living tissue. Despite this and its subsequent danger to wildlife, it has evaded a worldwide ban because it remains one of the most effective ways of controlling malaria. China and India were the biggest DDT users in 1999.

decomposer

any organism that breaks down dead matter. Decomposers play a vital role in the ecosystem by freeing important chemical substances, such as nitrogen compounds, locked up in dead organisms or excrement. They feed on some of the released organic matter, but leave the rest to filter back into the soil as dissolved nutrients, or pass in gas form into the atmosphere, for example as nitrogen and carbon dioxide.

The principal decomposers are bacteria and fungi, but earthworms and many other invertebrates are often included in this group. The nitrogen cycle relies on the actions of decomposers.

degeneration

change in the structure or chemical composition of a tissue or organ that interferes with its normal functioning. Examples of degeneration include fatty degeneration, fibroid degeneration (cirrhosis), and calcareous degeneration, all of which are part of natural changes that occur in old age.

The causes of degeneration are often unknown. Heredity often has a role in the degeneration of organs; for example, fibroid changes in the kidney can be seen in successive generations. Defective nutrition and continued stress on particular organs can cause degenerative changes. Alcoholism can result in cirrhosis of the liver and tuberculosis causes degeneration of the lungs.

denaturation

irreversible changes occurring in the structure of proteins such as enzymes, usually caused by changes in pH or temperature, by radiation or chemical treatments. An example is the heating of egg albumen resulting in solid egg white. The enzymes associated with digestion and metabolism become inactive if given abnormal conditions. Heat will damage their complex structure so that the usual interactions between enzyme and substrate can no longer occur.

denitrification

process occurring naturally in soil, where bacteria break down nitrates to give nitrogen gas, which returns to the atmosphere.

deoxyribonucleic acid

full name of DNA.

detritus

organic debris produced during the decomposition of animals and plants.

development

process whereby a living thing transforms itself from a single cell into a vastly complicated multicellular organism, with structures, such as limbs, and functions, such as respiration, all able to work correctly in relation to each other. Most of the details of this process remain unknown, although some of the central features are becoming understood.

Apart from the sex cells (gametes), each cell within an organism contains exactly the same genetic code. Whether a cell develops into a liver cell or a brain cell depends therefore not on which genes it contains, but on which genes are allowed to be expressed. The development of forms and patterns within an organism, and the production of different, highly specialized cells, is a problem of control, with genes being turned on and off according to the stage of development reached by the organism.

diabetes

disease *diabetes mellitus* in which a disorder of the islets of Langerhans in the pancreas prevents the body producing the hormone insulin, so that sugars cannot be used properly. Treatment is by strict dietary control and oral or injected insulin, depending on the type of diabetes.

There are two forms of diabetes: Type 1, or insulin-dependent diabetes, which usually begins in childhood (early onset) and is an autoimmune condition; and Type 2, or noninsulin-dependent diabetes, which occurs in later life (late onset).

Sugar accumulates first in the blood, then in the urine. The patient experiences thirst, weight loss, and copious voiding, along with degenerative changes in the capillary system. Without treatment, the patient may go blind, ulcerate, lapse into diabetic coma, and die. Early-onset diabetes tends to be more severe than that developing in later years, and its incidence has almost doubled in the last 20 years; it now affects 1 in 500 people. Before the discovery of insulin by Frederick Banting and Charles Best, severe diabetics did not survive.

diapause

period of suspended development that occurs in some species of insects and other invertebrates, characterized by greatly reduced metabolism. Periods of diapause are often timed to coincide with the winter months, and improve the animal's chances of surviving adverse conditions.

diet

range of foods eaten by an animal each day; it is also a particular selection of food, or the total amount and choice of food for a specific person or people. Most animals require seven kinds of food in their diet: proteins, carbohydrates, fats, vitamins, minerals, water, and roughage. A diet that contains all of these things in the correct amounts and proportions is termed a balanced diet. The amounts and proportions required varies with different animals, according to their size, age, and lifestyle. The digestive systems of animals have evolved to meet particular needs; they have also adapted to cope with the foods available in the surroundings in which they live. The necessity of finding and processing an appropriate diet is a very basic drive in animal evolution. *Dietetics* is the science of feeding individuals or groups; a dietition is a specialist in this science.

differentiation

in embryology, the process by which cells become increasingly different and specialized, giving rise to more complex structures that have particular functions in the adult organism. For instance, embryonic cells may develop into nerve, muscle, or bone cells.

diffusion

spontaneous and random movement of molecules or particles in a fluid (gas or liquid) from a region in which they are at a high concentration to a region of lower concentration, until a uniform concentration is achieved throughout. The difference in concentration between two such regions is called the *concentration gradient*. No mechanical mixing or stirring is involved. For instance, if a drop of ink is added to water, its molecules will diffuse until their colour becomes evenly distributed throughout. Diffusion occurs more rapidly across a higher concentration gradient and at higher temperature.

In biological systems, diffusion plays an essential role in the transport, over short distances, of molecules such as nutrients, respiratory gases, and neurotransmitters. It provides the means by which small molecules pass into and out of individual cells and micro-organisms, such as amoebae, that possess no circulatory system. Plant and animal organs whose function depends on diffusion – such as the lung – have a large surface area. Diffusion of water across a semi-permeable membrane is termed osmosis.

dihybrid inheritance

in genetics, a pattern of inheritance observed when two characteristics are studied in succeeding generations. The first experiments of this type, as well as in monohybrid inheritance, were carried out by Austrian biologist Gregor Mendel using pea plants.

diploblastic

having a body wall composed of two layers. The outer layer is the *ectoderm*, the inner layer is the *endoderm*. This pattern of development is shown by coelenterates.

diploid

having paired chromosomes in each cell. In sexually reproducing species, one set is derived from each parent, the gametes, or sex cells, of each parent being haploid (having only one set of chromosomes) due to meiosis (reduction cell division).

disaccharide

sugar made up of two monosaccharides or simple sugars. Sucrose, $C_{12}H_{22}O_{11}$, or table sugar, is a disaccharide.

dispersal

phase of reproduction during which gametes, eggs, seeds, or offspring move away from the parents into other areas. The result is that overcrowding is avoided and parents do not find themselves in competition with their own offspring. The mechanisms are various, including a reliance on wind or water currents and, in the case of animals, locomotion. The ability of a species to spread widely through an area and to colonize new habitats has survival value in evolution.

DNA abbreviation for deoxyribonucleic acid

molecular basis of heredity. A complex giant molecule that contains, in chemically coded form, the information needed for a cell to make proteins. DNA is a ladderlike double-stranded nucleic acid which forms the basis of genetic inheritance in all organisms, except for a few viruses that have only RNA. DNA is organized into chromosomes and, in organisms other than bacteria, it is found only in the cell nucleus.

Structure

DNA is made up of two chains of nucleotide subunits, with each nucleotide containing either a purine (adenine or guanine) or pyrimidine (cytosine or thymine) base.

The bases link up with each other (adenine linking with thymine, and cytosine with guanine) to form base pairs that connect the two strands of the DNA molecule like the rungs of a twisted ladder.

Heredity

The specific way in which the pairs form means that the base sequence is preserved from generation to generation. Hereditary information is stored as a specific sequence of bases. A set of three bases – known as a *codon* – acts as a blueprint for the manufacture of a particular amino acid, the subunit of a protein molecule.

Codons

Geneticists identify the codons by the initial letters of the constituent bases – for example, the base sequence of codon CAG is cytosine–adenine–guanine. The meaning of each of the codons in the genetic code has been worked out by molecular geneticists. There are four different bases, which means that there must be $4 \times 4 \times 4 = 64$ different codons. Proteins are usually made up of only 20 different amino acids, so many amino acids have more than one codon (for example, GGT, GGC, GGA, and GGG all code for the same amino acid, glycine). The first chromosome to have its DNA sequenced by geneticists was chromosome 22 (one of the smallest human chromosomes, but linked to schizophrenia), which had its estimated 800 genes and 33.5 million bases sequenced in 1999, leaving only a few gaps.

DNA fingerprinting or DNA profiling

another name for genetic fingerprinting.

dominance

in genetics, the masking of one allele (an alternative form of a gene) by another allele. For example, if a heterozygous person has one allele for blue eyes and one for brown eyes, his or her eye colour will be brown. The allele for blue eyes is described as recessive and the allele for brown eyes as dominant.

ductless gland

alternative name for an endocrine gland.

E. coli

abbreviation for *Escherichia coli*.

ecology

study of the relationship among organisms and the environments in which they live, including all living and nonliving components. The chief environmental factors governing the distribution of plants and animals are temperature, humidity, soil, light intensity, daylength, food supply, and interaction with other organisms. The term ecology was coined by the biologist Ernst Haeckel in 1866.

Ecology may be concerned with individual organisms (for example, behavioural ecology, feeding strategies), with populations (for example, population dynamics), or with entire communities (for example, competition between species for access to resources in an ecosystem, or predator–prey relationships). Applied ecology is concerned with the management and conservation of habitats and the consequences and control of pollution.

ecosystem

integrated unit consisting of a community of living organisms – bacteria, animals, and plants – and the physical environment – air, soil, water, and climate – that they inhabit. Individual organisms interact with each other and with their environment, or habitat, in a series of relationships that depends on the flow of energy and nutrients through the system. These relationships are usually complex and finely balanced, and in theory natural ecosystems are self-sustaining. However, major changes to an ecosystem, such as climate change, overpopulation, or the removal of a species, may threaten the system's sustainability and result in its eventual destruction. For instance, the removal of a major carnivore predator can result in the destruction of an ecosystem through overgrazing by herbivores.

Food chains

One of the main features of an ecosystem is its biodiversity. Members are usually classified as producers (those that can synthesize the organic materials they need from inorganic compounds in the environment) or consumers (those that are unable to manufacture their own food directly from these sources and depend upon producers to meet their needs). Thus plants, as producers, capture energy originating from the Sun through a process of photosynthesis and absorb nutrients from the soil and water; these stores of energy and nutrients then become available to the consumers – for example, they are passed via the herbivores that eat the plants, to the carnivores that feed on the herbivores. The sequence in which energy and nutrients pass through the system is known as a food chain, and the energy levels within a food chain are termed trophic levels. At each stage of assimilation, energy is lost by consumer functioning, and so there are always far fewer consumers at the end of the chain. This can be represented diagrammatically by a pyramid with the primary producers at the base, and is termed a pyramid of numbers. At each level of the chain, nutrients are returned to the soil through the decomposition of excrement and dead organisms, thus becoming once again available to plants, and completing a cycle crucial to the stability and survival of the ecosystem.

egg

in animals, the ovum, or female gamete (reproductive cell).

After fertilization by a sperm cell, it begins to divide to form an embryo. Eggs may be deposited by the female (ovipary) or they may develop within her body (vivipary and ovovivipary). In the oviparous reptiles and birds, the egg is protected by a shell and well supplied with nutrients in the form of yolk.

electron transport chain

arrangement of substances within the living cell that takes part in energy production. Electron transport is the means by which reduced flavoproteins (FP) and NAD are oxidized in steps, such that energy from certain steps can be used for the manufacture of ATP by oxidative phosphorylation.

electroporation

in biotechnology, technique of introducing foreign DNA into pollen with strong bursts of electricity which increase the permeability of cell membranes, used in genetic engineering.

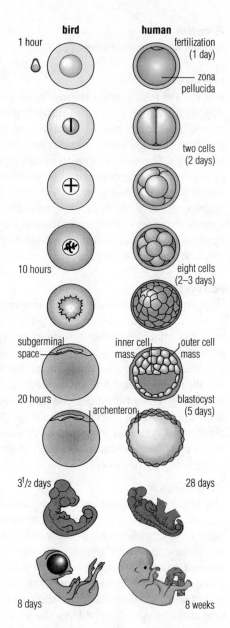

The development of a bird and a human embryo. In the human, division of the fertilized egg, or ovum, begins within hours of conception. Within a week, a hollow, fluid-containing ball – a blastocyst – with a mass of cells at one end has developed. After the third week, the embryo has changed from a mass of cells into a recognizable shape. At four weeks, the embryo is 3 mm/0.1 in long, with a large bulge for the heart and small pits for the ears. At six weeks, the embryo is 1.5 cm/0.6 in long with a pulsating heart and ear flaps. By the eighth week, the embryo (now technically a fetus) is 2.5 cm/1 in long and recognizably human, with eyelids and small fingers and toes.

embryo

early developmental stage of an animal or a plant following fertilization of an ovum (egg cell), or activation of an ovum by parthenogenesis. In humans, the term embryo describes the fertilized egg during its first seven weeks of existence; from the eighth week onwards it is referred to as a fetus.

In animals the embryo exists either within an egg (where it is nourished by food contained in the yolk), or in mammals, in the uterus of the mother. In mammals (except marsupials) the embryo is fed through the placenta. The plant embryo is found within the seed in higher plants. It sometimes consists of only a few cells, but usually includes a root, a shoot (or primary bud), and one or two cotyledons, which nourish the growing seedling.

emergent properties

features of a system that are due to the way in which its components are structured in relation to each other, rather than to the individual properties of those components. Thus the distinctive characteristics of chemical compounds are emergent properties of the way in which the constituent elements are organized, and cannot be explained by the particular properties of those elements taken in isolation. In biology, ecosystem stability is an emergent property of the interaction between the constituent species, and not a property of the species themselves.

endocrine gland

gland that secretes hormones into the bloodstream to regulate body processes. Endocrine glands are most highly developed in vertebrates, but are also found in other animals, notably insects. In humans the main endocrine glands are the pituitary, thyroid, parathyroid, adrenal, pancreas, ovary, and testis.

endoparasite

parasite that lives inside the body of its host.

endoplasm

inner, liquid part of a cell's cytoplasm.

endoplasmic reticulum (ER)

membranous system of tubes, channels, and flattened sacs that form compartments within eukaryotic cells. It stores and transports

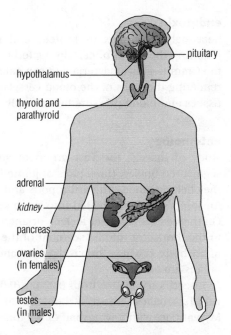

The main human endocrine glands. These glands produce hormones – chemical messengers – which travel in the bloodstream to stimulate certain cells.

proteins within cells and also carries various enzymes needed for the synthesis of fats. The ribosomes, or the organelles that carry out protein synthesis, are sometimes attached to parts of the ER.

Under the electron microscope, ER looks like a series of channels and vesicles, but it is in fact a large, sealed, baglike structure crumpled and folded into a convoluted mass. The interior of the 'bag', the ER lumen, stores various proteins needed elsewhere in the cell, then organizes them into transport vesicles formed by a small piece of ER membrane budding from the main membrane.

endorphin

natural substance (a polypeptide) that modifies the action of nerve cells. Endorphins are produced by the pituitary gland and hypothalamus of vertebrates. They lower the perception of pain by reducing the transmission of signals between nerve cells.

Endorphins not only regulate pain and hunger, but are also involved in the release of sex hormones from the pituitary gland. Opiates act in a similar way to endorphins, but are not rapidly degraded by the body, as natural endorphins are, and thus have a long-lasting effect on pain perception and mood. Endorphin release is stimulated by exercise.

endotoxin

heat stable complex of protein and lipopolysaccharide that is produced following the death of certain bacteria. Endotoxins are typically produced by the Gram negative bacteria and can cause fever. They can also cause shock by rendering the walls of the blood vessels permeable so that fluid leaks into the tissues and blood pressure falls sharply.

entomology

study of insects, the vast group of small invertebrate animals with hard, segmented bodies, three pairs of jointed legs, and, usually, two pairs of wings; they belong among the arthropods and are distributed throughout the world. An insect's body is divided into three segments: head, thorax, and abdomen. On the head is a pair of feelers, or antennae. The legs and wings are attached to the thorax, or middle segment of the body. The abdomen, or end segment of the body, is where food is digested and excreted and where the reproductive organs are located.

Insects vary in size from 0.02 cm/0.007 in to 35 cm/13.5 in in length. The world's smallest insect is believed to be a 'fairy fly' wasp in the family Mymaridae, with a wingspan of 0.2 mm/0.008 in. (Class Insecta.)

environment

in ecology, the sum of conditions affecting a particular organism, including physical surroundings, climate, and influences of other living organisms.

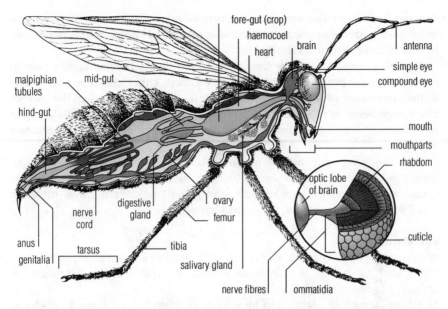

Body plan of an insect. The general features of the insect body include a segmented body divided into head, thorax, and abdomen, jointed legs, feelers or antennae, and usually two pairs of wings. Insects often have compound eyes with a large field of vision.

In common usage, 'the environment' often means the total global environment, without reference to any particular organism. In genetics, it is the external influences that affect an organism's development, and thus its phenotype.

environmentalism

theory emphasizing the primary influence of the environment on the development of groups or individuals. It stresses the importance of the physical, biological, psychological, or cultural environment as a factor influencing the structure or behaviour of animals, including humans.

In politics this has given rise in many countries to Green parties, which aim to 'preserve the planet and its people'.

enzyme

biological catalyst produced in cells, and capable of speeding up the chemical reactions necessary for life. They are large, complex proteins, and are highly specific, each chemical reaction requiring its own particular enzyme. The enzyme's specificity arises from its active site, an area with a shape corresponding to part of the molecule with which it reacts (the substrate). The enzyme and the substrate slot together forming an enzyme–substrate complex that allows the reaction to take place, after which the enzyme falls away unaltered.

The activity and efficiency of enzymes are influenced by various factors, including temperature and pH conditions. Temperatures above 60°C/140°F damage (denature) the intricate structure of enzymes, causing reactions to cease. Each enzyme operates best within a specific pH range, and is denatured by excessive acidity or alkalinity.

Digestive enzymes include amylases (which digest starch), lipases (which digest fats), and proteases (which digest protein). Other enzymes play a part in the conversion of food energy into ATP; the manufacture of all the molecular components of the body; the replication of DNA when a cell divides; the production of hormones; and the control of movement of substances into and out of cells.

Enzymes have many medical and industrial uses, from washing powders to drug production, and as research tools in molecular biology. They can be extracted from bacteria and moulds, and genetic engineering now makes it possible to tailor an enzyme for a specific purpose.

epidermis

outermost layer of cells on an organism's body. In plants and many invertebrates such as insects, it consists of a single layer of cells. In vertebrates, it consists of several layers of cells.

The epidermis of plants and invertebrates often has an outer noncellular cuticle that protects the organism from desiccation.

In vertebrates, such as reptiles, birds, and mammals, the outermost layer of cells is dead, forming a tough, waterproof layer, known as skin.

erythroblast

series of nucleated cells that go through various stages of development in the bone marrow until they form red blood cells (erythrocytes). This process is known as erythropoiesis. Erythroblasts can appear in the blood of people with blood cancers.

erythrocyte

another name for red blood cell.

Escherichia coli or colon bacillus

rod-shaped Gram-negative bacterium (see bacteria) that lives, usually harmlessly, in the colon of most warm-blooded animals. It is the commonest cause of urinary tract infections in humans. It is sometimes found in water or meat where faecal contamination has occurred and can cause severe gastric problems.

Escherichia coli is the only species in the bacterial family Enterobacteriaceae. The mapping of the genome of *E. coli*, consisting of 4,403 genes, was completed in 1997. It is probably the organism about which most molecular genetics is known, and is of pre-eminent importance in recombinant DNA research.

essential amino acid

water-soluble organic molecule vital to a healthy diet because it cannot be synthesized from other food molecules; see amino acid.

essential fatty acid

organic compound consisting of a hydrocarbon chain and important in the diet; see fatty acid.

ethology

comparative study of animal behaviour in its natural setting. Ethology is concerned with the causal mechanisms (both the stimuli that elicit behaviour and the physiological mechanisms controlling it), as well as the development of behaviour, its function, and its evolutionary history.

Ethology was pioneered during the 1930s by the Austrians Konrad Lorenz and Karl von Frisch who, with the Dutch zoologist Nikolaas Tinbergen, received a Nobel prize in 1973. Ethologists believe that the significance of an animal's behaviour can be understood only in its natural context, and emphasize the importance of field studies and an evolutionary perspective. A late 20th-century development within ethology is sociobiology, the study of the evolutionary function of social behaviour.

eugenics

study of ways in which the physical and mental characteristics of the human race may be improved. The eugenic principle was abused by the Nazi Party in Germany during the 1930s and early 1940s to justify the attempted extermination of entire social and ethnic groups and the establishment of selective breeding programmes. Modern eugenics is concerned mainly with the elimination of genetic disease.

The term was coined by the English scientist Francis Galton in 1883, and the concept was originally developed in the late 19th century with a view to improving human intelligence and behaviour.

eukaryote

one of the two major groupings (superkingdoms) into which all organisms are divided. Included are all organisms, except bacteria and cyanobacteria (blue-green algae), which belong to the prokaryote grouping.

The cells of eukaryotes possess a clearly defined nucleus, bounded by a membrane, within which DNA is formed into distinct chromosomes. Eukaryotic cells also contain mitochondria, chloroplasts, and other structures (organelles) that, together with a defined nucleus, are lacking in the cells of prokaryotes.

eusociality

form of social life found in insects such as honey bees and termites, in which the colony is made up of special castes (for example, workers, drones, and reproductives) whose membership is biologically determined. The worker castes do not usually reproduce. Only one mammal, the naked mole rat, has a social organization of this type. A eusocial shrimp was discovered in 1996 living in the coral reefs of Belize. *Synalpheus regalis* lives in colonies of up to 300 individuals, all the offspring of a single reproductive female.

evolution

slow, gradual process of change from one form to another, as in the evolution of the universe from its formation to its present state, or in the evolution of life on Earth. In biology, it is the process by which life has developed by stages from single-celled organisms into the multiplicity of animal and plant life, extinct and existing, that inhabit the Earth. The development of the concept of evolution is usually associated with the English naturalist Charles Darwin who attributed the main role in evolutionary change to natural selection acting on randomly occurring variations. However, these variations in species are now known to be adaptations produced by spontaneous changes or mutations in the genetic material of organisms.

Evolution and creationism

Organic evolution traces the development of simple unicellular forms to more complex forms, ultimately to the flowering plants and vertebrate animals, including humans. The Earth contains an immense diversity of living organisms: about a million different species of animals and half a million species of plants have so far been described. Some religions deny the theory of evolution considering it conflicts with their belief that God created all things. But most people accept that there is overwhelming evidence the diversity of life arose by a gradual process of evolutionary divergence and not by individual acts of divine creation. There are several lines of evidence: the fossil record, the existence of similarities or homologies between different groups of organisms, embryology, and geographical distribution.

Natural selection, sexual selection, and chance

The idea of continuous evolution can be traced as far back as Lucretius in the 1st century BC, but it did not gain wide acceptance until the 19th century following the work of Scottish geologist Charles Lyell, French naturalist Jean Baptiste Lamarck, Darwin together with Alfred Russel Wallace, and English biologist T H Huxley. Natural selection occurs because those individuals better adapted to their particular environments reproduce more effectively, thus contributing their characteristics (in the form of genes) to future generations. The current theory of evolution, neo-Darwinism, combines Darwin's theory of natural selection with the theories of Austrian biologist Gregor Mendel on genetics.

Currently, neither the general concept of evolution nor the importance of natural selection is doubted by biologists, but there still remains dispute over other possible processes involved in evolutionary change. Besides natural selection, artificial selection, and sexual selection, chance may play a large part in deciding which genes become characteristic of a population – a phenomenon called 'genetic drift'. It is now also clear that evolutionary change does not always occur at a constant rate, but that the process can have long periods of relative stability interspersed with periods of rapid change. This has led to new theories, such as the punctuated equilibrium model. See also adaptive radiation.

evolutionary stable strategy (ESS)

assemblage of behavioural or physical characters (collectively termed a 'strategy') of a population that is resistant to replacement by any forms bearing new traits, because the new traits will not be capable of successful reproduction.

ESS analysis is based on game theory and can be applied both to genetically determined physical characters (such as horn length), and to learned behavioural responses (for example, whether to fight or retreat from an opponent). An ESS may be conditional on the context, as in the rule 'fight if the opponent is smaller, but retreat if the opponent is larger'.

evolutionary toxicology

study of the effects of pollution on evolution. A polluted habitat may cause organisms to select for certain traits, as in *industrial melanism* for example, where some insects, such as the peppered moth, evolve to be darker in polluted areas, and therefore better camouflaged against predation.

Pollutants may also trigger mutations, for example, voles living around the Chernobyl exploded nuclear reactor have a very high mutation rate despite appearing healthy and reproducing successfully. Fish in polluted rivers also exhibit mutations.

excretion

removal of the waste products of metabolism from living organisms. In plants and simple animals, waste products are removed by diffusion. Plants, for example, excrete O_2, a product of photosynthesis. In mammals, waste products are removed by specialized excretory organs, principally the kidneys, which excrete urea. Water and metabolic wastes are also excreted in the faeces and, in humans, through the sweat glands in the skin; carbon dioxide and water are removed via the lungs. The liver excretes bile pigments.

exon

in genetics, a sequence of bases in DNA that codes for a protein. Exons make up only 2% of the body's total DNA. The remainder is made up of introns. During RNA processing the introns are cut out of the molecule and the exons spliced together.

extinction

complete disappearance of a species or higher taxon. Extinctions occur when an animal becomes unfit for survival in its natural habitat usually to be replaced by another, better-suited animal. An organism becomes ill-suited for survival because its environment is changed or because its relationship to other organisms is altered. For example, a predator's fitness for survival depends upon the availability of its prey.

Past extinctions

Mass extinctions are episodes during which large numbers of species have become extinct virtually simultaneously, the best known being that of the dinosaurs, other large reptiles, and various marine invertebrates about 65 million years ago between the end of the Cretaceous period and the beginning of the Tertiary period. The latter, known as the *K–T extinction*, has been attributed to catastrophic environmental changes following a meteor impact or unusually prolonged and voluminous volcanic eruptions.

Another mass extinction occurred about 10,000 years ago when many giant species of mammal died out. This is known as the 'Pleistocene overkill' because their disappearance was probably hastened by the hunting activities of prehistoric humans. The greatest mass extinction occurred about 250 million years ago, marking the Permian–Triassic boundary, when up to 96% of all living species became extinct. Mass extinctions apparently occur at periodic intervals of approximately 26 million years.

Current extinctions

Humans have the capacity to profoundly influence many habitats and today a large number of extinctions are attributable to human activity. Some species, such as the dodo of Mauritius, the moas of New Zealand, and the passenger pigeon of North America, were exterminated by hunting. Others became extinct when their habitat was destroyed. Endangered species are close to extinction. The rate of extinction is difficult to estimate, but appears to have been accelerated by humans. Conservative estimates put the rate of loss due to deforestation alone at 4,000 to 6,000 species a year. Overall, the rate could be as high as one species an hour, with the loss of one species putting those dependent on it at risk. Australia has the worst record for extinction: 18 mammals have disappeared since Europeans settled there, and 40 more are threatened.

extremophile

microbe able to thrive in extreme conditions, such as very high temperatures (thermophiles), low temperatures (psychrophiles), high acidity (acidophiles), or high alkalinity (alkaliphiles). Examples of extremophiles are found in both bacteria and Archaea.

fat

in the broadest sense, a mixture of lipids – chiefly triglycerides (lipids containing three fatty acid molecules linked to a molecule of glycerol). More specifically, the term refers to a lipid mixture that is solid at room temperature (20°C); lipid mixtures that are liquid at room temperature are called *oils*. The higher the proportion of saturated fatty acids in a mixture, the harder the fat.

Boiling fats in strong alkali forms soaps (saponification). Fats are essential constituents of food for many animals, with a calorific value twice that of carbohydrates; however, eating too much fat, especially fat of animal origin, has been linked with heart disease in humans. In many animals and plants, excess carbohydrates and proteins are converted into fats for storage. Mammals and other vertebrates store fats in specialized connective tissues (adipose tissues), which not only act as energy reserves but also insulate the body and cushion its organs.

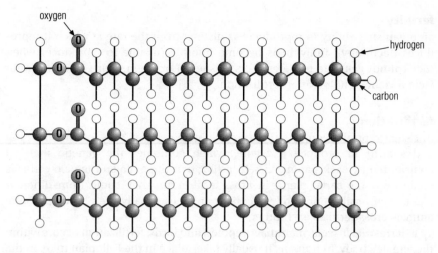

The molecular structure of typical fat. The molecule consists of three fatty acid molecules linked to a molecule of glycerol.

fatty acid or carboxylic acid

organic compound consisting of a hydrocarbon chain of an even number of carbon atoms, with a carboxyl group (–COOH) at one end. The covalent bonds between the carbon atoms may be single or double; where a double bond occurs the carbon atoms concerned carry one instead of two hydrogen atoms. Chains with only single bonds have all the hydrogen they can carry, so they are said to be *saturated* with hydrogen. Chains with one or more double bonds are said to be *unsaturated* (see polyunsaturate). Fatty acids are produced in the small intestine when fat is digested.

Saturated fatty acids include palmitic and stearic acids; unsaturated fatty acids include oleic (one double bond), linoleic (two double bonds), and linolenic (three double bonds). Linoleic acid accounts for more than one third of some margarines. Supermarket brands that say they are high in polyunsaturates may contain as much as 39%. Fatty acids are generally found combined with glycerol in lipids such as triglycerides.

fecundity

potential rate at which an organism reproduces, as distinct from its ability to reproduce (fertility). In vertebrates, it is usually measured as the number of offspring produced by a female each year. Specifically, it refers to the quantity of gametes (usually eggs) produced per female over a given time.

feedback

another term for biofeedback: the influence of the outcome of one process upon the functioning of another process.

fertility

an organism's ability to reproduce, as distinct from the rate at which it reproduces (fecundity). Individuals become infertile (unable to reproduce) when they cannot generate gametes (eggs or sperm) or when their gametes cannot yield a viable embryo after fertilization.

fertilization

in sexual reproduction, the union of two gametes (sex cells, often called egg and sperm) to produce a zygote, which combines the genetic material contributed by each parent. In self-fertilization the male and female gametes come from the same plant; in cross-fertilization they come from different plants. Self-fertilization rarely occurs in animals; usually even hermaphrodite animals cross-fertilize each other.

In terrestrial insects, mammals, reptiles, and birds, fertilization occurs within the female's body. In humans it usually takes place in the Fallopian tube. In the majority of fishes and amphibians, and most aquatic invertebrates, fertilization occurs externally, when both sexes release their gametes into the water. In most fungi, gametes are not released, but the hyphae of the two parents grow towards each other and fuse to achieve fertilization. In higher plants, pollination precedes fertilization.

fetus or foetus

stage in mammalian embryo development. The human embryo is usually termed a fetus after the eighth week of development, when the limbs and external features of the head are recognizable.

field studies

study of ecology, geography, geology, history, archaeology, and allied subjects, in the natural environment as opposed to the laboratory.

fitness

in genetic theory, a measure of the success with which a genetically determined character can spread in future generations. By convention, the normal character is assigned a fitness of one and variants (determined by other alleles) are then assigned fitness values relative to this. Those with fitness greater than one will spread more rapidly and will ultimately replace the normal allele; those with fitness less than one will gradually die out.

See also inclusive fitness.

flagellum

(plural flagella) small hairlike organ on the surface of certain cells. Flagella are the motile organs of certain protozoa and single-celled algae, and of the sperm cells of higher animals. Unlike cilia, flagella usually occur singly or in pairs; they are also longer and have a more complex whiplike action.

Each flagellum consists of contractile filaments producing snakelike movements that propel cells through fluids, or fluids past cells. Water movement inside sponges is also produced by flagella.

fluorescence microscopy

technique for examining samples under a microscope without slicing them into thin sections. Instead, fluorescent dyes are introduced into the tissue and used as a light source for imaging purposes. Fluorescent dyes can also be bonded to monoclonal antibodies and used to highlight areas where particular cell proteins occur.

folic acid

vitamin of the B complex. It is found in liver, legumes and green leafy vegetables, and whole grain foods, and is also synthesized by the intestinal bacteria. It is essential for growth, and plays many other roles in the body. Lack of folic acid causes anaemia because it is necessary for the synthesis of nucleic acids and the formation of red blood cells.

food

anything eaten by human beings and other animals and absorbed by plants to sustain life and health. The building blocks of food are nutrients, and humans can utilize the following nutrients: *carbohydrates* as starches found in bread, potatoes, and pasta; as simple sugars in sucrose and honey; and as fibres in cereals, fruit, and vegetables; *proteins* as from nuts, fish, meat, eggs, milk, and some vegetables; *fats* as found in most animal products (meat, lard, dairy products, fish), also in margarine, nuts and seeds, olives, and edible oils; *vitamins*, found in a wide variety of foods, except for vitamin B_{12}, which is found mainly in foods of animal origin; and *minerals*, found in a wide variety of foods (for example, calcium from milk and broccoli, iodine from seafood, and iron from liver and green vegetables).

Liquids consumed are principally *water*, ubiquitous in nature, and *alcohol*, found in fermented distilled beverages, from 40% in spirits to 0.01% in low-alcohol lagers and beers.

Food is needed both for energy, measured in calories or kilojoules, and nutrients, which are converted to body tissues. Some nutrients, such as fat, carbohydrate, and alcohol, provide mainly energy; other nutrients are important in other ways; for example, fibre is an aid to metabolism. Proteins provide energy and are necessary for building cell and tissue structure.

food chain

in ecology, a sequence showing the feeding relationships between organisms in a particular ecosystem. Each organism depends on the next lowest member of the chain for its food. A pyramid of numbers can be used to show the reduction in food energy at each step up the food chain.

Energy in the form of food is shown to be transferred from autotrophs, or producers, which are principally plants and photosynthetic micro-organisms, to a series of heterotrophs, or consumers. The heterotrophs comprise the herbivores, which feed on the producers; carnivores, which feed on the herbivores; and decomposers, which break down the dead bodies and waste products of all four groups (including their own), ready for recycling.

In reality, however, organisms have varied diets, relying on different kinds of foods, so that the food chain is an oversimplification. The more complex *food web* shows a greater variety of relationships, but again emphasizes that energy passes from plants to herbivores to carnivores.

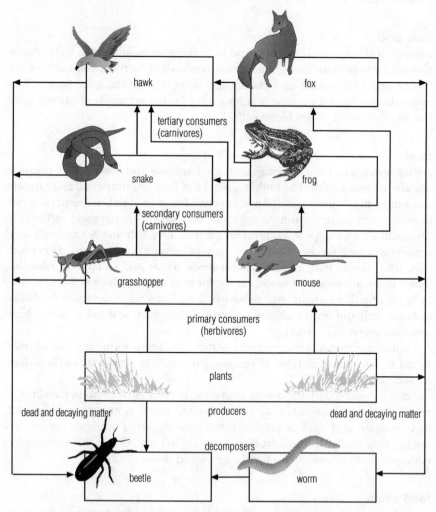

The complex interrelationships between animals and plants in a food web. A food web shows how different food chains are linked in an ecosystem. Note that the arrows indicate movement of energy through the web. For example, an arrow shows that energy moves from plants to the grasshopper, which eats the plants.

Environmentalists have used the concept of the food chain to show how poisons and other forms of pollution can pass from one animal to another, threatening rare species. For example, the pesticide DDT has been found in lethal concentrations in the bodies of animals at the top of the food chain, such as the golden eagle *Aquila chrysaetos*.

food irradiation

exposure of food to low-level irradiation to kill micro-organisms; a technique used in food technology. Irradiation is highly effective, and does not make the food any more radioactive than it is naturally. Irradiated food is used for astronauts and immunocompromised patients in hospitals. Some vitamins are partially destroyed, such as vitamin C, and it would be unwise to eat only irradiated fruit and vegetables.

freeze-drying

method of preserving food. The product to be dried is frozen and then put in a vacuum chamber that forces out the ice as water vapour, a process known as sublimation.

Many of the substances that give products such as coffee their typical flavour are volatile, and would be lost in a normal drying process because they would evaporate along with the water. In the freeze-drying process these volatile compounds do not pass into the ice that is to be sublimed, and are therefore largely retained.

fungus

any of a unique group of organisms that includes moulds, yeasts, rusts, smuts, mildews, mushrooms, and toadstools. There are around 70,000 species of fungi known to science, though there may be as many as 1.5 million actually in existence. They are not considered to be plants for three main reasons: they have no leaves or roots; they contain no chlorophyll (green colouring) and are therefore unable to make their own food by photosynthesis; and they reproduce by spores. Some fungi are edible but many are highly poisonous; they often cause damage and sometimes disease to the organic matter they live and feed on, but some fungi are exploited in the production of food and drink (for example, yeasts in baking and brewing) and in medicine (for example, penicillin).

Fungi are either parasites, existing on living plants or animals, or saprotrophs, living on dead matter. Many of the most serious plant diseases are caused by fungi, and several fungi attack humans and animals. Athlete's foot, thrush, and ringworm are fungal diseases. Endophytes are fungi that live inside plants. Almost all plants have endophytes and many have large numbers, for example the grass fescue has 400 species.

galactose ($C_6H_{12}O_6$)

one of the hexose sugars, an isomer of glucose and fructose.

gamete

cell that functions in sexual reproduction by merging with another gamete to form a zygote. Examples of gametes include sperm and egg cells. In most organisms, the gametes are haploid (they contain half the number of chromosomes of the parent), owing to reduction division or meiosis.

In higher organisms, gametes are of two distinct types: large immobile ones known as eggs or egg cells (see ovum) and small ones known as sperm. They come together at fertilization. In some lower organisms the gametes are all the same, or they may belong to different mating strains but have no obvious differences in size or appearance.

gas exchange

movement of gases between an organism and the atmosphere, principally oxygen and carbon dioxide. All aerobic organisms (most animals and plants) take in oxygen in order to burn food and manufacture ATP. The resultant oxidation reactions release carbon dioxide as a waste product to be passed out into the environment. Green plants also absorb carbon dioxide during photosynthesis, and release oxygen as a waste product.

Specialized respiratory surfaces have evolved during evolution to make gas exchange more efficient. In humans and other tetrapods (four-limbed vertebrates), gas exchange occurs in the lungs, aided by the breathing movements of the ribs. Many adult amphibia and terrestrial invertebrates can absorb oxygen directly through the skin. The bodies of insects and some spiders contain a system of air-filled tubes known as tracheae. Fish have gills as their main respiratory surface. In plants, gas exchange generally takes place via the stomata and the air-filled spaces between the cells in the interior of the leaf.

gene

unit of inherited material, encoded by a strand of DNA and transcribed by RNA. In higher organisms, genes are located on the chromosomes. A gene consistently affects a particular character in an individual – for example, the gene for eye colour. Also termed a Mendelian gene, after Austrian biologist Gregor Mendel, it occurs at a particular point, or locus, on a particular chromosome and may have several variants, or alleles, each specifying a particular form of that character – for example, the alleles for blue or brown eyes. Some alleles show dominance. These mask the effect of other alleles, known as recessive.

In the 1940s, it was established that a gene could be identified with a particular length of DNA, which coded for a complete protein molecule, leading to the 'one gene, one enzyme' principle. Later it was realized that proteins can be made up of several polypeptide chains, each with a separate gene, so this principle was modified to 'one gene, one polypeptide'. However, the fundamental idea remains the same, that genes produce their visible effects simply by coding for proteins; they control the structure of those proteins via the genetic code, as well as the amounts produced and the timing of production.

In modern genetics, the gene is identified either with the cistron (a set of codons that determines a complete polypeptide) or with the unit of selection (a Mendelian gene that determines a particular character in the organism on which natural selection can act). Genes undergo mutation and recombination to produce the variation on which natural selection operates.

gene amplification

technique by which selected DNA from a single cell can be duplicated indefinitely until there is a sufficient amount to analyse by conventional genetic techniques.

Gene amplification uses a procedure called the polymerase chain reaction. The sample of DNA is mixed with a solution of enzymes called polymerases, which enable it to replicate, and with a plentiful supply of nucleotides, the building blocks of DNA. The mixture is repeatedly heated and cooled. At each warming, the double-stranded DNA present separates into two single strands, and with each cooling the polymerase assembles a new paired strand for each single strand. Each cycle takes approximately 30 minutes to complete, so that after 10 hours there is one million times more DNA present than at the start.

The technique is used to test for genetic defects in a single cell taken from an embryo, before the embryo is reimplanted in in vitro fertilization.

gene bank

collection of seeds or other forms of genetic material, such as tubers, spores, bacterial or yeast cultures, live animals and plants, frozen sperm and eggs, or frozen embryos. These are stored for possible future use in agriculture, plant and animal breeding, or in medicine, genetic engineering, or the restocking of wild habitats where species have become extinct. Gene banks may be increasingly used as the rate of extinction increases, depleting the Earth's genetic variety (biodiversity).

gene imprinting

genetic phenomenon whereby a small number of genes function differently depending on whether they were inherited from the father or the mother. If two copies of an imprinted gene are inherited from one parent and none from the other, a genetic abnormality results, whereas no abnormality occurs if, as is normal, a copy is inherited from both parents. Gene imprinting is known to play a part in a number of genetic disorders and childhood diseases, for example, the Prader–Willi syndrome (characterized by mild mental retardation and compulsive eating).

gene pool

total sum of alleles (variants of genes) possessed by all the members of a given population or species alive at a particular time.

gene-splicing

see genetic engineering.

gene therapy

medical technique for curing or alleviating inherited diseases or defects that are due to a gene malfunction; certain infections, and several kinds of cancer in which affected cells from a sufferer are removed from the body, the DNA repaired in the laboratory (genetic engineering), and the normal functioning cells reintroduced. In 1990 a genetically engineered gene was used for the first time to treat a patient.

The first human being to undergo gene therapy, in 1990, was one of the so-called 'bubble babies' – a four-year-old American girl suffering from a rare enzyme (ADA) deficiency that cripples the immune system. Unable to fight off infection, such children are nursed in a germ-free bubble; they usually die in early childhood.

Cystic fibrosis is the commonest inherited disorder and the one most keenly targeted by genetic engineers; it has been pioneered in patients in the USA and UK. Gene therapy is not the final answer to inherited disease; it may cure the patient but it cannot prevent him or her from passing on the genetic defect to any children. However, it does hold out the promise of a cure for various other conditions, including heart disease and some cancers; US researchers have successfully used a gene gun to target specific tumour cells.

genetic code

way in which instructions for building proteins, the basic structural molecules of living matter, are 'written' in the genetic material DNA. This relationship between the sequence of bases (the subunits in a DNA molecule) and the sequence of amino acids (the subunits of a protein molecule) is the basis of heredity. The code employs codons of three bases each; it is the same in almost all organisms, except for a few minor differences recently discovered in some protozoa.

Only 2% of DNA is made up of base sequences, called *exons*, that code for proteins. The remaining DNA is known as 'junk' DNA or *introns*.

genetic engineering

all-inclusive term that describes the deliberate manipulation of genetic material by biochemical techniques. It is often achieved by the introduction of new DNA, usually by means of a virus or plasmid. This can be for pure research, gene therapy, or to breed functionally specific plants, animals, or bacteria. These organisms with a foreign gene added are said to be transgenic (see transgenic organism).

Practical uses

In genetic engineering, the splicing and reconciliation of genes is used to increase knowledge of cell function and reproduction, but it can also achieve practical ends. For example, plants grown for food could be given the ability to fix nitrogen, found in some bacteria, and so reduce the need for expensive fertilizers, or simple bacteria may be modified to produce rare drugs. A foreign gene can be inserted into laboratory cultures of bacteria to generate commercial biological products, such as synthetic insulin, hepatitis-B vaccine, and interferon. Gene splicing was invented in 1973 by the US scientists Stanley Cohen and Herbert Boyer, and patented in the USA in 1984.

US figures for the 1997 and 1998 performance of genetically modified crops of maize, cotton, and soya released by the US Department of Agriculture in July 1999, revealed that in two-thirds of the crops studied there was no real improvement in yield and in over half of those modified to be insect resistant farmers had still needed to use similar quantities of pesticide as required for unmodified crops.

New developments
Developments in genetic engineering have led to the production of growth hormone, and a number of other bone-marrow stimulating hormones. New strains of animals have also been produced; a new strain of mouse was patented in the USA in 1989 (the application was rejected in the European Patent Office). A vaccine against a sheep parasite (a larval tapeworm) has been developed by genetic engineering; most existing vaccines protect against bacteria and viruses.

The first genetically engineered food went on sale in 1994; the 'Flavr Savr' tomato, produced by the US biotechnology company Calgene, was available in California and Chicago.

Safety measures
There is a risk that when transplanting genes between different types of bacteria (*Escherichia coli*, which lives in the human intestine, is often used) new and harmful strains might be produced. For this reason strict safety precautions are observed, and the altered bacteria are disabled in some way so they are unable to exist outside the laboratory.

There are also concerns for the environmental consequences of genetically modified crops and in 1999 US ecologists found evidence that maize modified to contain the insecticidal *Bt* genes from the soil bacterium *Bacillus thuringiensis* maybe harmful to the monarch butterfly caterpillar. Monarchs feed on milkweed, which often grows near maize fields and some of the transgenic maize pollen is contaminating the milkweed.

In 1999 the UK Department of Environment, Transport and the Regions began a £3.3-million four-year trial to assess the risk to nature posed by genetically modified crops. Crops of genetically modified maize and oilseed rape were planted at six sites around Britain and biologists will monitor surrounding wildlife and plants. The trials are being severely hampered by sabotage by protestors.

genetic fingerprinting or genetic profiling
technique developed in the UK by Professor Alec Jeffreys (1950–), and now allowed as a means of legal identification. It determines the pattern of certain parts of the genetic material DNA that is unique to each individual. Like conventional fingerprinting, it can accurately distinguish humans from one another, with the exception of identical siblings from multiple births. It can be applied to as little material as a single cell.

Genetic fingerprinting involves isolating DNA from cells, then comparing and contrasting the sequences of component chemicals between individuals. The DNA pattern can be ascertained from a sample of skin, hair, or semen. Although differences are minimal (only 0.1% between unrelated people), certain regions of DNA, known as *hypervariable regions*, are unique to individuals.

Genetic fingerprinting is used in paternity testing, forensic medicine, and inbreeding studies.

genetics

branch of biology concerned with the study of heredity and variation; it attempts to explain how characteristics of living organisms are passed on from one generation to the next. The science of genetics is based on the work of Austrian biologist Gregor Mendel whose experiments with the cross-breeding (hybridization) of peas showed that the inheritance of characteristics and traits takes place by means of discrete 'particles' (genes). These are present in the cells of all organisms, and are now recognized as being the basic units of heredity. All organisms possess genotypes (sets of variable genes) and phenotypes (characteristics produced by certain genes). Modern geneticists investigate the structure, function, and transmission of genes.

Before the publication of Mendel's work in 1865, it had been assumed that the characteristics of both parents were blended during inheritance, but Mendel showed that the genes remain intact, although their combinations change. As a result of his experiments with the cultivation of the common garden pea, Mendel introduced the concept of hybridization (see monohybrid inheritance). Since Mendel, the study of genetics has advanced greatly, first through breeding experiments and light-microscope observations (classical genetics), later by means of biochemical and electron microscope studies (molecular genetics).

In 1944, Canadian-born bacteriologist Oswald Avery, together with his colleagues at the Rockefeller Institute, Colin McLeod and Maclyn McCarty, showed that the genetic material was deoxyribonucleic acid (DNA), and not protein as was previously thought. A further breakthrough was made in 1953 when James Watson and Francis Crick published their molecular model for the structure of DNA, the double helix, based on X-ray diffraction photographs. The following decade saw the cracking of the genetic code. The genetic code is said to be universal since the same code applies to all organisms from bacteria and viruses to higher plants and animals, including humans. Today the deliberate manipulation of genes by biochemical techniques, or genetic engineering, is commonplace.

genome

full complement of genes carried by a single (haploid) set of chromosomes. The term may be applied to the genetic information carried by an individual or to the range of genes found in a given species. The human genome is made up of approximately 100,000 genes.

genotype

particular set of alleles (variants of genes) possessed by a given organism. The term is usually used in conjunction with phenotype, which is the product of the genotype and all environmental effects. See also nature–nurture controversy.

genus plural genera

group of one or more species with many characteristics in common. Thus all doglike species (including dogs, wolves, and jackals) belong to the genus *Canis* (Latin 'dog'). Species of the same genus are thought to be descended from a common ancestor species. Related genera are grouped into families.

germination

in botany, the initial stages of growth in a seed, spore, or pollen grain. Seeds germinate when they are exposed to favourable external conditions of moisture, light, and temperature, and when any factors causing dormancy have been removed.

The process begins with the uptake of water by the seed. The embryonic root, or radicle, is normally the first organ to emerge, followed by the embryonic shoot, or plumule. Food reserves, either within the endosperm or from the cotyledons, are broken down to nourish the rapidly growing seedling. Germination is considered to have ended with the production of the first true leaves.

germ-line therapy

hypothetical application of gene therapy to sperm and egg cells to remove the risk of an inherited disease being passed to offspring. It is controversial because of the fear it will be used to produce 'designer babies', and may result in unforseen side effects.

gestation

in all mammals except the monotremes (platypus and spiny anteaters), the period from the time of implantation of the embryo in the uterus to birth. This period varies among species; in humans it is about 266 days, in elephants 18–22 months, in cats about 60 days, and in some species of marsupial (such as opossum) as short as 12 days.

gland

specialized organ of the body that manufactures and secretes enzymes, hormones, or other chemicals. In animals, glands vary in size from small (for example, tear glands) to large (for example, the pancreas), but in plants they are always small, and may consist of a single cell. Some glands discharge their products internally (endocrine glands) and others externally (exocrine glands). Lymph nodes are sometimes wrongly called glands.

glucagon

hormone secreted by the alpha cells of the islets of Langerhans in the pancreas, which increases the concentration of glucose in the blood by promoting the breakdown of glycogen in the liver. Secretion occurs in response to a lowering of blood glucose concentrations.

Glucagon injections can be issued to close relatives of patients with diabetes who are being treated with insulin. Hypoglycaemia may develop in such patients in the event of inadequate control of diabetes. An injection of glucagon can be used to reverse hypoglycaemia before serious symptoms, such as unconsciousness, develop.

glucose or dextrose or grape sugar ($C_6H_{12}O_6$)

sugar present in the blood and manufactured by green plants during photosynthesis. The respiration reactions inside cells involves the oxidation of glucose to produce ATP, the 'energy molecule' used to drive many of the body's biochemical reactions.

In humans and other vertebrates optimum blood glucose levels are maintained by the hormone insulin.

Glucose is prepared in syrup form by the hydrolysis of cane sugar or starch, and may be purified to a white crystalline powder. Glucose is a monosaccharide sugar (made up of a single sugar unit), unlike the more familiar sucrose (cane or beet sugar), which is a disaccharide (made up of two sugar units: glucose and fructose).

Golgi apparatus or Golgi body

stack of flattened membranous sacs found in the cells of eukaryotes. Many molecules travel through the Golgi apparatus on their way to other organelles or to the endoplasmic reticulum. Some are modified or assembled inside the sacs. The Golgi apparatus is named after the Italian physician Camillo Golgi. It produces the membranes that surround the cell vesicles or lysosomes.

growth

increase in size and weight during the development of an organism. Growth is an increase in biomass (mass of organic material, excluding water) and is associated with cell division by mitosis, and with the differentiation of cells to perform specific functions, for example red blood cells in mammals and root cells in plants. All organisms grow, although the rate of growth varies over a lifetime. Typically, an organism shows an S-shaped curve, in which growth is at first slow, then fast, then, towards the end of life, nonexistent. Growth may even be negative during the period before death, with decay occurring faster than cellular replacement. Growth is affected by genetic factors, which dictate the eventual size and appearance of an organism. It is dependent upon an adequate supply of water and nutrients, and, particularly in plants, appropriate conditions of light and temperature.

haemoglobin

protein used by all vertebrates and some invertebrates for oxygen transport because the two substances combine reversibly. In vertebrates it occurs in red blood cells (erythrocytes), giving them their colour.

In the lungs or gills where the concentration of oxygen is high, oxygen attaches to haemoglobin to form *oxyhaemoglobin*. This process effectively increases the amount of oxygen that can be carried in the bloodstream. The oxygen is later released in the body tissues where it is at a low concentration, and the deoxygenated blood returned to the lungs or gills. Haemoglobin will combine also with carbon monoxide to form carboxyhaemoglobin, but in this case the reaction is irreversible.

haploid

having a single set of chromosomes in each cell. Most higher organisms are diploid – that is, they have two sets – but their gametes (sex cells) are haploid. Some plants, such as mosses, liverworts, and many seaweeds, are haploid, and male honey bees are haploid because they develop from eggs that have not been fertilized. See also meiosis.

Hardy–Weinberg equilibrium

in population genetics, the theoretical relative frequency of different alleles within a given population of a species, when the stable endpoint of evolution in an undisturbed environment is reached.

herbivore

animal that feeds on green plants (or photosynthetic single-celled organisms) or their products, including seeds, fruit, and nectar. The most numerous type of herbivore is thought to be the zooplankton, tiny invertebrates in the surface waters of the oceans that feed on small photosynthetic algae. Herbivores are more numerous than other animals because their food is the most abundant. They form a vital link in the food chain between plants and carnivores.

Mammalian herbivores that rely on cellulose as a major part of their diet, for instance cows and sheep, generally possess millions of specialized bacteria in their gut. These are capable of producing the enzyme cellulase, necessary for digesting cellulose; no mammal is able to manufacture cellulase on its own.

heredity

transmission of traits from parent to offspring. See also genetics.

hermaphrodite

organism that has both male and female sex organs. Hermaphroditism is the norm in such species as earthworms and snails, and is common in flowering plants. Cross-fertilization is common among hermaphrodites, with the parents functioning as male and female simultaneously, or as one or the other sex at different stages in their development. Human hermaphrodites are extremely rare.

heterosis or hybrid vigour

improvement in physical capacities that sometimes occurs in the hybrid produced by mating two genetically different parents.

The parents may be of different strains or varieties within a species, or of different species, as in the mule, which is stronger and has a longer life span than either of its parents (donkey and horse). Heterosis is also exploited in hybrid varieties of maize, tomatoes, and other crops.

heterotroph

any living organism that obtains its energy from organic substances produced by other organisms. All animals and fungi are heterotrophs, and they include herbivores, carnivores, and saprotrophs (those that feed on dead animal and plant material).

heterozygous

having two different alleles for a given trait. In homozygous organisms, by contrast, both chromosomes carry the same allele. In an outbreeding population an individual organism will generally be heterozygous for some genes but homozygous for others.

For example, in humans, alleles for both blue- and brown-pigmented eyes exist, but the 'blue' allele is recessive to the dominant 'brown' allele.

Only individuals with blue eyes are predictably homozygous for this trait; brown-eyed people can be either homozygous or heterozygous.

histology

study of plant and animal tissue by visual examination, usually with a microscope.

Stains are often used to highlight structural characteristics such as the presence of starch or distribution of fats.

homeostasis

maintenance of a constant environment around living cells, particularly with regard to pH, salt concentration, temperature, and blood sugar levels. Stable conditions are important for the efficient functioning of the enzyme reactions within the cells. In humans, homeostasis in the blood (which provides fluid for all tissues) is ensured by several organs. The kidneys regulate pH, urea, and water concentration. The lungs regulate oxygen and carbon dioxide. Temperature is regulated by the liver and the skin (see temperature regulation). Glucose levels in the blood are regulated by the liver and the pancreas.

homologous

term describing an organ or structure possessed by members of different taxonomic groups (for example, species, genera, families, orders) that originally derived from the same structure in a common ancestor. The wing of a bat, the arm of a monkey, and the flipper of a seal are homologous because they all derive from the forelimb of an ancestral mammal.

homozygous

having two identical alleles for a given trait. Individuals homozygous for a trait always breed true; that is, they produce offspring that resemble them in appearance when bred with a genetically similar individual; inbred varieties or species are homozygous for almost all traits.

Recessive alleles are only expressed in the homozygous condition. See also heterozygous.

hormone

chemical secretion of the ductless endocrine glands and specialized nerve cells concerned with control of body functions. The major glands are the thyroid, parathyroid, pituitary, adrenal, pancreas, ovary, and testis. There are also hormone-secreting cells in the kidney, liver, gastrointestinal tract, thymus (in the neck), pineal (in the brain), and placenta. Hormones bring about changes in the functions of various organs according to the body's requirements. The hypothalamus, which adjoins the pituitary gland at the base of the brain, is a control centre for overall coordination of hormone secretion; the thyroid hormones determine the rate of general body chemistry; the adrenal hormones prepare the organism during stress for 'fight or flight'; and the sexual hormones such as oestrogen and testosterone govern reproductive functions.

The endocrine system, together with the nervous system, forms the neuro-endocrine system. Thus, chemical messages can be relayed to the appropriate part, or parts, of the body in response to stimulants either through nervous impulses via the nerves or through hormones secreted in the blood, or by both together. Hormones regulate homeostasis (a constant state within the body) and the body's responses to external and internal stimuli, and also control tissue development, morphogenesis (the development of an organism's form and structure), and reproduction. Many human diseases that are caused by hormone deficiency can be treated with hormone preparations.

In plants, hormones are organic chemicals, and are usually referred to as 'growth substances'. These are synthesized by plants, and the five major types are abscisic acid, auxin, cytokinin, ethylene (ethene), and gibberellin. These substances regulate growth and development, and are usually produced in a particular part of the plant, such as the shoot tip, and transported to other parts where they take effect.

host

organism that is parasitized by another. In commensalism, the partner that does not benefit may also be called the host.

Human Genome Project

research scheme to map the complete nucleotide (see nucleic acid) sequence of human DNA. It was begun in 1988 and a working draft of the genome (a mapping of 97% of the genome, sequencing of 85%, and completion of 24% of the human genome) was achieved in June 2000. The publicly-funded Human

Genome Organization (HUGO) is coordinating the $300 million project (the largest research project ever undertaken in the life sciences), which is taking place in over 20 centres around the world. Sequencing is also being carried out commercially by US biotechnology company Celera Genomics. The completed detailed mapping of the genome is scheduled for 2003.

There are probably between 50,000 and 150,000 different genes in the human genome, and one gene may contain more than 2 million nucleotides. The knowledge gained from mapping all these genes is expected to help prevent or treat many crippling and lethal diseases, but there are potential ethical problems associated with knowledge of an individual's genetic make-up, and fears that it will lead to genetic discrimination.

Sequencing

Each strand of DNA carries a sequence of chemical building blocks, the nucleotides. There are only four different types of nucleotide, but the number of possible combinations is immense. The different combinations of nucleotides produce different proteins in the cell, and thus determine the structure of the body and its individual variations. To establish the nucleotide sequence, DNA strands are broken into fragments, which are duplicated (by being introduced into cells of yeast or the bacterium *Escherichia coli*) and distributed to the research centres.

Genes account for only a small amount of the DNA sequence. Over 90% of DNA appears not to have any function, although it is perfectly replicated each time the cell divides, and handed on to the next generation. Many higher organisms have large amounts of redundant DNA and it may be that this is an advantage, in that a pool of DNA is available to form new genes if one is lost by mutation.

Whose genome?

The genome sequenced is not that of any one person. The HGP collected blood and sperm samples from a large number of donors and then processed the DNA of a small number (10–20) of these, ensuring that neither their scientists nor the donors would know whose DNA was finally used. As all humans share the same basic set of genes the information gained will be applicable to everyone.

human species, origins of

evolution of humans from ancestral primates. The African apes (gorilla and chimpanzee) are shown by anatomical and molecular comparisons to be the closest living relatives of humans. The oldest known *hominids* (of the human group), the australopithecines, found in Africa, date from 3.5–4.4 million years ago. The first to use tools came 2 million years later, and the first humanoids to use fire and move out of Africa appeared 1.7 million years ago. Neanderthals were not direct ancestors of the human species. Modern humans are all believed to descend from one African female of 200,000 years ago, although there is a rival theory that humans evolved in different parts of the world simultaneously.

Miocene apes

Genetic studies indicate that the last common ancestor between chimpanzees and humans lived 5 to 10 million years ago. There are only fragmentary remains of ape and hominid fossils from this period. Dispute continues over the hominid status of *Ramapithecus*, the jaws and teeth of which have been found in India and Kenya in late Miocene deposits, dated between 14 and 10 million years. The lower jaw of a fossil ape found in the Otavi Mountains, Namibia, comes from deposits dated between 10 and 15 million years ago, and is similar to finds from East Africa and Turkey. It is thought to be close to the initial divergence of the great apes and humans.

Australopithecines

Bones of the earliest known human ancestor were found in Ethiopia in 1998 and are dated as 5 million years old. *A. afarensis*, found in Ethiopia and Kenya, date from 3.9 to 4.4 million years ago. The most complete australopithecine skeleton to date was found in South Africa in April 2000, It is about 1.8 million years old and from a female *Australopithecus robustus*. These hominids walked upright and they were either direct ancestors or an offshoot of the line that led to modern humans. They may have been the ancestors of *Homo habilis* (considered by some to be a species of *Australopithecus*), who appeared about 2 million years later, had slightly larger bodies and brains, and were probably the first to use stone tools. Also living in Africa at the same time was *A. africanus*, a gracile hominid thought to be a meat-eater, and *A. robustus*, a hominid with robust bones, large teeth, heavy jaws, and thought to be a vegetarian. They are not generally considered to be our ancestors.

A new species of *Australopithecus* was discovered in Ethiopia in 1999. Named *A. garhi*, the fossils date from 2.5 million years ago and also share anatomical features with *Homo* species.

Homo erectus

Over 1.7 million years ago, *Homo erectus*, believed by some to be descended from *H. habilis*, appeared in Africa. *H. erectus* had prominent brow ridges, a flattened cranium, with the widest part of the skull low down, and jaws with a rounded tooth row, but the chin, characteristic of modern humans, is lacking. They also had much larger brains (900–1,200 cu cm), and were probably the first to use fire and the first to move out of Africa. Their remains are found as far afield as China, West Asia, Spain, and southern Britain. Modern human *H. sapiens sapiens* and the Neanderthals *H. sapiens neanderthalensis* are probably descended from *H. erectus*.

Australian palaeontologists announced the discovery of stone tools dated at about 800,000 to 900,000 years old and belonging to *H. erectus* on Flores, an island near Bali, in 1998. The discovery provides strong evidence that *H. erectus* were seafarers and had the language abilities and social structure to organize the movements of large groups to colonize new islands. In 2000 Japanese archaeologists discovered that *H. erectus* were probably building hut-like shelters around 500,000 years ago, the oldest known artificial structures.

Neanderthals

Neanderthals were large-brained and heavily built, probably adapted to the cold conditions of the ice ages. They lived in Europe and the Middle East, and disappeared about 40,000 years ago, leaving *H. sapiens sapiens* as the only remaining species of the hominid group. Possible intermediate forms between Neanderthals and *H. sapiens sapiens* have been found at Mount Carmel in Israel and at Broken Hill in Zambia, but it seems that *H. sapiens sapiens* appeared in Europe quite rapidly and either wiped out the Neanderthals or interbred with them.

Modern humans

There are currently two major views of human evolution: the *'out of Africa'* *model*, according to which *H. sapiens* emerged from *H. erectus*, or a descendant species, in Africa and then spread throughout the world; and the *multiregional model*, according to which selection pressures led to the emergence of similar advanced types of *H. sapiens* from *H. erectus* in different parts of the world at around the same time. Analysis of DNA in recent human populations suggests that *H. sapiens* originated about 200,000 years ago in Africa from a single female ancestor, 'Eve'. The oldest known fossils of *H.sapiens* also come from Africa, dating from 150,000–100,000 years ago. Separation of human populations would have occurred later, with separation of Asian, European, and Australian populations taking place between 100,000 and 50,000 years ago.

hybrid

offspring from a cross between individuals of two different species, or two inbred lines within a species. In most cases, hybrids between species are infertile and unable to reproduce sexually. In plants, however, doubling of the chromosomes (see polyploid) can restore the fertility of such hybrids.

Hybrids between different genera were believed to be extremely rare (an example is the *Cupressocyparis leylandii* cypress which, like some hybrids, shows exceptional vigour, or heterosis) but research in the late 1990s shows that hybridization is much more common than traditionally represented. One British evolutionary biologist estimated in 1999 that approximately 10% of animal species and 20% of plant species produced fertile offspring through interspecies mating. Blue whales, for example, hybridize with fin whales and different species of birds of paradise also hybridize. In the wild, a 'hybrid zone' may occur where the ranges of two related species meet.

hydroponics

cultivation of plants without soil, using specially prepared solutions of mineral salts. Beginning in the 1930s, large crops were grown by hydroponic methods, at first in California but since then in many other parts of the world.

ichthyology

study of fish, aquatic vertebrates that use gills to obtain oxygen from fresh or sea water. There are three main groups: the bony fishes or Osteichthyes

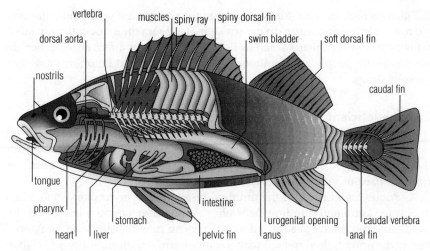

The anatomy of a fish. All fishes move through water using their fins for propulsion. The bony fishes, like the specimen shown here, constitute the largest group of fishes with about 20,000 species.

(goldfish, cod, tuna); the cartilaginous fishes or Chondrichthyes (sharks, rays); and the jawless fishes or Agnatha (hagfishes, lampreys).

Fishes of some form are found in virtually every body of water in the world except for the very salty water of the Dead Sea and some of the hot larval springs. Of the 30,000 fish species, approximately 2,500 are freshwater.

immunity

protection that organisms have against foreign micro-organisms, such as bacteria and viruses, and against cancerous cells. The cells that provide this protection are called white blood cells, or leucocytes, and make up the immune system. They include neutrophils and macrophages, which can engulf invading organisms and other unwanted material, and natural killer cells that destroy cells infected by viruses and cancerous cells. Some of the most important immune cells are the B cells and T cells. Immune cells coordinate their activities by means of chemical messengers or lymphokines, including the antiviral messenger interferon. The lymph nodes play a major role in organizing the immune response.

Immunity is also provided by a range of physical barriers such as the skin, tear fluid, acid in the stomach, and mucus in the airways. AIDS is one of many viral diseases in which the immune system is affected.

immunocompromised

lacking a fully effective immune system. The term is most often used in connection with infections such as AIDS where the virus interferes with the immune response (see immunity).

Other factors that can impair the immune response are pregnancy, diabetes, old age, malnutrition, and extreme stress, making someone susceptible to infections by micro-organisms (such as listeria) that do not affect normal, healthy people. Some people are immunodeficient; others could be on immunosuppressive drugs.

immunodeficient

lacking one or more elements of a working immune system. Immune deficiency is the term generally used for patients who are born with such a defect, while those who acquire such a deficiency later in life are referred to as *immunocompromised* or immunosuppressed.

A serious impairment of the immune system is sometimes known as SCID, or Severe Combined Immune Deficiency. At one time children born with this condition would have died in infancy. They can now be kept alive in a germ-free environment, then treated with a bone-marrow transplant from a relative, to replace the missing immune cells. At present, the success rate for this type of treatment is still fairly low. See also gene therapy.

imprinting

process whereby a young animal learns to recognize both specific individuals (for example, its mother) and its own species.

Imprinting is characteristically an automatic response to specific stimuli at a time when the animal is especially sensitive to those stimuli (the *sensitive period*). Thus, goslings learn to recognize their mother by following the first moving object they see after hatching; as a result, they can easily become imprinted on other species, or even inanimate objects, if these happen to move near them at this time. In chicks, imprinting occurs only between 10 and 20 hours after hatching. In mammals, the mother's attachment to her infant may be a form of imprinting made possible by a sensitive period; this period may be as short as the first hour after giving birth.

inbreeding

mating of closely related individuals. It is considered undesirable because it increases the risk that offspring will inherit copies of rare deleterious recessive alleles (genes) from both parents and so suffer from disabilities.

inclusive fitness

success with which a given variant (or allele) of a gene is passed on to future generations by a particular individual, after additional copies of the allele in the individual's relatives and their offspring have been taken into account.

The concept was formulated by W D Hamilton as a way of explaining the evolution of altruism in terms of natural selection. See also fitness and kin selection.

indicator species

plant or animal whose presence or absence in an area indicates certain environmental conditions, such as soil type, high levels of pollution, or, in rivers, low levels of dissolved oxygen. Many plants show a preference for either alkaline or acid soil conditions, while certain trees require aluminium, and are found only in soils where it is present. Some lichens are sensitive to sulphur dioxide in the air, and absence of these species indicates atmospheric pollution.

ingestion

process of taking food into the mouth. The method of food capture varies but may involve biting, sucking, or filtering. Many single-celled organisms have a region of their cell wall that acts as a mouth. In these cases surrounding tiny hairs (cilia) sweep food particles together, ready for ingestion.

inorganic compound

compound that does not contain carbon and is not manufactured by living organisms. Water, sodium chloride, and potassium are inorganic compounds because they are widely found outside living cells. However, carbon dioxide is considered inorganic, contains carbon, and is manufactured by organisms during respiration. See organic compound.

instinct

behaviour found in all equivalent members of a given species (for example, all the males, or all the females with young) that is presumed to be genetically determined.

Examples include a male robin's tendency to attack other male robins intruding on its territory and the tendency of many female mammals to care for their offspring. Instincts differ from reflexes in that they involve very much more complex actions, and learning often plays an important part in their development.

insulin

protein hormone, produced by specialized cells in the islets of Langerhans in the pancreas, that regulates the metabolism (rate of activity) of glucose, fats, and proteins. Insulin was discovered by Canadian physician Frederick Banting and Canadian physiologist Charles Best, who pioneered its use in treating diabetes.

Normally, insulin is secreted in response to rising blood sugar levels (after a meal, for example), stimulating the body's cells to store the excess. Failure of this regulatory mechanism in diabetes mellitus requires treatment with insulin injections or capsules taken by mouth. Types vary from pig and beef insulins to synthetic and bioengineered ones. They may be combined with other substances to make them longer- or shorter-acting. Implanted, battery-powered insulin pumps deliver the hormone at a preset rate, to eliminate the unnatural rises and falls that result from conventional, subcutaneous (under the skin) delivery. Human insulin has now been produced from bacteria by genetic engineering techniques, but may increase the chance of sudden, unpredictable hypoglycaemia, or low blood sugar.

interferon (IFN)

naturally occurring cellular protein that makes up part of mammalian defences against viral disease. Three types (alpha, beta, and gamma) are produced by infected cells and uninfected cells, making them immune to virus attack.

Interferon was discovered in 1957 by Scottish virologist Alick Isaacs. Interferons are cytokines, small molecules that carry signals from one cell to another. They can be divided into two main types: *type I* (alpha, beta, tau, and omega) interferons are more effective at bolstering cells' ability to resist infection; *type II* (gamma) interferon is more important to the normal functioning of the immune system. Alpha interferon may be used to treat some cancers; interferon beta 1b has been found useful in the treatment of multiple sclerosis.

interstitial

undifferentiated tissue that is interspersed with the characteristic tissue of an organ. It is often formed of fibrous tissue and supports the organ. Interstitial fluid refers to the fluid present in small amounts in the tissues of an organ.

intron or junk DNA

sequence of bases in DNA that carries no genetic information. Introns, discovered in 1977, make up approximately 98% of DNA (the rest is made up of exons). Introns may be present within genes but are removed during translation. Their function is unknown.

10% of the human genome is made up of one base sequence, *Alu*, that occurs in about 1 million separate locations. It is made up of 283 nucleotides, has no determinable function (though some do have an effect on nearby genes), and is a transposon ('jumping gene').

invertebrate

animal without a backbone. The invertebrates form all of the major divisions of the animal kingdom called phyla, with the exception of vertebrates. Invertebrates include the sponges, coelenterates, flatworms, nematodes, annelids, arthropods, molluscs, and echinoderms. Primitive aquatic chordates such as sea squirts and lancelets, which only have notochords and do not possess a vertebral column of cartilage or bone, are sometimes called invertebrate chordates, but this is misleading, since the notochord is the precursor of the backbone in advanced chordates.

in vitro process

biological experiment or technique carried out in a laboratory, outside the body of a living organism (literally 'in glass', for example in a test tube). By contrast, an in vivo process takes place within the body of an organism.

in vivo process

biological experiment or technique carried out within a living organism; by contrast, an in vitro process takes place outside the organism, in an artificial environment such as a laboratory.

involuntary action

behaviour not under conscious control, for example the contractions of the gut during peristalsis or the secretion of adrenaline by the adrenal glands. Breathing and urination reflexes are involuntary, although both can be controlled voluntarily to some extent. These processes are regulated by the autonomic nervous system.

iteroparity

repeated production of offspring at intervals throughout the life cycle. It is usually contrasted with semelparity, where each individual reproduces only once during its life.

junk DNA

another name for intron, a region of DNA that contains no genetic information.

karyotype

set of chromosomes characteristic of a given species. It is described as the number, shape, and size of the chromosomes in a single cell of an organism. In humans for example, the karyotype consists of 46 chromosomes, in mice 40, crayfish 200, and in fruit flies 8.

The diagrammatic representation of a complete chromosome set is called a *karyogram*.

kinesis

nondirectional movement in response to a stimulus; for example, woodlice move faster in drier surroundings. *Taxis* is a similar pattern of behaviour, but there the response is directional.

kingdom

primary division in biological classification. At one time, only two kingdoms were recognized: animals

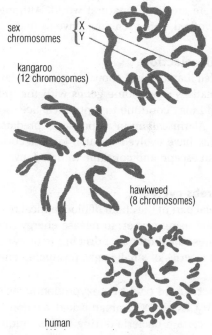

The characteristics, or karyotype, of the chromosomes vary according to species. The kangaroo has 12 chromosomes, the hawkweed has 8, and a human being has 46.

and plants. Today most biologists prefer a five-kingdom system, even though it still involves grouping together organisms that are probably unrelated. One widely accepted scheme is as follows: ***Kingdom Animalia*** (all multicellular animals); ***Kingdom Plantae*** (all plants, including seaweeds and other algae, except blue-green); ***Kingdom Fungi*** (all fungi, including the unicellular yeasts, but not slime moulds); ***Kingdom Protista*** or ***Protoctista*** (protozoa, diatoms, dinoflagellates, slime moulds, and various other lower organisms with eukaryotic cells); and ***Kingdom Monera*** (all prokaryotes – the bacteria and cyanobacteria, or blue-green algae). The first four of these kingdoms make up the eukaryotes.

When only two kingdoms were recognized, any organism with a rigid cell wall was a plant, and so bacteria and fungi were considered plants, despite their many differences. Other organisms, such as the photosynthetic flagellates (euglenoids), were claimed by both kingdoms. The unsatisfactory nature of the two-kingdom system became evident during the 19th century, and the biologist Ernst Haeckel was among the first to try to reform it. High-power microscopes have revealed more about the structure of cells; it has become clear that there is a fundamental difference between cells without a nucleus (prokaryotes) and those with a nucleus (eukaryotes). However, these differences are larger than those between animals and higher plants, and are unsuitable for use as kingdoms. At present there is no agreement on how many kingdoms there are in the natural world. Although the five-kingdom system is widely favoured, some schemes have as many as 20.

kin selection

idea that altruism shown to genetic relatives can be worthwhile, because those relatives share some genes with the individual that is behaving altruistically, and may continue to reproduce. See inclusive fitness.

Alarm-calling in response to predators is an example of a behaviour that may have evolved through kin selection: relatives that are warned of danger can escape and continue to breed, even if the alarm caller is caught.

Krebs cycle

final part of the chain of biochemical reactions by which organisms break down food using oxygen to release energy (respiration). It takes place within structures called mitochondria in the body's cells, and breaks down food molecules in a series of small steps, producing energy-rich molecules of ATP.

lactic acid or 2-hydroxypropanoic acid

$CH_3CHOHCOOH$ organic acid, a colourless, almost odourless liquid, produced by certain bacteria during fermentation and by active muscle cells when they are exercised hard and are experiencing oxygen debt. An accumulation of lactic acid in the muscles may cause cramp. It occurs in yogurt, buttermilk, sour cream, poor wine, and certain plant extracts, and is used in food preservation and in the preparation of pharmaceuticals.

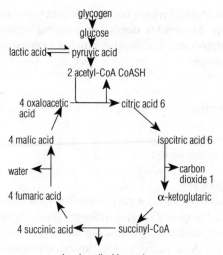

The purpose of the Krebs (or tricarboxylic acid) cycle is to complete the biochemical breakdown of food to produce energy-rich molecules, which the organism can use to fuel work. Acetyl coenzyme A (acetyl CoA) – produced by the breakdown of sugars, fatty acids, and some amino acids – reacts with oxaloacetic acid to produce citric acid, which is then converted in a series of enzyme-catalysed steps back to oxaloacetic acid. In the process, molecules of carbon dioxide and water are given off, and the precursors of the energy-rich molecules ATP are formed. (The numbers in the diagram indicate the number of carbon atoms in the principal compounds.)

lactose

white sugar, found in solution in milk; it forms 5% of cow's milk. It is commercially prepared from the whey obtained in cheese-making. Like table sugar (sucrose), it is a disaccharide, consisting of two basic sugar units (monosaccharides), in this case, glucose and galactose. Unlike sucrose, it is tasteless.

larva

stage between hatching and adulthood in those species in which the young have a different appearance and way of life from the adults. Examples include tadpoles (frogs) and caterpillars (butterflies and moths). Larvae are typical of the invertebrates, some of which (for example, shrimps) have two or more distinct larval stages. Among vertebrates, it is only the amphibians and some fishes that have a larval stage.

The process whereby the larva changes into another stage, such as a pupa (chrysalis) or adult, is known as metamorphosis.

lek

closely spaced set of very small territories each occupied by a single male during the mating season. Leks are found in the mating systems of several ground-dwelling birds (such as grouse) and a few antelopes, and in some insects.

The lek is a traditional site where both males and females congregate during the breeding season. The males display to passing females in the hope of attracting them to mate. Once mated, the females go elsewhere to lay their eggs or to complete gestation.

leucine
one of the nine essential amino acids.

leucocyte
another name for a white blood cell.

leukocyte also leucocyte
white blood cell. Leukocytes play a part in the body's defences and give immunity against disease. There are several different types. Some (phagocytes and macrophages) engulf invading micro-organisms, others kill infected cells, while lymphocytes produce more specific immune responses. Leukocytes are colorless, with clear or granulated cytoplasm, and are capable of independent amoeboid movement. They occur in the blood, lymph, and elsewhere in the body's tissues.

Unlike mammalian red blood cells, leukocytes possess a nucleus. Human blood contains about 11,000 leukocytes to the cubic millimetre – about 1 to every 500 red cells.

Leukocyte numbers may be reduced (leukopenia) by starvation, pernicious anemia, and certain infections, such as typhoid and malaria. An increase in the numbers (leukocytosis) is a reaction to normal events such as digestion, exertion, and pregnancy, and to abnormal ones such as loss of blood, cancer, and most infections.

leukotriene
group of naturally occurring substances that stimulate the activity, for example contraction, of smooth muscles.

life
ability to grow, reproduce, and respond to such stimuli as light, heat, and sound. Life on Earth may have began about 4 billion years ago when a chemical reaction produced the first organic substance. Over time, life has evolved from primitive single-celled organisms to complex multicellular ones. There are now some 10 million different species of plants and animals living on the Earth. The earliest fossil evidence of life is threadlike chains of cells discovered in 1980 in deposits in northwestern Australia; these 'stromatolites' have been dated as being 3.5 billion years old.

Biology is the study of living organisms – their evolution, structure, functioning, classification, and distribution – while biochemistry is the study of the chemistry of living organisms. Biochemistry is especially concerned with the function of the chemical components of organisms such as proteins, carbohydrates, lipids, and nucleic acids.

Life probably originated in the primitive oceans. The original atmosphere, 4 billion years ago, consisted of carbon dioxide, nitrogen, and water. Laboratory experiments have shown that more complex organic molecules, such as amino acids and nucleotides, can be produced from these ingredients by passing electric sparks through a mixture. The climate of the early atmosphere was probably very violent, with lightning a common feature, and these conditions could have resulted in the oceans becoming rich in organic molecules, producing the so-called 'primeval soup'. These molecules may then have organized themselves into clusters capable of reproducing and eventually developing into simple cells. Soon after life developed, photosynthesis would have become the primary source of energy for life. By this process, life would have substantially affected the chemistry of the atmosphere and, in turn, that of its own environment. Once the atmosphere had changed to its present composition, life could only be created by the replication of living organisms (a process called biogenesis).

life cycle

sequence of developmental stages through which members of a given species pass. Most vertebrates have a simple life cycle consisting of fertilization of sex cells or gametes, a period of development as an embryo, a period of juvenile growth after hatching or birth, an adulthood including sexual reproduction, and finally death. Invertebrate life cycles are generally more complex and may involve major reconstitution of the individual's appearance (metamorphosis) and completely different styles of life. Plants have a special type of life cycle with two distinct phases, known as alternation of generations. Many insects such as cicadas, dragonflies, and mayflies have a long larvae or pupae phase and a short adult phase. Dragonflies live an aquatic life as larvae and an aerial life during the adult phase. In many invertebrates and protozoa there is a sequence of stages in the life cycle, and in parasites different stages often occur in different host organisms.

linkage

association between two or more genes that tend to be inherited together because they are on the same chromosome.

The closer together they are on the chromosome, the less likely they are to be separated by crossing over (one of the processes of recombination) and they are then described as being 'tightly linked'.

lipase

enzyme responsible for breaking down fats into fatty acids and glycerol. It is produced by the pancreas and requires a slightly alkaline environment. The products of fat digestion are absorbed by the intestinal wall.

lipid

any of a large number of esters of fatty acids, commonly formed by the reaction of a fatty acid with glycerol. They are soluble in alcohol but not in water.

Lipids are the chief constituents of plant and animal waxes, fats, and oils. Phospholipids are lipids that also contain a phosphate group, usually linked to an organic base; they are major components of biological cell membranes.

liposome

minute droplet of oil that is separated from a medium containing water by a phospholipid layer. Drugs, such as cytotoxic agents, can be incorporated into liposomes and given by injection or by mouth. The liposomes allow the drug to reach the site of action, such as a tumour, without being broken down in the body.

liver

large organ of vertebrates, which has many regulatory and storage functions. The human liver is situated in the upper abdomen, and weighs about 2 kg/ 4.5 lb. It is divided into four lobes. The liver receives the products of digestion, converts glucose to glycogen (a long-chain carbohydrate used for storage), and then back to glucose when needed. In this way the liver regulates the level of glucose in the blood (see homeostasis). It removes excess amino acids from the blood, converting them to urea, which is excreted by the kidneys. The liver also synthesizes vitamins, produces bile and blood-clotting factors, and removes damaged red cells and toxins such as alcohol from the blood.

lymph

fluid found in the lymphatic system of vertebrates. Lymph is drained from the tissues by lymph capillaries, which empty into larger lymph vessels (lymphatics). These lead to lymph nodes (small, round bodies chiefly situated in the neck, armpit, groin, thorax, and abdomen), which process the lympho- cytes produced by the bone marrow, and filter out harmful substances and bacteria. From the lymph nodes, vessels carry the lymph to the thoracic duct and the right lymphatic duct, which drain into the large veins in the neck. Some vertebrates, such as amphibians, have a lymph heart, which pumps lymph through the lymph vessels.

Lymph carries some nutrients, and white blood cells to the tissues, and waste matter away from them. It exudes from capillaries into the tissue spaces between the cells and is similar in composition to blood plasma.

lymph nodes

small masses of lymphatic tissue in the body that occur at various points along the major lymphatic vessels. Tonsils and adenoids are large lymph nodes. As the lymph passes through them it is filtered, and bacteria and other micro- organisms are engulfed by cells known as macrophages.

lymphocyte

type of white blood cell with a large nucleus, produced in the bone marrow. Most occur in the lymph and blood, and around sites of infection. *B lymphocytes* or B cells are responsible for producing antibodies. *T lymphocytes* or T cells have several roles in the mechanism of immunity.

lymphokines
chemical messengers produced by lymphocytes that carry messages between the cells of the immune system (see immunity). Examples include interferon, which initiates defensive reactions to viruses, and the interleukins, which activate specific immune cells.

lysis
any process that destroys a cell by rupturing its membrane or cell wall (see lysosome).

lysosome
membrane-enclosed structure, or organelle, inside a cell, principally found in animal cells. Lysosomes contain enzymes that can break down proteins and other biological substances. They play a part in digestion, and in the white blood cells known as phagocytes the lysosome enzymes attack ingested bacteria.

macrophage
type of white blood cell, or leucocyte, found in all vertebrate animals. Macrophages specialize in the removal of bacteria and other micro-organisms, or of cell debris after injury. Like phagocytes, they engulf foreign matter, but they are larger than phagocytes and have a longer life span. They are found throughout the body, but mainly in the lymph and connective tissues, and especially the lungs, where they ingest dust, fibres, and other inhaled particles.

mammal
any of a large group of warm-blooded vertebrate animals characterized by having mammary glands in the female; these are used for suckling the young. Other features of mammals are hair (very reduced in some species, such as whales); a middle ear formed of three small bones (ossicles); a lower jaw consisting of two bones only; seven vertebrae in the neck; and no nucleus in the red blood cells. (Class Mammalia.)

Mammals are divided into three groups:
placental mammals, where the young develop inside the mother's body, in the uterus, receiving nourishment from the blood of the mother via the placenta;
marsupials, where the young are born at an early stage of development and develop further in a pouch on the mother's body where they are attached to and fed from a nipple; and
monotremes, where the young hatch from an egg outside the mother's body and are then nourished with milk.

The monotremes are the least evolved and have been largely displaced by more sophisticated marsupials and placentals, so that there are only a few types surviving (platypus and echidna). Placentals have spread to all parts of the globe, and where placentals have competed with marsupials, the placentals have in general displaced marsupial types. However, marsupials occupy many specialized niches in South America and, especially, Australasia.

According to the Red List of endangered species published by the World Conservation Union (IUCN) for 1996, 25% of mammal species are threatened with extinction.

marsupial

mammal in which the female has a pouch where she carries her young (born tiny and immature) for a considerable time after birth. Marsupials include omnivorous, herbivorous, and carnivorous species, among them the kangaroo, wombat, opossum, phalanger, bandicoot, dasyure, and wallaby.

The Australian marsupial anteater known as the numbat is an exception to the rule in that it has no pouch.

meiosis

process of cell division in which the number of chromosomes in the cell is halved. It only occurs in eukaryotic cells, and is part of a life cycle that involves sexual reproduction because it allows the genes of two parents to be combined without the total number of chromosomes increasing.

In sexually reproducing diploid animals (having two sets of chromosomes per cell), meiosis occurs during formation of the gametes (sex cells, sperm and egg), so that the gametes are haploid (having only one set of chromosomes). When the gametes unite during fertilization, the diploid condition is restored. In plants, meiosis occurs just before spore formation. Thus the spores are haploid and in lower plants such as mosses they develop into a haploid plant called a gametophyte which produces the gametes.

membrane

continuous layer, made up principally of fat molecules, that encloses a cell or organelles within a cell. Small molecules, such as water and sugars, can pass through the cell membrane by diffusion. Large molecules, such as proteins, are transported across the membrane via special channels, a process often involving energy input. The Golgi apparatus within the cell is thought to produce certain membranes.

In cell organelles, enzymes may be attached to the membrane at specific positions, often alongside other enzymes involved in the same process, like workers at a conveyor belt. Thus membranes help to make cellular processes more efficient.

Mendelism

theory of inheritance originally outlined by Austrian biologist Gregor Mendel. He suggested that, in sexually reproducing species, all characteristics are inherited through indivisible 'factors' (now identified with genes) contributed by each parent to its offspring.

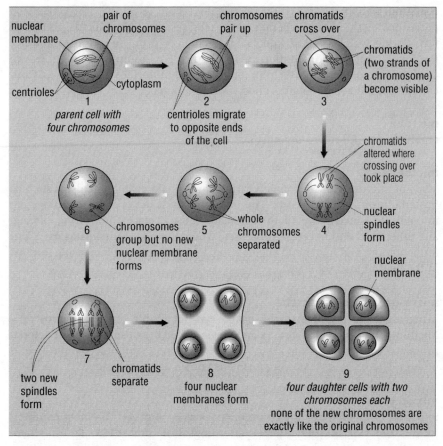

Meiosis is a type of cell division that produces gametes (sex cells, sperm and egg). This sequence shows an animal cell but only four chromosomes are shown in the parent cell (1). There are two stages in the division process. In the first stage (2–6), the chromosomes come together in pairs and exchange genetic material. This is called crossing over. In the second stage (7–9), the cell divides to produce four gamete cells, each with only one copy of each chromosome from the parent cell.

metabolism

chemical processes of living organisms enabling them to grow and to function. It involves a constant alternation of building up complex molecules (***anabolism***) and breaking them down (***catabolism***). For example, green plants build up complex organic substances from water, carbon dioxide, and mineral salts (photosynthesis); by digestion animals partially break down complex organic substances, ingested as food, and subsequently resynthesize them for use in their own bodies. Within cells, complex molecules are broken down by the process of respiration. The waste products of metabolism are removed by excretion.

metamorphosis

period during the life cycle of many invertebrates, most amphibians, and some fish, during which the individual's body changes from one form to another through a major reconstitution of its tissues. For example, adult frogs are produced by metamorphosis from tadpoles, and butterflies are produced from caterpillars following metamorphosis within a pupa.

microbe

another name for micro-organism.

microbiology

study of micro-organisms, mostly viruses and single-celled organisms such as bacteria, protozoa, and yeasts. The practical applications of microbiology are in medicine (since many micro-organisms cause disease); in brewing, baking, and other food and beverage processes, where the micro-organisms carry out fermentation; and in genetic engineering, which is creating increasing interest in the field of microbiology.

micro-organism or microbe

living organism invisible to the naked eye but visible under a microscope. Micro-organisms include viruses and single-celled organisms such as bacteria, protozoa, yeasts, and some algae. The term has no taxonomic significance in biology. The study of micro-organisms is known as microbiology.

mimicry

imitation of one species (or group of species) by another. The most common form is *Batesian mimicry* (named after English naturalist H W Bates), where the mimic resembles a model that is poisonous or unpleasant to eat, and has aposematic, or warning, coloration; the mimic thus benefits from the fact that predators have learned to avoid the model. Hoverflies that resemble bees or wasps are an example. Appearance is usually the basis for mimicry, but calls, songs, scents, and other signals can also be mimicked.

In *Mullerian mimicry*, two or more equally poisonous or distasteful species have a similar colour pattern, thereby reinforcing the warning each gives to predators. In some cases, mimicry is not for protection, but allows the mimic to prey on, or parasitize, the model.

mitochondria singular mitochondrion

membrane-enclosed organelles within eukaryotic cells, containing enzymes responsible for energy production during aerobic respiration. Mitochondria absorb O_2 and glucose and produce energy in the form of ATP by breaking down the glucose to CO_2 and H_2O. These rod-like or spherical bodies are thought to be derived from free-living bacteria that, at a very early stage in the history of life, invaded larger cells and took up a symbiotic way of life inside. Each still contains its own small loop of DNA called mitochondrial DNA, and new mitochondria arise by division of existing ones. Mitochondria each have 37 genes.

Mutations in mitochondrial genes are always inherited from the mother. These mutations have been linked to a number of disorders, mainly degenerative, including Alzheimer's disease and diabetes.

mitosis

process of cell division by which identical daughter cells are produced. During mitosis the DNA is duplicated and the chromosome number doubled, so new cells contain the same amount of DNA as the original cell.

The genetic material of eukaryotic cells is carried on a number of chromosomes. To control movements of chromosomes during cell division so that both new cells get the correct number, a system of protein tubules, known as the spindle, organizes the chromosomes into position in the middle of the cell

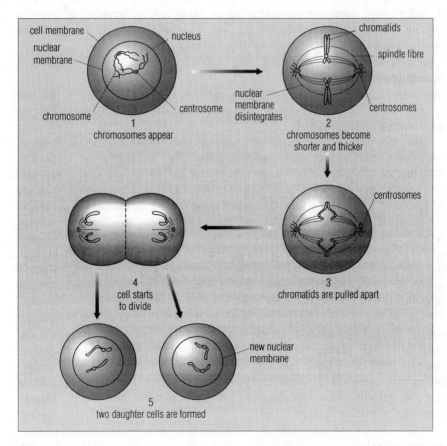

The stages of mitosis, the process of cell division that takes place when a plant or animal cell divides for growth or repair. The two daughter cells each receive the same number of chromosomes as were in the original cell.

before they replicate. The spindle then controls the movement of chromosomes as the cell goes through the stages of division: *interphase*, *prophase*, *metaphase*, *anaphase*, and *telophase*. See also meiosis.

molecular biology

study of the molecular basis of life, including the biochemistry of molecules such as DNA, RNA, and proteins, and the molecular structure and function of the various parts of living cells.

molecular clock

use of rates of mutation in genetic material to calculate the length of time elapsed since two related species diverged from each other during evolution. The method can be based on comparisons of the DNA or of widely occurring proteins, such as haemoglobin.

Since mutations are thought to occur at a constant rate, the length of time that must have elapsed in order to produce the difference between two species can be estimated. This information can be compared with the evidence obtained from palaeontology to reconstruct evolutionary events.

monohybrid inheritance

pattern of inheritance seen in simple genetics experiments, where the two animals (or two plants) being crossed are genetically identical except for one gene, which is heterozygous.

This gene may code for some obvious external features such as seed colour, with one parent having green seeds and the other having yellow seeds. The offspring are monohybrids, that is, hybrids for one gene only, having received one copy of the gene from each parent. Known as the F1 generation, they are all identical, and usually resemble one parent, whose version of the gene (the dominant allele) masks the effect of the other version (the recessive allele). Although the characteristic coded for by the recessive allele (for example, green seeds) completely disappears in this generation, it can reappear in offspring of the next generation if they have two recessive alleles. On average, this will occur in one out of four offspring from a cross between two of the monohybrids. The next generation (called F2) show a 3:1 ratio for the characteristic in question, 75% being like the original parent with the recessive allele. Austrian biologist Gregor Mendel first carried out experiments of this type (crossing varieties of artificially bred plants, such as peas) and they revealed the principles of genetics. The same basic mechanism underlies all inheritance, but in most plants and animals there are so many genetic differences interacting to produce the external appearance (phenotype) that such simple, clear-cut patterns of inheritance are not evident.

monophyletic

in biological classification, term describing a group of species composed of an ancestral species plus all of its descendant species. Examples of such groups are the mammals, birds, and insects. Monophyletic groups, or *clades*, are the basis of the system of classification known as cladistics.

If a group does not include all the descendants of a common ancestor, it is called paraphyletic; if it includes some or all of the descendants but not the common ancestor, it is called polyphyletic.

monosaccharide or simple sugar

carbohydrate that cannot be hydrolysed (split) into smaller carbohydrate units. Examples are glucose and fructose, both of which have the molecular formula $C_6H_{12}O_6$.

morphology

study of the physical structure and form of organisms, in particular their soft tissues.

motility

ability to move spontaneously. The term is often restricted to those cells that are capable of independent locomotion, such as spermatozoa. Many single-celled organisms are motile, for example, the amoeba. Research has shown that cells capable of movement, including vertebrate muscle cells, have certain biochemical features in common. Filaments of the proteins actin and myosin are associated with motility, as are the metabolic processes needed for breaking down the energy-rich compound ATP (adenosine triphosphate).

muscle

contractile animal tissue that produces locomotion and power, and maintains the movement of body substances. Muscle is made of long cells that can contract to between one-half and one-third of their relaxed length.

Striped (or striated) muscles are activated by motor nerves under voluntary control; their ends are usually attached via tendons to bones.

Involuntary or *smooth* muscles are controlled by motor nerves of the autonomic nervous system, and are located in the gut, blood vessels, iris, and various ducts.

Cardiac muscle occurs only in the heart, and is also controlled by the autonomic nervous system.

mutagen

any substance that increases the rate of gene mutation. A mutagen may also act as a carcinogen.

mutation

change in the genes produced by a change in the DNA that makes up the hereditary material of all living organisms. Mutations, the raw material of evolution, result from mistakes during replication (copying) of DNA molecules. Due to the redundancy built into genetic code many mutations have no effect upon DNA functions. Only a few improve the organism's performance and are therefore favoured by natural selection. Mutation rates are increased by certain chemicals and by radiation.

Common mutations include the omission or insertion of a base (one of the chemical subunits of DNA); these are known as *point mutations*. Larger-scale mutations include removal of a whole segment of DNA or its inversion within the DNA strand. Not all mutations affect the organism, because there is a certain amount of redundancy in the genetic information. If a mutation is 'translated' from DNA into the protein that makes up the organism's structure, it may be in a nonfunctional part of the protein and thus have no detectable effect. This is known as a *neutral mutation*, and is of importance in molecular clock studies because such mutations tend to accumulate gradually as time passes. Some mutations do affect genes that control protein production or functional parts of protein, and most of these are lethal to the organism.

mutualism
association between two organisms of different species whereby both profit from the relationship; see symbiosis.

natural selection
process whereby gene frequencies in a population change through certain individuals producing more descendants than others because they are better able to survive and reproduce in their environment.

The accumulated effect of natural selection is to produce adaptations such as the insulating coat of a polar bear or the spadelike forelimbs of a mole. The process is slow, relying firstly on random variation in the genes of an organism being produced by mutation and secondly on the genetic recombination of sexual reproduction. It was recognized by Charles Darwin and English naturalist Alfred Russel Wallace as the main process driving evolution.

nature–nurture controversy or environment–heredity controversy
long-standing dispute among philosophers and psychologists over the relative importance of environment, that is, upbringing, experience, and learning ('nurture'), and heredity, that is, genetic inheritance ('nature'), in determining the make-up of an organism, as related to human personality and intelligence. One area of contention is the reason for differences between individuals; for example, in performing intelligence tests. The environmentalist position assumes that individuals do not differ significantly in their inherited mental abilities and that subsequent differences are due to learning, or to differences in early experiences. Opponents insist that certain differences in the capacities of individuals (and hence their behaviour) can be attributed to inherited differences in their genetic make-up.

navigation, biological
ability of animals or insects to navigate. Although many animals navigate by following established routes or known landmarks, many animals can navigate

without such aids; for example, birds can fly several thousand miles back to their nest site, over unknown terrain.

Such feats may be based on compass information derived from the position of the Sun, Moon, or stars, or on the characteristic patterns of Earth's magnetic field.

Biological navigation refers to the ability to navigate both in long-distance migrations and over shorter distances when foraging (for example, the honey bee finding its way from the hive to a nectar site and back). Where reliant on known landmarks, birds may home on features that can be seen from very great distances (such as the cloud caps that often form above isolated mid-ocean islands). Even smells can act as a landmark. Aquatic species like salmon are believed to learn the characteristic taste of the river where they hatch and return to it, often many years later. Brain cells in some birds have been found to contain magnetite and may therefore be sensitive to the Earth's magnetic field.

nematode

any of a group of unsegmented worms that are pointed at both ends, with a tough, smooth outer skin. They include many free-living species found in soil and water, including the sea, but a large number are parasites, such as the roundworms and pinworms that live in humans, or the eelworms that attack plant roots. They differ from flatworms in that they have two openings to the gut (a mouth and an anus). (Phylum Nematoda.) The group includes *Caenorhabditis elegans* which is a model genetic organism and the first multi-cellular animal to have its complete genome sequenced.

neo-Darwinism

modern theory of evolution, built up since the 1930s by integrating the 19th-century English scientist Charles Darwin's theory of evolution through natural selection with the theory of genetic inheritance founded on the work of the Austrian biologist Gregor Mendel.

Neo-Darwinism asserts that evolution takes place because the environment is slowly changing, exerting a selection pressure on the individuals within a population. Those with characteristics that happen to adapt to the new environment are more likely to survive and have offspring and hence pass on these favourable characteristics. Over time the genetic make-up of the population changes and ultimately a new species is formed.

neoteny

retention of some juvenile characteristics in an animal that seems otherwise mature. An example is provided by the axolotl, a salamander that can reproduce sexually although still in its larval form.

It has been suggested that new species could arise in this way, and that our own species evolved from its apelike ancestors by neoteny, on the grounds that facially we resemble a young ape.

nerve

bundle of nerve cells enclosed in a sheath of connective tissue and transmitting nerve impulses to and from the brain and spinal cord. A single nerve may contain both motor and sensory nerve cells, but they function independently.

nerve cell or neuron

elongated cell, the basic functional unit of the nervous system that transmits information rapidly between different parts of the body. Each nerve cell has a cell body, containing the nucleus, from which trail processes called dendrites, responsible for receiving incoming signals. The unit of information is the *nerve impulse*, a travelling wave of chemical and electrical changes involving the membrane of the nerve cell. The cell's longest process, the axon, carries impulses away from the cell body.

The impulse involves the passage of sodium and potassium ions across the nerve-cell membrane. Sequential changes in the permeability of the membrane to positive sodium (Na^+) ions and potassium (K^+) ions produce electrical signals called action potentials. Impulses are received by the cell body and passed, as a pulse of electric charge, along the axon. The axon terminates at the synapse, a specialized area closely linked to the next cell (which may be another nerve cell or a specialized effector cell such as a muscle). On reaching the synapse, the impulse releases a chemical neurotransmitter, which diffuses across to the neighbouring cell and there stimulates another impulse or the action of the effector cell.

Nerve impulses travel quickly – in humans, they may reach speeds of 160 m/525 ft per second.

nervous system

system of interconnected nerve cells of most invertebrates and all vertebrates. It is composed of the central and autonomic nervous systems. It may be as simple as the nerve net of coelenterates (for example, jellyfishes) or as complex as the mammalian nervous system, with a central nervous system comprising brain and spinal cord and a peripheral nervous system connecting up with sensory organs, muscles, and glands.

Human nervous system

The human nervous system represents the product of millions of years of evolution, particularly in the degree of *encephalization* or brain complexity. It can be divided into central and peripheral parts for descriptive purposes, although there is both anatomical and functional continuity between the two parts. The central nervous system consists of the brain and the spinal cord. The peripheral nervous system is not so clearly subdivided, but its anatomical parts are: (1) the spinal nerves; (2) the cranial nerves; and (3) the autonomic nervous system.

neuron

another name for a nerve cell.

neurotransmitter

chemical that diffuses across a synapse, and thus transmits impulses between nerve cells, or between nerve cells and effector organs (for example, muscles). Common neurotransmitters are noradrenaline (which also acts as a hormone) and acetylcholine, the latter being most frequent at junctions between nerve and muscle. Nearly 50 different neurotransmitters have been identified.

niche

in ecology, the 'place' occupied by a species in its habitat, including all chemical, physical, and biological components, such as what it eats, the time of day at which the species feeds, temperature, moisture, the parts of the habitat that it uses (for example, trees or open grassland), the way it reproduces, and how it behaves.

It is believed that no two species can occupy exactly the same niche, because they would be in direct competition for the same resources at every stage of their life cycle.

nicotinamide adenine dinucleotide (NAD)

naturally occurring compound which acts as a coenzyme. It consists of two nucleotides, adenosine mononucleotide and nicotinamide mononucleotide, joined by a phosphate bridge. A similar compound, NAD phosphate, *NADP*, is produced by phosphorylating the ribose part of the adenosine mononucleotide. NAD takes part in oxidation–reduction reactions, being converted to $NADH_2$ by accepting two hydrogen atoms. In this form it is able to enter the electron transport chain where it is oxidized back to NAD, producing large quantities of ATP in the process. NADP is an important oxidation–reduction factor in fatty acid biosynthesis.

nitric oxide or nitrogen monoxide (NO)

colourless gas released when metallic copper reacts with nitric acid and when nitrogen and oxygen combine at high temperatures. It is oxidized to nitrogen dioxide on contact with air. Nitric oxide has a wide range of functions in the body. It is involved in the transmission of nerve impulses and the protection of nerve cells against stress. It is released by macrophages in the immune system in response to viral and bacterial infection or to the proliferation of cancer cells. It is also important in the control of blood pressure.

nitrification

process that takes place in soil when bacteria oxidize ammonia, turning it into nitrates. Nitrates can be absorbed by the roots of plants, so this is a vital stage in the nitrogen cycle.

nitrogen cycle

process of nitrogen passing through the ecosystem. Nitrogen, in the form of inorganic compounds (such as nitrates) in the soil, is absorbed by plants and

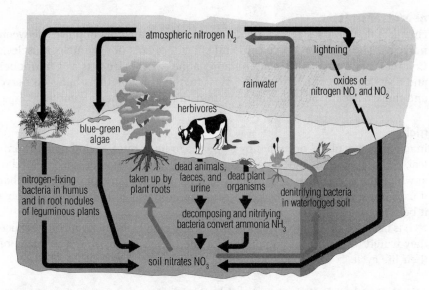

The nitrogen cycle is one of a number of cycles during which the chemicals necessary for life are recycled. The carbon, sulphur, and phosphorus cycles are others. Since there is only a limited amount of these chemicals in the Earth and its atmosphere, the chemicals must be continuously recycled if life is to go on.

turned into organic compounds (such as proteins) in plant tissue. A proportion of this nitrogen is eaten by herbivores, with some of this in turn being passed on to the carnivores, which feed on the herbivores. The nitrogen is ultimately returned to the soil as excrement and when organisms die and are converted back to inorganic form by decomposers.

Although about 78% of the atmosphere is nitrogen, this cannot be used directly by most organisms. However, certain bacteria and cyanobacteria are capable of nitrogen fixation. Some nitrogen-fixing bacteria live mutually with leguminous plants (peas and beans) or other plants (for example, alder), where they form characteristic nodules on the roots. The presence of such plants increases the nitrate content, and hence the fertility, of the soil.

nitrogen fixation

process by which nitrogen in the atmosphere is converted into nitrogenous compounds by the action of micro-organisms, such as cyanobacteria (see blue-green algae) and bacteria, in conjunction with certain legumes. Several chemical processes duplicate nitrogen fixation to produce fertilizers.

nucleic acid

complex organic acid made up of a long chain of nucleotides, present in the nucleus and sometimes the cytoplasm of the living cell. The two types, known as DNA (deoxyribonucleic acid) and RNA (ribonucleic acid), form the basis of heredity. The nucleotides are made up of a sugar (deoxyribose or ribose), a phosphate group, and one of four purine or pyrimidine bases. The order of the bases along the nucleic acid strand contains the genetic code.

nucleolus

RNA-rich structure found in the nucleus of eukaryotic cells. It produces the RNA that makes up the ribosomes, from instructions in the DNA.

nucleotide

organic compound consisting of a purine (adenine or guanine) or a pyrimidine (thymine, uracil, or cytosine) base linked to a sugar (deoxyribose or ribose) and a phosphate group. DNA and RNA are made up of long chains of nucleotides.

nucleus

central, membrane-enclosed part of a eukaryotic cell, containing threads of DNA. During cell division these coil up to form chromosomes. The nucleus controls the function of the cell by determining which proteins are produced within it (see DNA for details of this process). Because proteins are the chief structural molecules of living matter and, as enzymes, regulate all aspects of metabolism, it may be seen that the genetic code within the nucleus is effectively responsible for building and controlling the whole organism.

The nucleus contains the *nucleolus*, the part of the cell where ribosomes are produced. Movement of molecules into and out of the nucleus occurs through the nuclear pores. An average mammalian nucleus has approximately 3,000 pores.

oestrogen

any of a group of hormones produced by the ovaries of vertebrates; the term is also used for various synthetic hormones that mimic their effects. The principal oestrogen in mammals is oestradiol. Oestrogens control female sexual development, promote the growth of female secondary sexual characteristics, stimulate egg production, and, in mammals, prepare the lining of the uterus for pregnancy.

Oestrogens are used therapeutically for some hormone disorders and to inhibit lactation; they also form the basis of oral contraceptives. US researchers in 1995 observed that oestrogen plays a role in the healing of damaged blood vessels. It has also been found that women recover more quickly from strokes if given a low oestrogen dose.

omnivore

animal that feeds on both plant and animal material. Omnivores have digestive adaptations intermediate between those of herbivores and carnivores, with relatively unspecialized digestive systems and gut micro-organisms that can digest a variety of foodstuffs. Omnivores include humans, the chimpanzee, the cockroach, and the ant.

oncogene

gene carried by a virus that induces a cell to divide abnormally, giving rise to a cancer. Oncogenes arise from mutations in genes (proto-oncogenes) found in all normal cells. They are usually also found in viruses that are capable of transforming normal cells to tumour cells. Such viruses are able to insert their oncogenes into the host cell's DNA, causing it to divide uncontrollably. More than one oncogene may be necessary to transform a cell in this way.

In 1989 US scientists J Michael Bishop and Harold Varmus were jointly awarded the Nobel Prize for Physiology or Medicine for their concept of oncogenes, although credit for the discovery was claimed by a French cancer specialist, Dominique Stehelin.

ontogeny

process of development of a living organism, including the part of development that takes place after hatching or birth. The idea that 'ontogeny recapitulates phylogeny' (the development of an organism goes through the same stages as its evolutionary history), proposed by the German scientist Ernst Heinrich Haeckel, is now discredited.

oocyte

immature ovum. Only a fraction of the oocytes produced in the ovary survive until puberty and not all of these undergo meiosis to become an ovum that can be fertilized by a sperm.

operon

group of genes that are found next to each other on a chromosome, and are turned on and off as an integrated unit. They usually produce enzymes that control different steps in the same biochemical pathway by a single operator gene. Operons were discovered in 1961 (by the French biochemists François Jacob and Jacques Monod) in bacteria.

They are less common in higher organisms where the control of metabolism is a more complex process.

order

in biological classification, a group of related families. For example, the horse, rhinoceros, and tapir families are grouped in the order Perissodactyla, the odd-toed ungulates, because they all have either one or three toes on each foot. The names of orders are not shown in italic (unlike genus and species names) and by convention they have the ending '-formes' in birds and fish; '-a' in mammals, amphibians, reptiles, and other animals; and '-ales' in fungi and plants. Related orders are grouped together in a class.

organ

part of a living body that has a distinctive function or set of functions. Examples include the liver or brain in animals, or the leaf in plants. An organ is composed of a group of coordinated tissues. A group of organs working together to perform a function is called an *organ system,* for example, the digestive system comprises a number of organs including the stomach, the small intestine, the colon, the pancreas, and the liver.

organelle

discrete and specialized structure in a living cell; organelles include mitochondria, chloroplasts, lysosomes, ribosomes, and the nucleus.

organic compound

class of compounds that contain carbon. The original distinction between organic and inorganic compounds was based on the belief that the molecules of living systems were unique, and could not be synthesized in the laboratory. Today it is routine to manufacture thousands of organic chemicals both in research and in the drug industry. Certain simple compounds of carbon, such as carbonates, oxides of carbon, carbon disulphide, and carbides are usually treated in inorganic chemistry.

organizer

in embryology, a part of the embryo that causes changes to occur in another part, through induction, thus 'organizing' development and differentiation.

ornithophily

pollination of flowers by birds. Ornithophilous flowers are typically brightly coloured, often red or orange. They produce large quantities of thin, watery nectar, and are scentless because most birds do not respond well to smell. They are found mostly in tropical areas, with hummingbirds being important pollinators in North and South America, and the sunbirds in Africa and Asia.

osmosis

movement of water through a selectively permeable membrane separating solutions of different concentrations. Water passes by diffusion from a *weak solution* (high water concentration) to a *strong solution* (low water concentration) until the two concentrations are equal. The selectively permeable membrane allows the diffusion of water but not of the solute (for example, sugar molecules). Many cell membranes behave in this way, and osmosis is a vital mechanism in the transport of fluids in living organisms – for example, in the transport of water from soil (weak solution) into the roots of plants (stronger solution of cell sap).

osmoregulation

Excessive flow of water into a cell by osmosis can burst the cell. Cells protect against this using processes of osmoregulation. If external pressure is applied to the stronger solution, osmosis is arrested. By this mechanism plant cells can osmoregulate, since the cell wall of a fully turgid cell exerts pressure on the solution within the cell. Animal cells such as the red blood cell cannot osmoregulate in this way since they have no cell wall. Instead, the correct concentration of plasma is maintained by the kidneys.

ovary

in female animals, the organ that generates the ovum. In humans, the ovaries are two whitish rounded bodies about 25 mm/1 in by 35 mm/1.5 in, located in the lower abdomen to either side of the uterus. Every month, from puberty to the onset of the menopause, an ovum is released from the ovary. This is called ovulation, and forms part of the menstrual cycle. In botany, an ovary is the expanded basal portion of the carpel of flowering plants, containing one or more ovules. It is hollow with a thick wall to protect the ovules. Following fertilization of the ovum, it develops into the fruit wall or pericarp.

The ovaries of female animals secrete the hormones responsible for the secondary sexual characteristics of the female, such as smooth, hairless facial skin and enlarged breasts. An ovary in a half-grown human fetus contains 5 million eggs, and so the unborn baby already possesses the female genetic information for the next generation.

In botany, the relative position of the ovary to the other floral parts is often a distinguishing character in classification; it may be either inferior or superior, depending on whether the petals and sepals are inserted above or below.

ovoviviparous

method of animal reproduction in which fertilized eggs develop within the female (unlike oviparous), and the embryo gains no nutritional substances from the female (unlike viviparous). It occurs in some invertebrates, fishes, and reptiles.

ovulation

in female animals, the process of releasing egg cells (ova) from the ovary. In mammals it occurs as part of the menstrual cycle.

ovum plural ova

female gamete (sex cell) before fertilization. In animals it is called an egg, and is produced in the ovaries. In plants, where it is also known as an egg cell or oosphere, the ovum is produced in an ovule. The ovum is nonmotile. It must be fertilized by a male gamete before it can develop further, except in cases of parthenogenesis.

oxygen

colourless, odourless, tasteless, nonmetallic, gaseous element, symbol O, atomic number 8, relative atomic mass 15.9994. It is the most abundant element in the Earth's crust (almost 50% by mass), forms about 21% by volume of the atmosphere, and is present in combined form in water and many other substances. Oxygen is a by-product of photosynthesis and the basis for respiration in plants and animals.

pancreas

in vertebrates, an accessory gland of the digestive system located close to the duodenum. When stimulated by the hormone secretin, it releases enzymes into the duodenum that digest starches, proteins, and fats. In humans, it is about 18 cm/7 in long, and lies behind and below the stomach. It contains groups of cells called the *islets of Langerhans*, which secrete the hormones insulin and glucagon that regulate the blood sugar level.

paraphyletic

in biological classification, term describing a group of species that includes the most recent common ancestor of all its members but not all of its descendants. For example, the class Reptilia is a paraphyletic group because it includes the reptiles' sauropsid ancestor but not birds, which are also its descendants. Other examples are invertebrates and fish.

If a group consists of all the descendants of a common ancestor plus the ancestor itself, it is called monophyletic; if it includes some or all of the descendants but not their common ancestor, it is called polyphyletic. Distinguishing between such groups is an integral part of the system of classification known as cladistics, which seeks to classify organisms into a hierarchy of monophyletic groups, or *clades*.

parasite

organism that lives on or in another organism (called the host) and depends on it for nutrition, often at the expense of the host's welfare. Parasites that live inside the host, such as liver flukes and tapeworms, are called *endoparasites*; those that live on the exterior, such as fleas and lice, are called *ectoparasites*. Parasitic wasps, such as ichneumons, are more correctly *parisitoids*, as they ultimately kill their hosts.

parental care

time and energy spent by a parent in order to rear its offspring to maturity. Among animals, it ranges from the simple provision of a food supply for the hatching young at the time the eggs are laid (for example, many wasps) to feeding and protection of the young after hatching or birth, as in birds and mammals. In the more social species, parental care may include the teaching of skills – for example, female cats teach their kittens to hunt.

parental generation

in genetic crosses, the set of individuals at the start of a test, providing the first set of gametes from which subsequent generations (known as the F1 and F2) will arise.

parthenogenesis

development of an ovum (egg) without any genetic contribution from a male. Parthenogenesis is the normal means of reproduction in a few plants (for example, dandelions) and animals (for example, certain fish). Some sexually

During spring and summer female aphids such as this Macrosiphum cholodkovskyi *produce a continuous succession of offspring by parthenogenesis, but mate and lay eggs before the onset of winter.* Premaphotos Wildlife

reproducing species, such as aphids, show parthenogenesis at some stage in their life cycle to accelerate reproduction to take advantage of good conditions. In most cases, there is no fertilization at all, but in a few the stimulus of being fertilized by a sperm is needed to initiate development, although the male's chromosomes are not absorbed into the nucleus of the ovum. Parthenogenesis can be artificially induced in many animals (such as rabbits) by cooling, pricking, or applying acid to an egg.

Pasteur effect
modification in the process of energy production in certain organisms. A bacterium or facultative cell which normally produces its ATP anaerobically, that is, without the use of oxygen, does so by means of glycolysis. In this process the yield of ATP per molecule of glucose is low, so the cell uses up a great deal of its glucose for its energy requirements. An aerobic organism, which uses oxygen, can employ the Krebs cycle to produce its energy, and the yield of ATP per molecule of glucose is much greater. The Pasteur effect occurs when a facultative anaerobic cell is provided with oxygen, so that its high rate of glucose metabolism is slowed down. It then produces energy from glucose far more efficiently because Krebs cycle is used, and in addition the production of lactic acid, a normal product of anaerobic glycolysis, is automatically stopped.

pathogen

any micro-organism that causes disease. Most pathogens are parasites, and the diseases they cause are incidental to their search for food or shelter inside the host. Nonparasitic organisms, such as soil bacteria or those living in the human gut and feeding on waste foodstuffs, can also become pathogenic to a person whose immune system or liver is damaged. The larger parasites that can cause disease, such as nematode worms, are not usually described as pathogens.

pentadactyl limb

typical limb of the mammals, birds, reptiles, and amphibians. These vertebrates (animals with backbone) are all descended from primitive amphibians whose immediate ancestors were fleshy-finned fish. The limb which evolved in those amphibians had three parts: a 'hand/foot' with five digits (fingers/toes), a lower limb containing two bones, and an upper limb containing one bone.

This basic pattern has persisted in all the terrestrial vertebrates, and those aquatic vertebrates (such as seals) which are descended from them. Natural selection has modified the pattern to fit different ways of life. In flying animals (birds and bats) it is greatly altered and in some vertebrates, such as whales and snakes, the limbs are greatly reduced or lost. Pentadactyl limbs of different species are an example of homologous organs.

peptide

molecule comprising two or more amino acid molecules (not necessarily different) joined by *peptide bonds*, whereby the acid group of one acid is linked to the amino group of the other (–CO.NH). The number of amino acid molecules in the peptide is indicated by referring to it as a di-, tri-, or polypeptide (two, three, or many amino acids).

Proteins are built up of interacting polypeptide chains with various types of bonds occurring between the chains. Incomplete hydrolysis (splitting up) of a protein yields a mixture of peptides, examination of which helps to determine the sequence in which the amino acids occur within the protein.

pest

any insect, fungus, rodent, or other living organism that has a harmful effect on human beings, other than those that directly cause human diseases. Most pests damage crops or livestock, but the term also covers those that damage buildings, destroy food stores, and spread disease.

phage

another name for a bacteriophage, a virus that attacks bacteria.

phagocyte

type of leukocyte, or white blood cell, that can engulf a bacterium or other invading micro-organism. Phagocytes are found in blood, lymph, and other body tissues, where they also ingest foreign matter and dead tissue. A macrophage differs in size and life span.

phenotype

visible traits, those actually displayed by an organism. The phenotype is not a direct reflection of the genotype because some alleles are masked by the presence of other, dominant alleles (see dominance). The phenotype is further modified by the effects of the environment (for example, poor nutrition stunts growth).

pheromone

chemical signal (such as an odour) that is emitted by one animal and affects the behaviour of others. Pheromones are used by many animal species to attract mates.

phospholipid

any lipid consisting of a glycerol backbone, a phosphate group, and two long chains. Phospholipids are found everywhere in living systems as the basis for biological membranes.

One of the long chains tends to be hydrophobic and the other hydrophilic (that is, they interrelate with water in opposite ways). This means that phospholipids will line up the same way round when in solution.

photochemical reaction

any chemical reaction in which light is produced or light initiates the reaction. Light can initiate reactions by exciting atoms or molecules and making them more reactive: the light energy becomes converted to chemical energy. Many photochemical reactions set up a chain reaction and produce free radicals.

This type of reaction is seen in the bleaching of dyes or the yellowing of paper by sunlight. It is harnessed by plants in photosynthesis and by humans in photography.

Chemical reactions that produce light are most commonly seen when materials are burned. Light-emitting reactions are used by living organisms in bioluminescence. One photochemical reaction is the action of sunlight on car exhaust fumes, which results in the production of ozone. Some large cities, such as Los Angeles, USA, and Santiago, Chile, now suffer serious pollution due to photochemical smog.

photoperiodism

biological mechanism that determines the timing of certain activities by responding to changes in day length. The flowering of many plants is initiated in this way. Photoperiodism in plants is regulated by a light-sensitive pigment, *phytochrome*. The breeding seasons of many temperate-zone animals are also triggered by increasing or declining day length, as part of their biorhythms.

Autumn-flowering plants (for example, chrysanthemum and soybean) and autumn-breeding mammals (such as goats and deer) require days that are shorter than a critical length; spring-flowering and spring-breeding ones (such as radish and lettuce, and birds) are triggered by longer days.

photosynthesis

process by which green plants trap light energy from the Sun. This energy is used to drive a series of chemical reactions which lead to the formation of carbohydrates. The carbohydrates occur in the form of simple sugar, or glucose, which provides the basic food for both plants and animals. For photosynthesis to occur, the plant must possess chlorophyll and must have a supply of carbon dioxide and water. Photosynthesis takes place inside chloroplasts which are found mainly in the leaf cells of plants.

The by-product of photosynthesis, oxygen, is of great importance to all living organisms, and virtually all atmospheric oxygen has originated by photosynthesis.

Chloroplasts contain the enzymes and chlorophyll necessary for photosynthesis, and the leaf structure of plants is specially adapted to this purpose.

Leaf structure

In the lower epidermis on the leaf underside are stomata (pores; see stoma), each of which is surrounded by a pair of guard cells that control their opening and closing. These guard cells contain chloroplasts. The central layer of the leaf

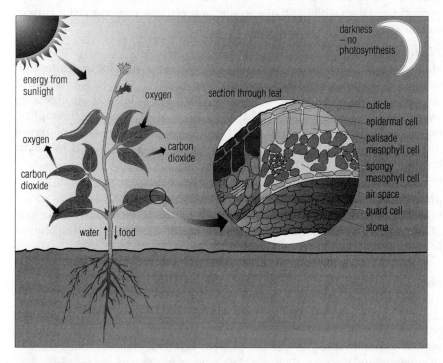

Process by which green plants and some bacteria manufacture carbohydrates from water and atmospheric carbon dioxide, using the energy of sunlight. Photosynthesis depends on the ability of chlorophyll molecules within plant cells to trap the energy of light to split water molecules, giving off oxygen as a by-product. The hydrogen of the water molecules is then used to reduce carbon dioxide to simple carbohydrates.

between the layers of epidermis is called the mesophyll, and all the cells in this tissue contain chloroplasts. Running through the mesophyll are the veins, each of which contains large, thick-walled xylem vessels for carrying water, and smaller, thin-walled phloem tubes for transporting the food produced by the leaf. Most of the glucose that forms during photosynthesis is stored in the chloroplasts as starch. As plant-eating animals eat the leaves they too are dependent on plant photosynthesis to supply their basic energy needs.

Chemical process

The chemical reactions of photosynthesis occur in two stages. During the *light reaction* sunlight is used to split water (H_2O) into oxygen (O_2), protons (hydrogen ions, H^+), and electrons, and oxygen is given off as a by-product. In the *dark reaction*, for which sunlight is not required, the protons and electrons are used to convert carbon dioxide (CO_2) into carbohydrates ($C_m(H_2O)_n$). So the whole process can be summarized by the equation:

$$CO_2 + 2H_2O \rightarrow C_m(H_2O)_n + H_2O + O_2$$

Photosynthesis depends on the ability of chlorophyll to capture the energy of sunlight and to use it to split water molecules. The initial charge separation occurs in less than a billionth of a second, a speed that compares with current computers.

Plant pigments

Photosynthetic pigments are the plant pigments responsible for capturing light energy during photosynthesis. The primary pigment is chlorophyll, which absorbs blue and red light. Other pigments, such as carotenoids, are accessory pigments which also capture light energy and pass it on to chlorophyll. Photosynthesis by cyanobacteria was responsible for the appearance of oxygen in the Earth's atmosphere 2 billion years ago, and photosynthesis by plants maintains the oxygen levels today.

phylogeny

historical sequence of changes that occurs in a given species during the course of its evolution. It was once erroneously associated with ontogeny (the process of development of a living organism).

phylum

major grouping in biological classification. Mammals, birds, reptiles, amphibians, fishes, and tunicates belong to the phylum Chordata; the phylum Mollusca consists of snails, slugs, mussels, clams, squid, and octopuses; the phylum Porifera contains sponges; and the phylum Echinodermata includes starfish, sea urchins, and sea cucumbers. In classifying plants (where the term 'division' often takes the place of 'phylum'), there are between four and nine phyla depending on the criteria used; all flowering plants belong to a single phylum, Angiospermata, and all conifers to another, Gymnospermata. Related phyla are grouped together in a kingdom; phyla are subdivided into classes.

There are 36 different phyla. The most recently identified is the Cyclophora described in 1995. It contains a single known species, *Symbion pandora*, that lives on lobsters.

physiology

branch of biology that deals with the functioning of living organisms, as opposed to anatomy, which studies their structures.

pineal body

cone-shaped outgrowth of the vertebrate brain. In some lower vertebrates, it develops a rudimentary lens and retina, which show it to be derived from an eye, or pair of eyes, situated on the top of the head in ancestral vertebrates. In fishes that can change colour to match their background, the pineal perceives the light level and controls the colour change. In birds, the pineal detects changes in daylight and stimulates breeding behaviour as spring approaches. Mammals also have a pineal gland, but it is located deeper within the brain. It secretes a hormone, melatonin, thought to influence rhythms of activity. In humans, it is a small piece of tissue attached by a stalk to the rear wall of the third ventricle of the brain.

pioneer species

in ecology, those species that are the first to colonize and thrive in new areas. Coal tips, recently cleared woodland, and new roadsides are areas where pioneer species will quickly appear. As the habitat matures other species take over, a process known as *succession*.

pituitary gland

major endocrine gland of vertebrates, situated in the centre of the brain. It is attached to the hypothalamus by a stalk. The pituitary consists of two lobes. The posterior lobe is an extension of the hypothalamus, and is in effect nervous tissue. It stores two hormones synthesized in the hypothalamus: ADH and oxytocin. The anterior lobe secretes six hormones, some of which control the activities of other glands (thyroid, gonads, and adrenal cortex); others are direct-acting hormones affecting milk secretion and controlling growth.

plant classification

taxonomy or classification of plants. Originally the plant kingdom included bacteria, diatoms, dinoflagellates, fungi, and slime moulds, but these are not now thought of as plants. The groups that are always classified as plants are the bryophytes (mosses and liverworts), pteridophytes (ferns, horsetails, and club mosses), gymnosperms (conifers, yews, cycads, and ginkgos), and angiosperms (flowering plants). The angiosperms are split into monocotyledons (for example, orchids, grasses, lilies) and dicotyledons (for example, oak, buttercup, geranium, and daisy).

The basis of plant classification was established by the Swedish naturalist Carolus Linnaeus. Among the angiosperms, it is largely based on the number and arrangement of the flower parts.

The unicellular algae, such as *Chlamydomonas*, are often now put with the protists (single-celled organisms) instead of the plants. Some classification schemes even classify the multicellular algae (seaweeds and freshwater weeds) in a new kingdom, the Protoctista, along with the protists.

plasma

liquid component of the blood. It is a straw-coloured fluid, largely composed of water (around 90%), in which a number of substances are dissolved. These include a variety of proteins (around 7%) such as fibrinogen (important in blood clotting), inorganic mineral salts such as sodium and calcium, waste products such as urea, traces of hormones, and antibodies to defend against infection.

plasmid

small, mobile piece of DNA found in bacteria that, for example, confers antibiotic resistance, used in genetic engineering. Plasmids are separate from the bacterial chromosome but still multiply during cell growth. Their size ranges from 3% to 20% of the size of the chromosome. Some plasmids carry 'fertility genes' that enable them to move from one bacterium to another and transfer genetic information between strains. Plasmid genes determine a wide variety of bacterial properties including resistance to antibiotics and the ability to produce toxins.

pleiotropy

process whereby a given gene influences several different observed characteristics of an organism. For example, in the fruit fly *Drosophila* the vestigial gene reduces the size of wings, modifies the halteres, changes the number of egg strings in the ovaries, and changes the direction of certain bristles. Many human syndromes are caused by pleiotropic genes, for example Marfan's syndrome where the slender physique, hypermobility of the joints, elongation of the limbs, dislocation of the lens, and susceptibility to heart disease are all caused by one gene.

poikilothermy

condition in which an animal's body temperature is largely dependent on the temperature of the air or water in which it lives. It is characteristic of all animals except birds and mammals, which maintain their body temperatures by homeothermy (they are 'warm-blooded').

Poikilotherms have behavioural means of temperature control; they can warm themselves up by basking in the sun, or shivering, and can cool themselves down by sheltering from the sun under a rock or by bathing in water.

Poikilotherms are often referred to as 'cold-blooded animals', but this is not really correct: their internal temperatures, regulated by behavioural means, are often as high as those of birds and mammals during the times they need to be active for feeding and reproductive purposes, and may be higher, for example in very hot climates. The main difference is that their body temperatures fluctuate more than those of homeotherms.

polyembryony

reproductive strategy in which one sexually produced embryo is split into a number of genetically identical offspring. Most of the approximately 18 poly-embryonic animals are parasitic, including various parasitic wasp species. Two species of armadillo also reproduce by polyembryony.

polymerase chain reaction (PCR)

technique developed during the 1980s to clone short strands of DNA from the genome of an organism, to produce enough of the DNA to be able to sequence and identify it. It was developed by US biochemist Kary Mullis of San Diego in 1983.

polymorphism

coexistence of several distinctly different types in a population (groups of animals of one species). Examples include the different blood groups in humans, different colour forms in some butterflies, and snail shell size, length, shape, colour, and stripiness.

polyphyletic

in biological classification, term describing a group of species that does not include its members' most recent common ancestor. Such groupings are avoided in most modern systems of classification. Examples are the marine mammals, trees, and algae.

If a group consists of all the descendants of a common ancestor plus the ancestor itself, it is called monophyletic; if it includes its members' common ancestor but not all of its descendants it is called paraphyletic. Distinguishing between such groups is an important part of the system of classification known as cladistics, which seeks to classify organisms into monophyletic groups, or *clades*.

polyploid

in genetics, possessing three or more sets of chromosomes in cases where the normal complement is two sets (diploid). Polyploidy arises spontaneously and is common in plants (mainly among flowering plants), but rare in animals. Many crop plants are natural polyploids, including wheat, which has four sets of chromosomes per cell (durum wheat) or six sets (common wheat).

Plant breeders can induce the formation of polyploids by treatment with a chemical, colchicine.

Matings between polyploid individuals and normal diploid ones are invariably sterile. Hence, an individual that develops polyploidy through a genetic aberration can initially only reproduce vegetatively, by parthenogenesis, or by self-fertilization (modes of reproduction that are common only among plants). Once a polyploid population is established, however, they can reproduce sexually. An example is cord-grass *Spartina anglica*, which is a polyploid of a European grass and a related North American grass, accidentally introduced. The resulting polyploid has spread dramatically.

polysaccharide

long-chain carbohydrate made up of hundreds or thousands of linked simple sugars (monosaccharides) such as glucose and closely related molecules.

The polysaccharides are natural polymers. They either act as energy-rich food stores in plants (starch) and animals (glycogen), or have structural roles in the plant cell wall (cellulose, pectin) or the tough outer skeleton of insects and similar creatures (chitin).

A typical polysaccharide molecule, glycogen (animal starch), is formed from linked glucose ($C_6H_{12}O_6$) molecules. A glycogen molecule has 100–1,000 linked glucose units.

polyunsaturate

type of fat or oil containing a high proportion of triglyceride molecules whose fatty acid chains contain several double bonds. By contrast, the fatty-acid chains of the triglycerides in saturated fats (such as lard) contain only single bonds. Medical evidence suggests that polyunsaturated fats, used widely in margarines and cooking fats, are less likely to contribute to cardiovascular disease than saturated fats, but there is also some evidence that they may have adverse effects on health.

The more double bonds the fatty-acid chains contain, the lower the melting point of the fat. Unsaturated chains with several double bonds produce oils, such as vegetable and fish oils, which are liquids at room temperature. Saturated fats, with no double bonds, are solids at room temperature. The polyunsaturated fats used for margarines are produced by taking a vegetable or fish oil and turning some of the double bonds to single bonds, so that the product is semi-solid at room temperature. This is done by bubbling hydrogen through the oil in the presence of a catalyst, such as platinum. The catalyst is later removed.

Monounsaturated oils, such as olive oil, whose fatty-acid chains contain a single double bond, are probably healthier than either saturated or polyunsaturated fats. Butter contains both saturated and unsaturated fats, together with cholesterol, which also plays a role in heart disease.

population

group of animals of one species, living in a certain area and able to interbreed; the members of a given species in a community of living things.

population cycle

regular fluctuations in the size of a population, as seen in lemmings, for example. Such cycles are often caused by density-dependent mortality: high mortality due to overcrowding causes a sudden decline in the population, which then gradually builds up again. Population cycles may also result from an interaction between a predator and its prey.

population genetics

branch of genetics that studies the way in which the frequencies of different alleles (alternative forms of a gene) in populations of organisms change, as a result of natural selection and other processes.

preadaptation

fortuitous possession of a character that allows an organism to exploit a new situation. In many cases, the character evolves to solve a particular problem that a species encounters in its preferred habitat, but once evolved may allow the organism to exploit an entirely different situation. The ability to extract oxygen directly from the air evolved in some early fishes, probably in response to life in stagnant, deoxygenated pools; this later made it possible for their descendants to spend time on land, so giving rise eventually to the air-breathing amphibians.

preservative

substance (additive) added to a food in order to inhibit the growth of bacteria, yeasts, moulds, and other micro-organisms, and therefore extend its shelf life. The term sometimes refers to anti-oxidants (substances added to oils and fats to prevent their becoming rancid) as well. All preservatives are potentially damaging to health if eaten in sufficient quantity. Both the amount used, and the foods in which they can be used, are restricted by law.

Alternatives to preservatives include faster turnover of food stocks, refrigeration, better hygiene in preparation, sterilization, and pasteurization.

prion acronym for proteinaceous infectious particle

infectious agent, a hundred times smaller than a virus. Composed of protein, and without any detectable nucleic acid (genetic material), it is strongly linked to a number of fatal degenerative brain diseases in mammals, such as bovine spongiform encephalopathy (BSE) in cattle, scrapie in sheep, and Creutzfeldt–Jakob disease (CJD) and kuru in humans.

The existence of prions was postulated by US neurologist Stanley Prusiner in 1982, when he and his colleagues isolated a single infectious agent for scrapie that consisted only of protein and had no associated nucleic acid (RNA or DNA). His theory remains unproven but has been upheld by subsequent research, which has identified the protein concerned as well as a mechanism for its action.

productivity, biological

in an ecosystem, the amount of material in the food chain produced by the primary producers (plants) that is available for consumption by animals. Plants turn carbon dioxide and water into sugars and other complex carbon compounds by means of photosynthesis. Their net productivity is defined as the quantity of carbon compounds formed, less the quantity used up by the respiration of the plant itself.

progesterone

steroid hormone that occurs in vertebrates. In mammals, it regulates the menstrual cycle and pregnancy. Progesterone is secreted by the corpus luteum (the ruptured Graafian follicle of a discharged ovum).

prokaryote

organism whose cells lack organelles (specialized segregated structures such as nuclei, mitochondria, and chloroplasts). Prokaryote DNA is not arranged in chromosomes but forms a coiled structure called a nucleoid. The prokaryotes comprise only the *bacteria* and *cyanobacteria*; all other organisms are eukaryotes.

protein

complex, biologically important substance composed of amino acids joined by peptide bonds. Proteins are essential to all living organisms. As enzymes they regulate all aspects of metabolism. Structural proteins such as *keratin* and *collagen* make up the skin, claws, bones, tendons, and ligaments; *muscle*

amino acids, where R is one of many possible side chains

peptide – this is one made of just three amino acid units. Proteins consist of very large numbers of amino acid units in long chains, folded up in specific ways

A protein molecule is a long chain of amino acids linked by peptide bonds. The properties of a protein are determined by the order, or sequence, of amino acids in its molecule, and by the three-dimensional structure of the molecular chain. The chain folds and twists, often forming a spiral shape.

proteins produce movement; *haemoglobin* transports oxygen; and *membrane* proteins regulate the movement of substances into and out of cells. For humans, protein is an essential part of the diet, and is found in greatest quantity in soy beans and other grain legumes, meat, eggs, and cheese.

Other types of bond, such as sulphur–sulphur bonds, hydrogen bonds, and cation bridges between acid sites, are responsible for creating the protein's characteristic three-dimensional structure, which may be fibrous, globular, or pleated. Protein provides 4 kcal of energy per gram (60 g per day is required).

protein engineering
creation of synthetic proteins designed to carry out specific tasks. For example, an enzyme may be designed to remove grease from soiled clothes and remain stable at the high temperatures in a washing machine.

protein synthesis
manufacture, within the cytoplasm of the cell, of the proteins an organism needs. The building blocks of proteins are amino acids, of which there are 20 types. The pattern in which the amino acids are linked decides what kind of protein is produced. In turn it is the genetic code, contained within DNA, that determines the precise order in which the amino acids are linked up during protein manufacture.

Interestingly, DNA is found only in the nucleus, yet protein synthesis occurs only in the cytoplasm. The information necessary for making the proteins is carried from the nucleus to the cytoplasm by another nucleic acid, RNA.

protist
single-celled organism which has a eukaryotic cell, but which is not a member of the plant, fungal, or animal kingdoms. The main protists are protozoa.

Single-celled photosynthetic organisms, such as diatoms and dinoflagellates, are classified as protists or algae. Recently the term has also been used for members of the kingdom Protista, which features in certain five-kingdom classifications of the living world (see also plant classification). This kingdom may include slime moulds, all algae (seaweeds as well as unicellular forms), and protozoa.

protoplasm
contents of a living cell. Strictly speaking it includes all the discrete structures (organelles) in a cell, but it is often used simply to mean the jellylike material in which these float. The contents of a cell outside the nucleus are called cytoplasm.

protozoa
group of single-celled organisms without rigid cell walls. Some, such as amoeba, ingest other cells, but most are saprotrophs or parasites. The group is polyphyletic (containing organisms which have different evolutionary origins).

punctuated equilibrium model

evolutionary theory developed by Niles Eldredge and US palaeontologist Stephen Jay Gould in 1972 to explain discontinuities in the fossil record. It claims that evolution continues through periods of rapid change alternating with periods of relative stability (stasis), and that the appearance of new lineages is a separate process from the gradual evolution of adaptive changes within a species.

The pattern of stasis and more rapid change is now widely accepted, but the second part of the theory remains unsubstantiated.

The *turnover pulse hypothesis* of US biologist Elisabeth Vrba postulates that the periods of rapid evolutionary change are triggered by environmental changes, particularly changes in climate.

punnett square

graphic technique used in genetics for determining the likely outcome, in statistical terms, of a genetic cross. It resembles a game of noughts and crosses, in which the genotypes of the parental generation gametes are entered first, so that the subsequent combinations can then be calculated.

pyramid of numbers

in ecology, a diagram that shows quantities of plants and animals at different levels of a food chain. This may be measured in terms of numbers (how many animals) or biomass (total mass of living matter), though in terms of showing transfer of food, biomass is a more useful measure. There is always far less biomass at the top of the chain than at the bottom, because only about 10% of the food an animal eats is turned into flesh – the rest is lost through metabolism and excretion. The amount of food flowing through the chain therefore drops with each step up the chain, hence the characteristic 'pyramid' shape.

In a pyramid of biomass, the primary producers (usually plants) are represented at the bottom by a broad band, the plant-eaters are shown above by a narrower band, and the animals that prey on them by a narrower band still. At the top of the pyramid are the 'top carnivores' such as lions and sharks.

quadrat

in environmental studies, a square structure used to study the distribution of plants in a particular place, for instance a field, rocky shore, or mountainside. The size varies, but is usually 0.5 or 1 metre square, small enough to be carried easily. The quadrat is placed on the ground and the abundance of species estimated. By making such measurements a reliable understanding of species distribution is obtained.

radiation biology

study of how living things are affected by radioactive (ionizing) emissions and by electromagnetic (nonionizing) radiation (electromagnetic waves). Both are potentially harmful and can cause mutations as well as leukaemia and other cancers; even low levels of radioactivity are very dangerous. Both however, are used therapeutically, for example to treat cancer, when the radiation dose is very carefully controlled (*radiotherapy* or X-ray therapy).

Radioactive emissions are more harmful. Exposure to high levels produces radiation burns and radiation sickness, plus genetic damage (resulting in birth defects) and cancers in the longer term. Exposure to low-level ionizing radiation can also cause genetic damage and cancers, particularly leukaemia.

Electromagnetic radiation is usually harmful only if exposure is to high-energy emissions, for example close to powerful radio transmitters or near radar-wave sources. Such exposure can cause organ damage, cataracts, loss of hearing, leukaemia and other cancers, or premature ageing. It may also affect the nervous system and brain, distorting their electrical nerve signals and leading to depression, disorientiation, headaches, and other symptoms. Individual sensitivity varies and some people are affected by electrical equipment, such as televisions, computers, and refrigerators.

Background radiation is the natural radiation produced by cosmic rays and radioactive rocks such as granite, and this must be taken into account when calculating the effects of nuclear accidents or contamination from power stations.

receptor

discrete areas of cell membranes or areas within cells with which neurotransmitters, hormones, and drugs interact. Such interactions control the activities of the body. For example, adrenaline transmits nervous impulses to receptors in the sympathetic nervous system which initiates the characteristic response to excitement and fear in an individual.

Other types of receptors, such as the proprioceptors, are located in muscles, tendons, and joints. They relay information on the position of the body and the state of muscle contraction to the brain.

recessive gene

in genetics, an allele (alternative form of a gene) that will show in the phenotype (observed characteristics of an organism) only if its partner allele on the paired chromosome is similarly recessive. Such an allele will not show if its partner is dominant, that is if the organism is heterozygous for a particular characteristic. Alleles for blue eyes in humans and for shortness in pea plants are recessive. Most mutant alleles are recessive and therefore are only rarely expressed.

recombinant DNA

in genetic engineering, DNA formed by splicing together genes from different sources into new combinations.

recombination

any process that recombines, or 'shuffles', the genetic material, thus increasing genetic variation in the offspring. The two main processes of recombination both occur during meiosis (reduction division of cells). One is *crossing over*, in which chromosome pairs exchange segments; the other is the random reassortment of chromosomes that occurs when each gamete (sperm or egg) receives only one of each chromosome pair.

red blood cell or erythrocyte

most common type of blood cell, responsible for transporting oxygen around the body. It contains haemoglobin, which combines with oxygen from the lungs to form oxyhaemoglobin. When transported to the tissues, these cells are able to release the oxygen because the oxyhaemoglobin splits into its original constituents.

Mammalian erythrocytes are disc-shaped with a depression in the centre and no nucleus; they are manufactured in the bone marrow and, in humans, last for only four months before being destroyed in the liver and spleen. Those of other vertebrates are oval and nucleated.

Red Data List

report published by the World Conservation Union (IUCN) and regularly updated that lists animal species by their conservation status. Categories of risk include *extinct in the wild*, *critically endangered*, *endangered*, *vulnerable*, and *lower risk* (divided into three subcategories).

regeneration

regrowth of a new organ or tissue after the loss or removal of the original. It is common in plants, where a new individual can often be produced from a 'cutting' of the original. In animals, regeneration of major structures is limited to lower organisms; certain lizards can regrow their tails if these are lost, and new flatworms can grow from a tiny fragment of an old one. In mammals, regeneration is limited to the repair of tissue in wound healing and the regrowth of peripheral nerves following damage.

replication

production of copies of the genetic material DNA; it occurs during cell division (mitosis and meiosis). Most mutations are caused by mistakes during replication.

During replication the paired strands of DNA separate, exposing the bases. Nucleotides floating in the cell matrix pair with the exposed bases, adenine pairing with thymine, and cytosine with guanine.

reproduction

process by which a living organism produces other organisms more or less similar to itself. The ways in which species reproduce differ, but the two main methods are by asexual reproduction and sexual reproduction. Asexual reproduction involves only one parent without the formation of gametes: the parent's cells divide by mitosis to produce new cells with the same number and kind of chromosomes as its own. Thus offspring produced asexually are clones of the parent and there is no variation. Sexual reproduction involves two parents, one male and one female. The parents' sex cells divide by meiosis producing gametes, which contain only half the number of chromosomes of the parent cell. In this way, when two sets of chromosomes combine during fertilization, a new combination of genes is produced. Hence the new organism will differ from both parents, and variation is introduced. The ability to reproduce is considered one of the fundamental attributes of living things.

Sexual reproductive systems

The plant organs concerned with sexual reproduction are found in the flowers. These consist of the stamens (male organ) and carpels (female organ). In male mammals the reproductive system consists of the testes, which produce sperm, epididymis, sperm duct, and penis, and in the females the ovaries, which produce eggs, Fallopian tubes, and uterus.

Hermaphrodites

These are bisexual organisms, such as earthworms, that have both male and female reproductive organs, or plants whose flowers contain both stamens and carpels. This is the normal arrangement in most plants. Some plant species, such as maize and birch, which have separate male and female flowers on the same plants are described as *monoeious*; in *dioecious* species, such as willow and holly, the male and female flowers are on separate plants.

reproduction rate or fecundity

in ecology, the rate at which a population or species reproduces itself.

respiration

metabolic process in organisms in which food molecules are broken down to release energy. The cells of all living organisms need a continuous supply of energy, and in most plants and animals this is obtained by *aerobic* respiration. In this process, oxygen is used to break down the glucose molecules in food. This releases energy in the form of energy-carrying molecules (ATP), and produces carbon dioxide and water as by-products. Respiration sometimes occurs without oxygen, and this is called *anaerobic* respiration. In this case, the end products are energy and either lactose acid or ethanol (alcohol) and carbon dioxide; this process is termed fermentation.

The exchange of oxygen and carbon dioxide between body tissues and the environment is termed 'external respiration', or ventilation. In air-breathing vertebrates the exchange takes place in the alveoli of the lungs, aided by the muscular movements of breathing. Respiration at the cellular level is termed *internal respiration*, and in all higher organisms occurs in the mitochondria. This takes place in two stages: the first stage, which does not require oxygen, is a form of anaerobic respiration; the second stage is the main energy-producing stage and does require oxygen. This is termed the Krebs cycle. In some bacteria the oxidant is the nitrate or sulphate ion.

respiratory surface

area used by an organism for the exchange of gases, for example the lungs, gills or, in plants, the leaf interior. The gases oxygen and carbon dioxide are both usually involved in respiration and photosynthesis. Although organisms have evolved different types of respiratory surface according to need, there are certain features in common. These include thinness and moistness, so that the gas can dissolve in a membrane and then diffuse into the body of the organism. In many animals the gas is then transported away from the surface and towards interior cells by the blood system.

response

any change in an organism occurring as a result of a stimulus. There are many different types of response, some involving the entire organism, others only groups of cells or tissues. Examples include the muscular contractions in an animal, the movement of leaves towards the light, and the onset of hibernation by small mammals at the start of winter.

restriction enzyme or endonuclease

bacterial enzyme that breaks a chain of DNA into two pieces at a specific point; used in genetic engineering. The point along the DNA chain at which the enzyme can work is restricted to places where a specific sequence of base pairs occurs. Different restriction enzymes will break a DNA chain at different points. The overlap between the fragments is used in determining the sequence of base pairs in the DNA chain.

rhesus factor

group of antigens on the surface of red blood cells of humans which characterize the rhesus blood group system. Most individuals possess the main rhesus factor (Rh+), but those without this factor (Rh−) produce antibodies if they come into contact with it. The name comes from rhesus monkeys, in whose blood rhesus factors were first found.

If an Rh− mother carries an Rh+ fetus, she may produce antibodies if fetal blood crosses the placenta. This is not normally a problem with the first infant because antibodies are only produced slowly. However, the antibodies continue to build up after birth, and a second Rh+ child may be attacked by antibodies passing from mother to fetus, causing the child to contract anaemia, heart failure, or brain damage. In such cases, the blood of the infant has to be changed for Rh− blood; a badly affected fetus may be treated in the womb. The problem can be circumvented by giving the mother anti-Rh globulin just after the first pregnancy, preventing the formation of antibodies.

ribonucleic acid

full name of RNA.

ribosome

protein-making machinery of the cell. Ribosomes are located on the endoplasmic reticulum (ER) of eukaryotic cells, and are made of proteins and a special type of RNA, ribosomal RNA. They receive messenger RNA (copied from the DNA) and amino acids, and 'translate' the messenger RNA by using its chemically coded instructions to link amino acids in a specific order, to make a strand of a particular protein.

RNA abbreviation for ribonucleic acid

nucleic acid involved in the process of translating the genetic material DNA into proteins. It is usually single-stranded, unlike the double-stranded DNA, and consists of a large number of nucleotides strung together, each of which comprises the sugar ribose, a phosphate group, and one of four bases (uracil, cytosine, adenine, or guanine). RNA is copied from DNA by the formation of base pairs, with uracil taking the place of thymine.

RNA occurs in three major forms, each with a different function in the synthesis of protein molecules. *Messenger RNA* (mRNA) acts as the template for protein synthesis. Each codon (a set of three bases) on the RNA molecule is matched up with the corresponding amino acid, in accordance with the genetic code. This process (translation) takes place in the ribosomes, which are made up of proteins and *ribosomal RNA* (rRNA). *Transfer RNA* (tRNA) is responsible for combining with specific amino acids, and then matching up a special 'anticodon' sequence of its own with a codon on the mRNA. This is how the genetic code is translated.

Although RNA is normally associated only with the process of protein synthesis, it makes up the hereditary material itself in some viruses, such as retroviruses.

ruminant

any even-toed hoofed mammal with a rumen, the 'first stomach' of its complex digestive system. Plant food is stored and fermented before being brought back to the mouth for chewing (chewing the cud) and then is swallowed to the next stomach. Ruminants include cattle, antelopes, goats, deer, and giraffes, all with a four-chambered stomach. Camels are also ruminants, but they have a three-chambered stomach.

salmonella

any of a very varied group of bacteria, genus *Salmonella*, that colonize the intestines of humans and some animals. Some strains cause typhoid and paratyphoid fevers, while others cause salmonella food poisoning, which is characterized by stomach pains, vomiting, diarrhoea, and headache. It can be fatal in elderly people, but others usually recover in a few days without antibiotics. Most cases are caused by contaminated animal products, especially poultry meat.

Human carriers of the disease may be well themselves but pass the bacteria on to others through unhygienic preparation of food. Domestic pets can also carry the bacteria while appearing healthy.

saltation

idea that an abrupt genetic change can occur in an individual, which then gives rise to a new species. The idea has now been largely discredited, although the appearance of polyploid individuals can be considered an example.

saturated fatty acid

fatty acid in which there are no double bonds in the hydrocarbon chain.

secondary sexual characteristic

external feature of an organism that is indicative of its gender (male or female), but not the reproductive organs themselves. They include facial hair in men and breasts in women, combs in cockerels, brightly coloured plumage in many male birds, and manes in male lions. In many cases, they are involved in displays and contests for mates and have evolved by sexual selection. Their development is stimulated by sex hormones.

In humans the development of secondary sexual characteristics is stimu-lated at puberty by the hormone oestrogen in women and testosterone in men. Women develop breasts; men develop a deeper voice and facial hair; and both develop hair in underarm and genital regions.

secretion

any substance (normally a fluid) produced by a cell or specialized gland, for example, sweat, saliva, enzymes, and hormones. The process whereby the substance is discharged from the cell is also known as secretion.

semelparity

occurrence of a single act of reproduction during an organism's lifetime. Most semelparous species produce very large numbers of offspring when they do reproduce, and normally die soon afterwards. Examples include the Pacific salmon and the pine looper moth. Many plants are semelparous, or mono-carpic. Repeated reproduction is called iteroparity.

senescence

deterioration in physical and (sometimes) mental capacities that occurs with ageing.

sensitivity

ability of an organism, or part of an organism, to detect changes in the envi-ronment. All living things are capable of some sensitivity, and any change detected by an organism is called a stimulus. Plant response to stimuli (for example, light, heat, moisture) is by directional growth (tropism). In animals, the body cells that detect the stimuli are called receptors, and these are often contained within a sense organ. For example, the eye is a sense organ, within which the retina contains rod and cone cells which are receptors. The part of the body that responds to a stimulus, such as a muscle, is called an effector, and the communication of stimuli from receptors to effectors is termed 'coordination'; messages are passed from receptors to effectors either via the nerves or by means of chemicals called hormones. Rapid communication and response to stimuli, such as light, sound, and scent, can be essential to an animal's well-being and survival, and evolution has led to the development of highly complex mechanisms for this purpose.

Nervous systems

Most animals have a nervous system that coordinates communication between stimulus and response. Nervous systems consist of special cells called neurones (see nerve cell) which are fundamentally the same as other body cells in that each contains a nucleus, cytoplasm, and cell membrane. In addition, in order to receive and pass messages, they also have long thin fibres of cytoplasm extending out from the cell body termed 'nerve fibres'. The longest of these, which can be more than a metre long, are called *axons*. The shorter fibres are called *dendrites*.

Nerve nets

Small animals, such as jellyfish, which do not need to coordinate complex messages between stimuli and response mechanisms, have simple nervous systems, termed 'nerve nets'. In a nerve net, each neurone is connected by fibres to adjacent neurones, so that a message received in any one part of the nervous system is relayed from neurone to neurone throughout the whole of the organism's body.

Central nervous systems

The evolution of larger and more complex animals, such as humans, has necessitated the development of far more elaborate nervous systems, and most animals have a central nervous system (CNS). The main difference between a simple nerve net and a central nervous system is the addition of a brain and spinal cord to coordinate and relay messages between receptors and the appropriate effectors, without involving the whole body. Thus rapid responses to specific stimuli are triggered.

sequencing

determining the sequence of chemical subunits within a large molecule. Techniques for sequencing amino acids in proteins were established in the 1950s, insulin being the first for which the sequence was completed. The Human Genome Project is attempting to determine the sequence of the 3 billion base pairs within human DNA. A rough draft of the whole genome had been sequenced by June 2000.

serum

clear fluid that separates out from clotted blood. It is blood plasma with the anticoagulant proteins removed, and contains antibodies and other proteins, as well as the fats and sugars of the blood. It can be produced synthetically, and is used to protect against disease.

sex chromosome

chromosome that differs between the sexes and that serves to determine the sex of the individual. In humans, females have two X chromosomes and males have an X and a Y chromosome.

sex determination

process by which the sex of an organism is determined. In many species, the sex of an individual is dictated by the two sex chromosomes (X and Y) it receives from its parents. In mammals, some plants, and a few insects, males are XY, and females XX; in birds, reptiles, some amphibians, and butterflies the reverse is the case. In bees and wasps, males are produced from unfertilized eggs, females from fertilized eggs. In 1991 it was shown that maleness is caused by a single gene, 14 base pairs long, on the Y chromosome.

Environmental factors can affect some fish and reptiles, such as turtles, where sex is influenced by the temperature at which the eggs develop.

Most fish have a very flexible system of sex determination, which can be affected by external factors. For example, in wrasse all individuals develop into females, but the largest individual in each area or school changes sex to become the local breeding male.

sex hormone

steroid hormone produced and secreted by the gonads (testes and ovaries). Sex hormones control development and reproductive functions and influence sexual and other behaviour.

sex linkage

in genetics, the tendency for certain characteristics to occur exclusively, or predominantly, in one sex only. Human examples include red-green colour blindness and haemophilia, both found predominantly in males. In both cases, these characteristics are recessive and are determined by genes on the X chromosome.

Since females possess two X chromosomes, any such recessive allele on one of them is likely to be masked by the corresponding allele on the other. In males (who have only one X chromosome paired with a largely inert Y chromosome) any gene on the X chromosome will automatically be expressed. Colour blindness and haemophilia can appear in females, but only if they are homozygous for these traits, due to inbreeding, for example.

sexual reproduction

reproductive process in organisms that requires the union, or fertilization, of gametes (such as eggs and sperm). These are usually produced by two different individuals, although self-fertilization occurs in a few hermaphrodites such as tapeworms. Most organisms other than bacteria and cyanobacteria (blue-green algae) show some sort of sexual process. Except in some lower organisms, the gametes are of two distinct types called eggs and sperm. The organisms producing the eggs are called females, and those producing the sperm, males. The fusion of a male and female gamete produces a *zygote*, from which a new individual develops. See reproduction.

The alternatives to sexual reproduction are parthenogenesis and asexual reproduction by means of spores.

sexual selection

process similar to natural selection but relating exclusively to success in finding a mate for the purpose of sexual reproduction and producing offspring. Sexual selection occurs when one sex (usually but not always the female) invests more effort in producing young than the other. Members of the other sex compete for access to this limited resource (usually males competing for the chance to mate with females).

Sexual selection often favours features that increase a male's attractiveness to females (such as the pheasant's tail) or enable males to fight with one another (such as a deer's antlers). More subtly, it can produce hormonal effects by which the male makes the female unreceptive to other males, causes the abortion of fetuses already conceived, or removes the sperm of males who have already mated with a female.

sickle-cell disease also called sickle-cell anaemia

hereditary chronic blood disorder common among people of black African descent; also found in the eastern Mediterranean, parts of the Persian Gulf, and in northeastern India. It is characterized by distortion and fragility of the red blood cells, which are lost too rapidly from the circulation. This often results in anaemia.

People with this disease have abnormal red blood cells (sickle cells), containing a defective haemoglobin. The presence of sickle cells in the blood is called *sicklemia*.

The disease is caused by a recessive allele. Those with two copies of the allele suffer debilitating anaemia; those with a single copy paired with the normal allele, suffer with only mild anaemia and have a degree of protection against malaria because fewer normal red blood cells are available to the parasites for infection.

sociobiology

study of the biological basis of all social behaviour, including the application of population genetics to the evolution of behaviour. It builds on the concept of inclusive fitness, contained in the notion of the 'selfish gene'. Contrary to some popular interpretations, it does not assume that all behaviour is genetically determined.

The New Zealand biologist W D Hamilton introduced the concept of inclusive fitness, which emphasizes that the evolutionary function of behaviour is to allow an organism to contribute as many of its own alleles as it can to future generations: this idea is encapsulated in the British zoologist Richard Dawkins's notion of the 'selfish gene'.

speciation

emergence of a new species during evolutionary history. One cause of speciation is the geographical separation of populations of the parent species, followed by reproductive isolation and selection for different environments so that they no longer produce viable offspring when they interbreed. Other causes are assortative mating and the establishment of a polyploid population.

species

distinguishable group of organisms that resemble each other or consist of a few distinctive types (as in polymorphism), and that can all interbreed to produce fertile offspring. Species are the lowest level in the system of biological classification.

Related species are grouped together in a genus. Within a species there are usually two or more separate populations, which may in time become distinctive enough to be designated subspecies or varieties, and could eventually give rise to new species through speciation. Around 1.4 million species have been identified so far, of which 750,000 are insects, 250,000 are plants, and 41,000 are vertebrates. In tropical regions there are roughly two species for each temperate-zone species. It is estimated that one species becomes extinct every day through habitat destruction.

A *native* species is a species that has existed in that country at least from prehistoric times; a *naturalized* species is one known to have been introduced by humans from another country, but which now maintains itself; while an *exotic* species is one that requires human intervention to survive.

sperm or semen

fluid containing the male gametes (sperm cells) of animals. Usually, each sperm cell has a head capsule containing a nucleus, a middle portion containing mitochondria (which provide energy), and a long tail (flagellum).

In most animals, sperm cells (sometimes called 'sperm' for short) are motile, and are propelled by a long flagellum, but in some (such as crabs and lobsters) they are nonmotile. The term is sometimes used for the motile male gametes (antherozoids) of lower plants. The human sperm cell is 0.0002 in/0.005 mm long and can survive inside the female for 2–9 days. Mammalian sperm cells have receptor cells identical to some of those found in the lining of the nose. These may help in navigating towards the egg.

spermatophore

small capsule containing sperm and other nutrients produced in invertebrates, newts, and cephalopods.

sterilization

killing or removal of living organisms such as bacteria and fungi. A sterile environment is necessary in medicine, food processing, and some scientific experiments. Methods include heat treatment (such as boiling), the use of chemicals (such as disinfectants), irradiation with gamma rays, and filtration.

steroid

any of a group of cyclic, unsaturated alcohols (lipids without fatty acid components), which, like sterols, have a complex molecular structure consisting of four carbon rings. Steroids include the sex hormones, such as testosterone, the corticosteroid hormones produced by the adrenal gland, bile acids, and cholesterol.

The term is commonly used to refer to anabolic steroid. In medicine, synthetic steroids are used to treat a wide range of conditions.

Steroids are also found in plants. The most widespread are the *brassinosteroids*, necessary for normal plant growth.

stimulus

any agency, such as noise, light, heat, or pressure, that can be detected by an organism's receptors. See sensitivity.

substrate

in biochemistry, a compound or mixture of compounds acted on by an enzyme. The term also refers to a substance such as agar that provides the nutrients for the metabolism of micro-organisms. Since the enzyme systems of micro-organisms regulate their metabolism, the essential meaning is the same.

succession

in ecology, a series of changes that occur in the structure and composition of the vegetation in a given area from the time it is first colonized by plants (*primary succession*), or after it has been disturbed by fire, flood, or clearing (*secondary succession*).

If allowed to proceed undisturbed, succession leads naturally to a stable climax community (for example, oak and hickory forest or savannah grassland) that is determined by the climate and soil characteristics of the area.

sucrose or cane sugar or beet sugar ($C_{12}H_{22}O_{11}$)

sugar found in the pith of sugar cane and in sugar beets. It is popularly known as sugar.

Sucrose is a disaccharide sugar, each of its molecules being made up of two simple sugar (monosaccharide) units: glucose and fructose.

symbiosis

any close relationship between two organisms of different species, and one where both partners benefit from the association. A well-known example is the pollination relationship between insects and flowers, where the insects feed on nectar and carry pollen from one flower to another. This is sometimes known as mutualism.

Symbiosis in a broader sense includes commensalism, parasitism, and inquilinism (one animal living in the home of another and sharing its food).

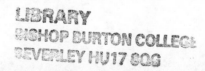

systematics

science of naming and identifying species, and determining their degree of relatedness. It plays an important role in preserving biodiversity; only a small fraction of existing species have been named and described. See also classification.

taxonomy

another name for the classification of living organisms.

telomere

chromosome tip. Telomeres prevent chromosomes sticking together. Like DNA they are made up of nucleotides, usually rich in thymine and guanine. Every time a cell divides, the telomeres shorten. They trigger the cell's senescence (inability to reproduce) when they reach a threshold length. This process is prevented from happening during the replication of cancer cells by the presence of the enzyme *telomerase*. Telomerase replaces the segments of the telomeres, maintaining their length so that cell replication is no longer controlled.

temperature regulation

ability of an organism to control its internal body temperature. Animals that rely on their environment for their body temperature (and therefore have a variable temperature) are known as *ectotherms* or 'cold-blooded' animals (for example, lizard). Animals with a constant body temperature irrespective of their environment are known as *endotherms* or 'warm-blooded' animals (for example, birds and mammals). Their temperature is regulated by the medulla in the brain.

Ectotherms have behavioural means of temperature control; they can warm themselves up by basking in the sun, or shivering, and can cool themselves down by sheltering from the sun under a rock or by bathing in water. In cold weather their metabolism slows and they become less active.

Endotherms too can regulate temperature by behavioural means (for example, seeking sun or shade), but also make use of physical and metabolic processes of regulation. The skin plays an important role – heat can be lost by sweating, whereby the water secreted evaporates from the skin and causes cooling. Heat can also be lost through capillaries near the surface of the skin, which flush with blood and lose heat by radiation. In the same way, heat can be retained by diverting blood from the surface capillaries, which gives the skin a paler colour in the cold. Heat can also be retained by hairs which become erect and trap an insulating layer of air next to the skin (producing 'goose bumps'). In some animals, there is a more specialized insulating layer such as fur, feathers, or blubber. Endotherms can also gain heat metabolically through shivering, whereby involuntary muscle contractions release heat, and by an increased metabolism in the liver.

test cross

in genetics, a breeding experiment used to discover the genotype of an individual organism. By crossing with a double recessive of the same species, the offspring will indicate whether the test individual is homozygous or heterozygous for the characteristic in question. In peas, a tall plant under investigation would be crossed with a double recessive short plant with known genotype tt. The results of the cross will be all tall plants if the test plant is TT. If the individual is in fact Tt then there will be some short plants (genotype tt) among the offspring.

tissue

any kind of cellular fabric that occurs in an organism's body. Several kinds of tissue can usually be distinguished, each consisting of cells of a particular kind bound together by cell walls (in plants) or extracellular matrix (in animals). Thus, nerve and muscle are different kinds of tissue in animals, as are parenchyma and sclerenchyma in plants.

tissue culture

process by which cells from a plant or animal are removed from the organism and grown under controlled conditions in a sterile medium containing all the necessary nutrients. Tissue culture can provide information on cell growth and differentiation, and is also used in plant propagation and drug production.

toxin

any poison produced by another living organism (usually a bacterium) that can damage the living body. In vertebrates, toxins are broken down by enzyme action, mainly in the liver.

trace element

chemical element necessary in minute quantities for the health of a plant or animal. For example, magnesium, which occurs in chlorophyll, is essential to photosynthesis, and iodine is needed by the thyroid gland of mammals for making hormones that control growth and body chemistry.

transcription

process by which the information for the synthesis of a protein is transferred from the DNA strand on which it is carried to the messenger RNA strand involved in the actual synthesis. It occurs by the formation of base pairs when a single strand of unwound DNA serves as a template for assembling the complementary nucleotides that make up the new RNA strand.

transduction

transfer of genetic material between cells by an infectious mobile genetic element such as a virus. Transduction is used in genetic engineering to produce new varieties of bacteria.

transfusion

intravenous delivery of blood or blood products (plasma, red cells) into a patient's circulation to make up for deficiencies due to disease, injury, or surgical intervention.

Cross-matching is carried out to ensure the patient receives the right blood group. Because of worries about blood-borne disease, there is a growing interest in autologous transfusion with units of the patient's own blood 'donated' over the weeks before an operation.

Blood is rarely transfused whole. Blood cells and platelets are separated and resuspended in solution. Plasma can be frozen and is used to treat clotting deficiencies.

Blood transfusion, first successfully pioneered in humans in 1818, remained highly risky until the discovery of blood groups, by Austrian-born immunologist Karl Landsteiner in 1900, which indicated the need for compatibility of donated blood.

transgenic organism

plant, animal, bacterium, or other living organism which has had a foreign gene added to it by means of genetic engineering.

translation

process by which proteins are synthesized. During translation, the information coded as a sequence of nucleotides in messenger RNA is transformed into a sequence of amino acids in a peptide chain. The process involves the 'translation' of the genetic code. See also transcription.

translocation

exchange of genetic material between chromosomes. It is responsible for congenital abnormalities, such as Down's syndrome.

transposon or jumping gene

segment of DNA able to move within or between chromosomes. Transposons trigger changes in gene expression by shutting off genes or causing insertion mutations.

The origins of transposons are obscure, but geneticists believe some may be the remnants of viruses that have permanently integrated their genes with those of their hosts. They were first identified by US geneticist Barbara McClintock in 1947.

triglyceride

chemical name for fat comprising three fatty acids reacted with a glycerol.

triploblastic

having a body wall composed of three layers. The outer layer is the *ectoderm*, the middle layer the *mesoderm*, and the inner layer the *endoderm*. This pattern of development is shown by most multicellular animals (including humans).

tropism or tropic movement

directional growth of a plant, or part of a plant, in response to an external stimulus such as gravity or light. If the movement is directed towards the stimulus it is described as positive; if away from it, it is negative. *Geotropism* for example, the response of plants to gravity, causes the root (positively geotropic) to grow downwards, and the stem (negatively geotropic) to grow upwards.

Phototropism occurs in response to light, *hydrotropism* to water, *chemotropism* to a chemical stimulus, and *thigmotropism*, or *haptotropism*, to physical contact, as in the tendrils of climbing plants when they touch a support and then grow around it.

Tropic movements are the result of greater rate of growth on one side of the plant organ than the other. Tropism differs from a nastic movement in being influenced by the direction of the stimulus.

trypsin

enzyme in the vertebrate gut responsible for the digestion of protein molecules. It is secreted by the pancreas but in an inactive form known as trypsinogen. Activation into working trypsin occurs only in the small intestine, owing to the action of another enzyme enterokinase, secreted by the wall of the duodenum. Unlike the digestive enzyme pepsin, found in the stomach, trypsin does not require an acid environment.

tumour

overproduction of cells in a specific area of the body, often leading to a swelling or lump. Tumours are classified as *benign* or *malignant*. Benign tumours grow more slowly, do not invade surrounding tissues, do not spread to other parts of the body, and do not usually recur after removal. However, benign tumours can be dangerous in areas such as the brain. The most familiar types of benign tumour are warts on the skin. In some cases, there is no sharp dividing line between benign and malignant tumours.

unicellular organism

animal or plant consisting of a single cell. Most are invisible without a microscope but a few, such as the giant amoeba, may be visible to the naked eye. The main groups of unicellular organisms are bacteria, protozoa, unicellular algae, and unicellular fungi or yeasts. Some become disease-causing agents (pathogens).

urea ($CO(NH_2)_2$)

waste product formed in the mammalian liver when nitrogen compounds are broken down. It is filtered from the blood by the kidneys, and stored in the bladder as urine prior to release. When purified, it is a white, crystalline solid. In industry it is used to make urea-formaldehyde plastics (or resins), pharmaceuticals, and fertilizers.

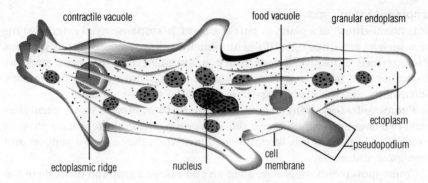

The amoebae are among the simplest living organisms, consisting of a single cell. Within the cell, there is a nucleus, which controls cell activity, and many other microscopic bodies and vacuoles (fluid-filled spaces surrounded by a membrane) with specialized functions. Amoebae eat by flowing around food particles, engulfing the particle; a process called phagocytosis.

urea cycle

biochemical process discovered by German-born British biochemist Hans Krebs and Henseleit in 1932, by which nitrogenous waste is converted into urea, which is easily excreted. When proteins and amino acids break down, ammonia, which is highly toxic, is formed. Most of the ammonia is converted into glutamate, and becomes usable for the synthesis of more amino acids and proteins. Any excess is converted into the water-soluble compound, urea, which can be excreted as urine. Free ammonia, carbon dioxide, and ATP react to form carbamyl phosphate. This compound then forms citrulline by reacting with the amino acid ornithine, which can then accept another amino group giving arginine. Arginine can then break down, giving urea, for excretion, and ornithine, which can take part in the cycle again.

uric acid $(C_5H_4N_4O_3)$

nitrogen-containing waste substance, formed from the breakdown of food and body protein.

It is only slightly soluble in water. Uric acid is the normal means by which most land animals that develop in a shell (birds, reptiles, insects, and land gastropods) deposit their waste products. The young are unable to get rid of their excretory products while in the shell and therefore store them in this insoluble form.

Humans and other primates produce some uric acid as well as urea, the normal nitrogenous waste product of mammals, adult amphibians, and many marine fishes. If formed in excess and not excreted, uric acid may be deposited in sharp crystals in the joints and other tissues, causing gout; or it may form stones (calculi) in the kidneys or bladder.

urinary system

system of organs that removes nitrogenous waste products and excess water from the bodies of animals. In vertebrates, it consists of a pair of kidneys, which produce urine; ureters, which drain the kidneys; and (in bony fishes, amphibians, some reptiles, and mammals) a bladder that stores the urine before its discharge. In mammals, the urine is expelled through the urethra; in other vertebrates, the urine drains into a common excretory chamber called a cloaca, and the urine is not discharged separately.

vaccine

any preparation of modified pathogens (viruses or bacteria) that is introduced into the body, usually either orally or by a hypodermic syringe, to induce the specific antibody reaction that produces immunity against a particular disease.

vacuole

fluid-filled, membrane-bound cavity inside a cell. It may be a reservoir for fluids that the cell will secrete to the outside, or may be filled with excretory products or essential nutrients that the cell needs to store. Plant cells usually have a large central vacuole containing sap (sugar and salts in solution) which serves both as a store of food and as a key factor in maintaining turgor. In amoebae (single-celled animals), vacuoles are the sites of digestion of engulfed food particles.

vegetative reproduction

type of asexual reproduction in plants that relies not on spores, but on multicellular structures formed by the parent plant. Some of the main types are stolons and runners, gemmae, bulbils, sucker shoots produced from roots (such as in the creeping thistle *Cirsium arvense*), tubers, bulbs, corms, and rhizomes. Vegetative reproduction has long been exploited in horticulture and agriculture, with various methods employed to multiply stocks of plants.

ventral surface

front of an animal. In vertebrates, the side furthest from the backbone; in invertebrates, the side closest to the ground. The positioning of the main nerve pathways on the ventral side is a characteristic of invertebrates.

vertebrate

any animal with a backbone. The 41,000 species of vertebrates include mammals, birds, reptiles, amphibians, and fishes. They include most of the larger animals, but in terms of numbers of species are only a tiny proportion of the world's animals. The zoological taxonomic group Vertebrata is a subgroup of the phylum Chordata.

A giant fossil conodont (an eel-like organism from the Cambrian period) was discovered in South Africa in 1995, and is believed to be one of the first vertebrates. Conodonts evolved 520 million years ago, predating the earliest fish by about 50 million years.

vestigial organ

organ that remains in diminished form after it has ceased to have any significant function in the adult organism. In humans, the appendix is vestigial, having once had a digestive function in our ancestors.

virus

infectious particle consisting of a core of nucleic acid (DNA or RNA) enclosed in a protein shell. Viruses are acellular and able to function and reproduce only if they can invade a living cell to use the cell's system to replicate themselves. In the process they may disrupt or alter the host cell's own DNA. The healthy human body reacts by producing an antiviral protein, interferon, which prevents the infection spreading to adjacent cells.

There are around 5,000 species of virus known to science (1998), though there may be as many as 0.5 million actually in existence.

Many viruses mutate continuously so that the host's body has little chance of developing permanent resistance; others transfer between species, with the new host similarly unable to develop resistance. The viruses that cause AIDS and Lassa fever are both thought to have 'jumped' to humans from other mammalian hosts.

Among diseases caused by viruses are canine distemper, chickenpox, common cold, herpes, influenza, rabies, smallpox, yellow fever, AIDS, and many plant diseases. Recent evidence implicates viruses in the development of some forms of cancer. *Bacteriophages* are viruses that infect bacterial cells.

Retroviruses are of special interest because they have an RNA genome and can produce DNA from this RNA by a process called reverse transcription.

Viroids, discovered in 1971, are even smaller than viruses; they consist of a single strand of nucleic acid with no protein coat. They may cause stunting in plants and some rare diseases in animals, including humans.

It is debatable whether viruses and viroids are truly living organisms, since they are incapable of an independent existence. Outside the cell of another organism they remain completely inert. The origin of viruses is also unclear, but it is believed that they are degenerate forms of life, derived from cellular organisms, or pieces of nucleic acid that have broken away from the genome of some higher organism and taken up a parasitic existence.

Antiviral drugs are difficult to develop because viruses replicate by using the genetic machinery of host cells, so that drugs tend to affect the host cell as well as the virus. Acyclovir (used against the herpes group of diseases) is one of the few drugs so far developed that is successfully selective in its action. It is converted to its active form by an enzyme that is specific to the virus, and it then specifically inhibits viral replication. Some viruses have shown developing resistance to the few antiviral drugs available.

Viruses have recently been found to be very abundant in seas and lakes, with between 5 and 10 million per millilitre of water at most sites tested, but up to 250 million per millilitre in one polluted lake. These viruses infect bacteria and, possibly, single-celled algae. They may play a crucial role in controlling the survival of bacteria and algae in the plankton.

vitalism

idea that living organisms derive their characteristic properties from a universal life force. In the 20th century, this view was associated with the French philosopher Henri Bergson.

vitamin

any of various chemically unrelated organic compounds that are necessary in small quantities for the normal functioning of the human body. Many act as coenzymes, small molecules that enable enzymes to function effectively. Vitamins must be supplied by the diet because the body generally cannot make them. They are normally present in adequate amounts in a balanced diet. Deficiency of a vitamin may lead to a metabolic disorder ('deficiency disease'), which can be remedied by sufficient intake of the vitamin. They are generally classified as *water-soluble* (B and C) or *fat-soluble* (A, D, E, and K).

Scurvy (the result of vitamin C deficiency) was observed at least 3,500 years ago, and sailors from the 1600s were given fresh sprouting cereals or citrus-fruit juices to prevent or cure it. The concept of scurvy as a deficiency disease, however, caused by the absence of a specific substance, emerged later. In the 1890s a Dutch doctor, Christiaan Eijkman, discovered that he could cure hens suffering from a condition like beriberi by feeding them on whole-grain, rather than polished, rice. In 1912 Casimir Funk, a Polish-born biochemist, had proposed the existence of what he called 'vitamines' (vital amines), but it was not fully established until about 1915 that several deficiency diseases were preventable and curable by extracts from certain foods. By then it was known that two groups of factors were involved, one being water-soluble and present, for example, in yeast, rice-polishings, and wheat germ, and the other being fat-soluble and present in egg yolk, butter, and fish-liver oils. The water-soluble substance, known to be effective against beriberi, was named vitamin B. The fat-soluble vitamin complex was at first called vitamin A. As a result of analytical techniques these have been subsequently separated into their various components, and others have been discovered.

Megavitamin therapy (the consumption of large doses of certain vitamins, for example vitamin C to prevent colds) has yielded at best unproven effects; some vitamins (A, for example) are extremely toxic in high doses.

Other animals may also need vitamins, but not necessarily the same ones. For example, choline, which humans can synthesize, is essential to rats and some birds, which cannot produce sufficient for themselves.

vivisection

literally, cutting into a living animal. Used originally to mean experimental surgery or dissection practised on a live subject, the term is often used by anti-vivisection campaigners to include any experiment on animals, surgical or otherwise.

Britain's 1876 Cruelty to Animals Act was the world's first legislation specifically to protect laboratory animals. By the end of the 20th century, public opinion was becoming increasingly divided on the question of animal experimentation.

water

chemical compound of hydrogen and oxygen elements, H_2O. It can exist as a solid (ice), liquid (water), or gas (water vapour). Water is the most common element on Earth and vital to all living organisms: it helps cells to maintain their form; as a solvent, it dissolves salts, sugars, proteins, and many other substances that are involved in metabolism and the digestion of food; it enables the transportation of bodily wastes, and the maintenance of a stable body temperature through perspiration and evaporation. But too much water can be dangerous. The process that maintains an equable balance of water content in an organism is osmoregulation. Organisms gain water in a number of ways – by osmosis, in food, and by respiration. They lose water by evaporation, in urine, and by osmosis. In humans, the kidneys play a very important role in the regulation of water balance.

Water makes up 60–70% of the human body or about 40 l/70 pt of which 25 l/53 pt are inside the cells, 15 l/26 pt outside (12 l/21 pt in tissue fluid, and 3 l/5 pt in blood plasma). A loss of 4 1/7 pt may cause hallucinations; a loss of 8–10 l/14–18 pt may cause death. About 1.5 l/2.6 pt a day are lost through breathing, perspiration, and faeces, and the additional amount lost in urine is the amount needed to keep the balance between input and output. In temperate climates, people cannot survive more than five or six days without water, or two or three days in a hot environment.

white blood cell or leucocyte

one of a number of different cells that play a part in the body's defences and give immunity against disease. Some (neutrophils and macrophages) engulf invading micro-organisms, others kill infected cells, while lymphocytes produce more specific immune responses. White blood cells are colourless, with clear or granulated cytoplasm, and are capable of independent amoeboid movement. They occur in the blood, lymph, and elsewhere in the body's tissues. Unlike mammalian red blood cells, they possess a nucleus. Human blood contains about 11,000 leucocytes to the cubic millimetre – about one to every 500 red cells.

White blood cell numbers may be reduced (leucopenia) by starvation, pernicious anaemia, and certain infections, such as typhoid and malaria. An increase in their numbers (leucocytosis) is a reaction to normal events such as digestion, exertion, and pregnancy, and to abnormal ones such as loss of blood, cancer, and most infections.

wild type

in genetics, the naturally occurring gene for a particular character that is typical of most individuals of a given species, as distinct from new genes that arise by mutation.

X chromosome

larger of the two sex chromosomes, the smaller being the Y chromosome. These two chromosomes are involved in sex determination. Females have two X chromosomes, males have an X and a Y. Genes carried on the X chromosome produce the phenomenon of sex linkage.

Early in the development of a female embryo, one of the X chromosomes becomes condensed so that most of its genes are inactivated. If this inactivation is incomplete, skeletal defects and mental retardation result.

Y chromosome

smaller of the two sex chromosomes. In male mammals it occurs paired with the other type of sex chromosome (X), which carries far more genes. The Y chromosome is the smallest of all the mammalian chromosomes and is considered to be largely inert (that is, without direct effect on the physical body), apart from containing the genes that control the development of the testes. There are only 20 genes discovered so far on the human Y chromosome, much fewer than on all other human chromosomes. See also sex determination.

In humans, about one in 300 males inherits two Y chromosomes at conception, making him an XYY triploid. Few if any differences from normal XY males exist in these individuals, although at one time they were thought to be emotionally unstable and abnormally aggressive. In 1989 the gene determining that a human being is male was found to occur on the X as well as on the Y chromosome; however, it is not activated in the female.

yeast

one of various single-celled fungi (see fungus) that form masses of tiny round or oval cells by budding. When placed in a sugar solution the cells multiply and convert the sugar into alcohol and carbon dioxide. Yeasts are used as fermenting agents in baking, brewing, and the making of wine and spirits. Brewer's yeast (*Saccharomyces cerevisiae*) is a rich source of vitamin B.

yeast artificial chromosome (YAC)

fragment of DNA from the human genome inserted into a yeast cell. The yeast replicates the fragment along with its own DNA. In this way the fragments are copied to be preserved in a gene library. YACs are characteristically between 250,000 and 1 million base pairs in length. A cosmid works in the same way.

zoology

branch of biology concerned with the study of animals. It includes any aspect of the study of animal form and function – description of present-day animals, the study of evolution of animal forms, anatomy, physiology, embryology, behaviour, and geographical distribution.

Appendix

Nobel Prize for Physiology or Medicine

Year	Winner(s)[1]	Awarded for
1901	Emil von Behring (Germany)	discovery that the body produces antitoxins, and development of serum therapy for diseases such as diphtheria
1902	Ronald Ross (UK)	work on the role of the *Anopheles* mosquito in transmitting malaria
1903	Niels Finsen (Denmark)	discovery of the use of ultraviolet light to treat skin diseases
1904	Ivan Pavlov (Russia)	discovery of the physiology of digestion
1905	Robert Koch (Germany)	investigations and discoveries in relation to tuberculosis
1906	Camillo Golgi (Italy) and Santiago Ramón y Cajal (Spain)	discovery of the fine structure of the nervous system
1907	Charles Laveran (France)	discovery that certain protozoa can cause disease
1908	Ilya Mechnikov (Russia) and Paul Ehrlich (Germany)	work on immunity
1909	Emil Kocher (Switzerland)	work on the physiology, pathology, and surgery of the thyroid gland
1910	Albrecht Kossel (Germany)	study of cell proteins and nucleic acids
1911	Allvar Gullstrand (Sweden)	work on the refraction of light through the different components of the eye
1912	Alexis Carrel (France)	work on the techniques for connecting severed blood vessels and transplanting organs
1913	Charles Richet (France)	work on allergic responses

Year	Winner(s)[1]	Awarded for
1914	Robert Bárány (Austria-Hungary)	work on the physiology and pathology of the equilibrium organs of the inner ear
1915		no award
1916		no award
1917		no award
1918		no award
1919	Jules Bordet (Belgium)	work on immunity
1920	August Krogh (Denmark)	discovery of the mechanism regulating the dilation and constriction of blood capillaries
1921		no award
1922	Archibald Hill (UK)	work in the production of heat in contracting muscle
	Otto Meyerhof (Germany)	work in the relationship between oxygen consumption and metabolism of lactic acid in muscle
1923	Frederick Banting (Canada) and John Macleod (UK)	discovery and isolation of the hormone insulin
1924	Willem Einthoven (Netherlands)	invention of the electrocardiograph
1925		no award
1926	Johannes Fibiger (Denmark)	discovery of a parasite *Spiroptera carcinoma* that causes cancer
1927	Julius Wagner-Jauregg (Austria)	use of induced malarial fever to treat paralysis caused by mental deterioration
1928	Charles Nicolle (France)	work on the role of the body louse in transmitting typhus
1929	Christiaan Eijkman (Netherlands)	discovery of a cure for beriberi, a vitamin-deficiency disease
	Frederick Hopkins (UK)	discovery of trace substances, now known as vitamins, that stimulate growth

Year	Winner(s)[1]	Awarded for
1930	Karl Landsteiner (USA)	discovery of human blood groups
1931	Otto Warburg (Germany)	discovery of respiratory enzymes that enable cells to process oxygen
1932	Charles Sherrington (UK) and Edgar Adrian (UK)	discovery of function of neurons (nerve cells)
1933	Thomas Morgan (USA)	work on the role of chromosomes in heredity
1934	George Whipple (USA), George Minot (USA), and William Murphy (USA)	work on treatment of pernicious anaemia by increasing the amount of liver in the diet
1935	Hans Spemann (Germany)	organizer effect in embryonic development
1936	Henry Dale (UK) and Otto Loewi (Germany)	chemical transmission of nerve impulses
1937	Albert Szent-Györgyi (Hungary)	investigation of biological oxidation processes and of the action of ascorbic acid (vitamin C)
1938	Corneille Heymans (Belgium)	mechanisms regulating respiration
1939	Gerhard Domagk (Germany)	discovery of the first antibacterial sulphonamide drug
1940	no award	
1941	no award	
1942	no award	
1943	Henrik Dam (Denmark)	discovery of vitamin K
	Edward Doisy (USA)	chemical nature of vitamin K
1944	Joseph Erlanger (USA) and Herbert Gasser (USA)	transmission of impulses by nerve fibres
1945	Alexander Fleming (UK)	discovery of the bactericidal effect of penicillin
	Ernst Chain (UK) and Howard Florey (Australia)	isolation of penicillin and its development as an antibiotic drug

Year	Winner(s)[1]	Awarded for
1946	Hermann Muller (USA)	discovery that X-ray irradiation can cause mutation
1947	Carl Cori (USA) and Gerty Cori (USA)	production and breakdown of glycogen (animal starch)
	Bernardo Houssay (Argentina)	function of the pituitary gland in sugar metabolism
1948	Paul Müller (Switzerland)	discovery of the first synthetic contact insecticide DDT
1949	Walter Hess (Switzerland)	mapping areas of the midbrain that control the activities of certain body organs
	Antonio Egas Moniz (Portugal)	therapeutic value of prefrontal leucotomy in certain psychoses
1950	Edward Kendall (USA), Tadeus Reichstein (Switzerland), and Philip Hench (USA)	structure and biological effects of hormones of the adrenal cortex
1951	Max Theiler (South Africa)	discovery of a vaccine against yellow fever
1952	Selman Waksman (USA)	discovery of streptomycin, the first antibiotic effective against tuberculosis
1953	Hans Krebs (UK)	discovery of the Krebs cycle
	Fritz Lipmann (USA)	discovery of coenzyme A, a nonprotein compound that acts in conjunction with enzymes to catalyse metabolic reactions leading up to the Krebs cycle
1954	John Enders (USA), Thomas Weller (USA), and Frederick Robbins (USA)	cultivation of the polio virus in the laboratory
1955	Hugo Theorell (Sweden)	work on the nature and action of oxidation enzymes
1956	André Cournand (USA), Werner Forssmann (West Germany), and Dickinson Richards (USA)	work on the technique for passing a catheter into the heart for diagnostic purposes

Year	Winner(s)[1]	Awarded for
1957	Daniel Bovet (Italy)	discovery of synthetic drugs used as muscle relaxants in anaesthesia
1958	George Beadle (USA) and Edward Tatum (USA)	discovery that genes regulate precise chemical effects
	Joshua Lederberg (USA)	work on genetic recombination and the organization of bacterial genetic material
1959	Severo Ochoa (USA) and Arthur Kornberg (USA)	discovery of enzymes that catalyse the formation of RNA (ribonucleic acid) and DNA (deoxyribonucleic acid)
1960	Macfarlane Burnet (Australia) and Peter Medawar (UK)	acquired immunological tolerance of transplanted tissues
1961	Georg von Békésy (USA)	investigations into the mechanism of hearing within the cochlea of the inner ear
1962	Francis Crick (UK), James Watson (USA), and Maurice Wilkins (UK)	discovery of the double-helical structure of DNA and of the significance of this structure in the replication and transfer of genetic information
1963	John Eccles (Australia), Alan Hodgkin (UK), and Andrew Huxley (UK)	ionic mechanisms involved in the communication or inhibition of impulses across neuron (nerve cell) membranes
1964	Konrad Bloch (USA) and Feodor Lynen (West Germany)	work on the cholesterol and fatty-acid metabolism
1965	François Jacob (France), André Lwoff (France), and Jacques Monod (France)	genetic control of enzyme and virus synthesis
1966	Peyton Rous (USA)	discovery of tumour-inducing viruses
	Charles Huggins (USA)	hormonal treatment of prostatic cancer
1967	Ragnar Granit (Sweden), Haldan Hartline (USA), and George Wald (USA)	physiology and chemistry of vision
1968	Robert Holley (USA), Har Gobind Khorana	interpretation of genetic code and its function in protein synthesis

Year	Winner(s)[1]	Awarded for
	(USA), and Marshall Nirenberg (USA)	
1969	Max Delbrück (USA), Alfred Hershey (USA), and Salvador Luria (USA)	replication mechanism and genetic structure of viruses
1970	Bernard Katz (UK), Ulf von Euler (Sweden), and Julius Axelrod (USA)	work on the storage, release, and inactivation of neurotransmitters
1971	Earl Sutherland (USA)	discovery of cyclic AMP, a chemical messenger that plays a role in the action of many hormones
1972	Gerald Edelman (USA) and Rodney Porter (UK)	work on the chemical structure of antibodies
1973	Karl von Frisch (Austria), Konrad Lorenz (Austria), and Nikolaas Tinbergen (UK)	work in animal behaviour patterns
1974	Albert Claude (USA), Christian de Duve (Belgium), and George Palade (USA)	work in structural and functional organization of the cell
1975	David Baltimore (USA), Renato Dulbecco (USA), and Howard Temin (USA)	work on interactions between tumour-inducing viruses and the genetic material of the cell
1976	Baruch Blumberg (USA) and Carleton Gajdusek (USA)	new mechanisms for the origin and transmission of infectious diseases
1977	Roger Guillemin (USA) and Andrew Schally (USA)	discovery of hormones produced by the hypothalamus region of the brain
	Rosalyn Yalow (USA)	radioimmunoassay techniques by which minute quantities of hormone may be detected
1978	Werner Arber (Switzerland), Daniel Nathans (USA), and Hamilton Smith (USA)	discovery of restriction enzymes and their application to molecular genetics

Year	Winner(s)[1]	Awarded for
1979	Allan Cormack (USA) and Godfrey Hounsfield (UK)	development of the computerized axial tomography (CAT) scan
1980	Baruj Benacerraf (USA), Jean Dausset (France), and George Snell (USA)	work on genetically determined structures on the cell surface that regulate immunological reactions
1981	Roger Sperry (USA)	functional specialization of the brain's cerebral hemispheres
	David Hubel (USA) and Torsten Wiesel (Sweden)	work on visual perception
1982	Sune Bergström (Sweden), Bengt Samuelsson (Sweden), and John Vane (UK)	discovery of prostaglandins and related biologically active substances
1983	Barbara McClintock (USA)	discovery of mobile genetic elements
1984	Niels Jerne (Denmark-UK), Georges Köhler (West Germany), and César Milstein (Argentina)	work on immunity and discovery of a technique for producing highly specific, monoclonal antibodies
1985	Michael Brown (USA) and Joseph L Goldstein (USA)	work on the regulation of cholesterol metabolism
1986	Stanley Cohen (USA) and Rita Levi-Montalcini (USA-Italy)	discovery of factors that promote the growth of nerve and epidermal cells
1987	Susumu Tonegawa (Japan)	work on the process by which genes alter to produce a range of different antibodies
1988	James Black (UK), Gertrude Elion (USA), and George Hitchings (USA)	work on the principles governing the design of new drug treatment
1989	Michael Bishop (USA) and Harold Varmus (USA)	discovery of oncogenes, genes carried by viruses that can trigger cancerous growth in normal cells

Year	Winner(s)[1]	Awarded for
1990	Joseph Murray (USA) and Donnall Thomas (USA)	pioneering work in organ and cell transplants
1991	Erwin Neher (Germany) and Bert Sakmann (Germany)	discovery of how gatelike structures (ion channels) regulate the flow of ions into and out of cells
1992	Edmond Fischer (USA) and Edwin Krebs (USA)	isolating and describing the action of the enzyme responsible for reversible protein phosphorylation, a major biological control mechanism
1993	Phillip Sharp (USA) and Richard Roberts (UK)	discovery of split genes (genes interrupted by nonsense segments of DNA)
1994	Alfred Gilman (USA) and Martin Rodbell (USA)	discovery of a family of proteins (G-proteins) that translate messages – in the form of hormones or other chemical signals – into action inside cells
1995	Edward Lewis (USA), Eric Wieschaus (USA), and Christiane Nüsslein-Volhard (Germany)	discovery of genes which control the early stages of the body's development
1996	Peter Doherty (Australia) and Rolf Zinkernagel (Switzerland)	discovery of how the immune system recognizes virus-infected cells
1997	Stanley Prusiner (USA)	discoveries, including the 'prion' theory, that could lead to new treatments of dementia-related diseases, including Alzheimer's and Parkinson's diseases
1998	Robert Furchgott (USA), Ferid Murad (USA), and Louis Ignarro (USA)	discovery that nitric oxide (NO) acts as a key chemical messenger between cells
1999	Günter Blobel (USA)	discovery that proteins have intrinsic signals that govern their transport and localization in the cell
2000	Arvid Carlsson (Sweden), Paul Greengard (USA), and Eric Kandel (USA)	elucidation of how signals are transmitted between nerve cells

[1] Nationality given is the citizenship of recipient at the time award was made.

Index

Note: page numbers in *italics* refer to illustrations